Also by Jonathan Raban

Driving Home
Surveillance
My Holy War
Waxwings
Passage to Juneau
Bad Land
The Oxford Book of the Sea
Hunting Mister Heartbreak
God, Man and Mrs Thatcher
For Love & Money
Coasting
Foreign Land
Old Glory
Arabia Through the Looking Glass
Soft City
The Society of the Poem
Mark Twain: Huckleberry Finn
The Technique of Modern Fiction

Father and Son

JONATHAN RABAN

Father and Son

A Memoir

Alfred A. Knopf
New York
2023

THIS IS A BORZOI BOOK
PUBLISHED BY ALFRED A. KNOPF

Copyright © 2023 by The Estate of Jonathan Raban

All rights reserved. Published in the United States by Alfred A. Knopf, a
division of Penguin Random House LLC, New York, and distributed in
Canada by Penguin Random House Canada Limited, Toronto.

www.aaknopf.com

Knopf, Borzoi Books, and the colophon are registered
trademarks of Penguin Random House LLC.

Grateful acknowledgment is made to *The Countryman* for
permission to reprint an excerpt from a poem by Field Marshal Earl
Wavell, originally published in *The Countryman* (Winter 1948).

Library of Congress Cataloging-in-Publication Data
Names: Raban, Jonathan, author.
Title: Father and son : a memoir / Jonathan Raban.
Description: First edition. | New York : Alfred A. Knopf, 2023.
Identifiers: LCCN 2022054048 (print) | LCCN 2022054049 (ebook) |
ISBN 9780375422454 (hardcover) | ISBN 9780593537367 (ebook)
Subjects: LCSH: Raban, Jonathan—Health. | Cerebrovascular disease—Patients—
Washington (State)—Seattle—Biography. | Raban, Jonathan—Family. |
Raban, Peter, 1918–1996. | Fathers and sons—Biography. | Seattle (Wash.)—Biography.
Classification: LCC RC388.5 R323 2023 (print) |
LCC RC388.5 (ebook) | DDC 616.8/10092 [B]—dc23/eng/20230321
LC record available at https://lccn.loc.gov/2022054048
LC ebook record available at https://lccn.loc.gov/2022054049

Jacket images: (inset left) Peter Raban and (background) postcard, courtesy
of Julia Raban; (inset right) Jonathan Raban by Eamonn McCabe/
Getty Images; (airmail pattern) whitemay/Getty Images
Jacket design by Jenny Carrow

Manufactured in the United States of America

First Edition

Father and Son

Chapter 1

—————————

I WAS TRANSFORMED into an old man quite suddenly, on June 11, 2011, three days short of my sixty-ninth birthday.

That dull midsummer Saturday, I woke soon after eight feeling inexplicably under the weather. It wasn't a hangover, though it seemed to have hangover symptoms (headache, mild nausea). I stepped groggily out of bed and dressed, fumbling with my shirt buttons, before rescuing the blue-sheathed *New York Times* from where it had been tossed on the steps that led down to the yard. The sky was low, the clouds like pumice stone. I had to hold on to the handrail to steady myself as I went back up to the second floor, and when I climbed the interior stairs to the big all-purpose room on the third floor, my left shoulder kept on bumping against the wall. My sense of balance had somehow slid off-center, and I felt queasy: I shook my head and swallowed several times to rid myself of what was obviously a slight malfunction of the inner ear.

Coffee cures most things in the early morning. I got the machine going and spread the paper on the dining table. Downstairs, my daughter, Julia, slept on in the bedroom next door to mine. This weekend belonged to her: yesterday had been her last day of high school; she'd been at a party last night, and her official graduation was on Tuesday. Today we were due to go to the Apple store and pick a new laptop for her to take to college in September. This inner ear thing was a distraction that I could well have done without. Swigging down coffee, I made myself concentrate on the news.

In Iowa, Newt Gingrich's campaign staff for his presidential run had deserted him. Big forest fire in Arizona. In Tripoli, Damascus, Cairo . . . I settled to reading the long and handsome obit of Patrick Leigh Fermor, who had finally handed in his dinner pail, aged ninety-six. Feeling at least half-restored, I refilled the coffee mug and went downstairs to my workroom, walking quietly so as not to wake Julia. On my computer screen was the unsatisfactory first page of a review essay about the Seattle billionaire Paul Allen, whose memoir was so oddly arranged that he might have written it himself, but probably hadn't. The book lay open on the floor; my piece was already late, but I always work badly at weekends, so I escaped onto the internet to browse Allen's many hobbies—his spacecraft, his sports teams, his brain institute, his rock music museum, his deepwater submarine. I wished I felt more kinship with these enthusiasms, which struck me as unappealingly schoolboyish, like collecting birds' eggs or trainspotting, and were conducted on an equally unappealing plutocratic scale.

Julia showed up in the doorway, wrapped in a faded pink bathrobe. Sleep had left her looking vague, her face not yet fully assembled. She had a question: Would I mind postponing our visit to the Apple store till tomorrow? She wanted more time to mull over the rival claims of the Air and the Pro. I masked my relief.

So much of life is acting. Being "well" requires impersonation. Acting the part of a fit person, I proposed lunch at a Mexican restaurant, and we agreed to meet up in an hour. In the interim, I tried to put myself back together as best I could, and when Julia next appeared I was splashed with Eau Sauvage, in a clean shirt and clean hacking jacket, as if we were off to lunch at somewhere grand and not the down-at-heel Mexican place with its quarter-in-the-slot candy dispensers and torn Naugahyde seats in the booths.

I drove. Handling the car took more concentration than usual. Self-consciously, I repeatedly checked the rearview mirror; changing gear, I made a mess of going from second into third, getting a note of shrill complaint from the gearbox. The three-mile drive seemed far longer and I was disinclined to talk as we rode in heavy traffic through Ballard and Crown Hill.

The restaurant was a friendly spot. A margarita for me and a Diet Coke for Julia came unordered. We had a halting conversation about laptops—never my strong subject—and when the food came to the table, she ate while I picked without appetite at a roasted lamb shank and left the margarita untouched. My attempt to appear well was beginning to come apart at the seams: it wasn't until we were back at the house that I remembered I'd failed to leave a tip. This lapse of manners troubled me, it was so out of character. I phoned the restaurant, asking them to put $7.50 on my credit card, then resumed my listless pursuit of Paul Allen.

Toward the end of the long, sluggish afternoon, the sky brightened and the trees beside the window suddenly sprang into chiaroscuro: sunlit leaves fluttering against stolid blocks of shadow. But this change in the external weather failed to rouse me from the lethargy that was gathering like fog. I visited the London *Times* online crossword and solved one clue. I was no stranger to wasted days, but this one felt more comprehensively wasted than any within recent memory.

Upstairs again, I was joined by Julia, who'd been occupied in her room. So long as she was around, it was possible to keep up my pretense of normality, or so I hoped. We had in the fridge a cast-iron Dutch oven full of chicken korma cooked the night before, but when I tried to lift it out it seemed that my right hand had gone to sleep, and the heavy pot threatened to empty itself over the floor. I had to ask Julia to move it to the stove. I measured, rinsed, and drained the rice using only my left hand.

We sat down to eat. Trying to marshal the rice with the knife in my right hand, I watched the blade as it slid feebly over the rice pile on the plate, barely grazing the surface of the grains. I tried again and got the same result. The knife flatly refused to carry out the order transmitted to it from my brain. Its insubordination made me at last acknowledge to myself that I was having a stroke. When I shared this news—in carefully toned-down form—with Julia, she said "hospital" and reached for her iPhone.*

I have a secret sympathy with Mary Baker Eddy, the founder of Christian Science, who thought all illness "error" and told her followers to avoid medical treatment at any cost. Doctors and hospitals exist

* Julia herself says otherwise, telling me that she had been surreptitiously busy on her phone for at least half an hour before I said anything, alternately Googling "stroke symptoms" and texting her mother about how to compel me to go to an emergency room right away.

to kill you is my own opinion, and on this occasion I thought that a good night's sleep would cure me of my error, and, besides, Julia and I had our date to visit the Apple store on Sunday morning, limp hand notwithstanding. I told her that the emergency rooms of Seattle would be crammed to their bursting point on this Saturday night with the victims of drug overdoses, stabbings, shootings, and the like. Much better to leave the whole business till tomorrow, when in all probability my temporary weakness would be gone.

"Well, you know what I think you should do."

Her lip was trembling and I saw she was attempting, and failing, to hold back tears. In eighteen years, she'd had plenty of opportunity to show frustration with me, but I'd never seen it so plainly registered on her face. It was infectious. I felt frustrated with me too.

"Okay, but not a downtown hospital, where it'd probably take hours to get seen."

The iPhone yielded as many hospitals in the area as it did restaurants. I picked one in Edmonds, a town a few miles north that in my mind's eye was populated by retired people, drawn there by its tranquil views of Puget Sound, and where there shouldn't be too much bloody mayhem to fill the ER on a Saturday night. The phone was immediately answered (good sign) by a woman's voice.

I asked if they were busy and said that I believed I was having a "ministroke."

"Are you a physician?"

"No."

"Then why would you think that?"

"Because I've gone sort of asymmetrical. My left side is normal but my right arm and leg are suddenly weak."

"Do you want me to call an ambulance for you?"

"No, I have transport."

"You have somebody to drive you?"

I slung Paul Allen's memoir, my Kindle, and my old cheap laptop into a satchel and we left the house. The steps outside had grown more hazardous since the morning, and the path to the gate was a trial: aiming to stick to the concrete, I kept lurching into the grass like a vaudeville drunk. Swaying in the road, I said, "Which car shall we take?"

For the first time, Julia's mother, who'd just bought a new car, had lent her the old one for the weekend, and the Subaru Forester was now parked outside our house, nose to nose with my Mazda MX-5. "Mine," Julia said.

She'd just passed her test, and I'd never been her passenger before except in the Mazda, where I'd failed to teach her how to stick-shift with any aplomb. I struggled with my seat belt. My right arm twitched feebly on my lap when I tried to lift it, and I couldn't feed the tongue of the belt into the slot with only my left hand. After I had made a series of bosh shots, Julia took care of it, making me remember how I used to strap her into her child seat.

"Mom doesn't like smoking in the car, but I'm sure she'd be okay with you smoking now if you keep your window down."

Obedient to my daughter, I fished out of my top pocket a partially smoked Upmann demitasse cigar and lit up, conscious that Julia must know very well that my incessant smoking was the obvious cause of this journey to the ER, and silently thanked her for she drove with a precision that surprised me, moving out confidently into the fast lane on 99, past the neon motel signs and the warnings to motorists not to curb-crawl for hookers. It was just after sunset now, and the old road to British Columbia and California was taking on its customary, garish nighttime colors. I'd always warmed to its air of old-fashioned vice and thievery, how it put the lie to Seattle's besetting niceness and tameness. I'd never been inside the strip clubs of 99, and rarely visited its bars, but I valued their promise of a life so near and yet so unexplored.

Julia and I maintained an easy, bantering talk that kept our severe destination as far as possible at bay. She'd entered the hospital's address on her iPhone, and I watched as it approached us like a fate. "Take the next left," I said.

No one was in sight on the hospital campus, the parking lot largely empty of cars. It was just as I'd hoped: the usual tribal festivities of a Saturday night evidently didn't happen in Edmonds. Grabbing at lampposts for stability wherever they offered themselves, I stumbled across the lot to the emergency room, brushing off Julia's offer of help, determined to make it on my own. The tarmac tilted and fell beneath my feet like the deck of a ship in a moderately heavy sea.

A form to fill in, signature required. Then a nurse put me through a short quiz, to which the answers came fast and readily: Jonathan Raban; Saturday, June 11, 2011; Barack Obama. She asked me to smile; I did so. She told me to raise my arms above my head; I managed to crook my right elbow, but my forearm wouldn't rise above waist level, and the hand dangled from the wrist.

She escorted the two of us to a consulting room, where another nurse took charge, helping me to climb aboard a gurney before she checked my temperature, pulse rate, and blood pressure. The result made her frown and repeat the exercise. She left the room, but quickly returned with a doctor in tow.

"How long has this been going on?" He gave me two pills to ease the pressure of the blood as it fizzed through my arteries.

I said that I'd been feeling off-color all day but had developed real symptoms only an hour or so before this.

"You should have come in before: the earlier we get to see a patient with a stroke, the more we can do."

I said that if I reported to a hospital every time I felt slightly unwell, I'd be a permanent resident there. The doctor said he'd need a brain scan, for which I'd need to change my street clothes for a hospital gown—an item that had been through the wash so many times that it was hardly more substantial than a spiritualist's supernatural ectoplasm. It was a struggle to feed my dead right arm into and down the sleeve of this ghostly piece of apparel.

An orderly was summoned, who wheeled me down a corridor and into a technician's studio, where the main item of furniture appeared to be a tilted silver rocket launcher. I was fed feetfirst inside the barrel of the thing by the techie, who dealt with me as affably and impersonally as if he were a checkout clerk and I was a barcode. When he closed the top of his machine, I was in darkness, with just a small dot of red light for company. This light began to slowly circle my skull.

Locked in the scanner, watching the light disappear on the far periphery of my vision, I felt an irrational and involuntary swell of elation. Everything was out of my hands now; I had no more autonomy than a parcel being sorted by the postal service. The sheer novelty of the hospital, its people and peculiar technologies, worked on me as trips into unfamiliar country had done in the past: strangeness, as always, even in this circumstance, a surefire source of pleasure. Inside the scanner I felt lightweight, free of responsibilities (not least the responsibility of reviewing Paul Allen), back on my travels.

Flat on my back on the gurney, I was pushed down the corridor, wheels rattling, to the consulting room, where the doctor was already looking at a picture of the left side of my brain on a portable video monitor, and Julia sat with a short story anthology on her knees, opened at the first page of Raymond Carver's "Cathedral." The doctor said, "Ischemic stroke. Two bloodings. See?"

I didn't see. The picture on the screen was a monochrome study in shades of gray, like a weathered landscape swept by rain. Squeamishness made me not want to look at it too closely.

"Bloodings," I said, and explained that I'd only ever heard the word used in the context of foxhunting, where it was the name of an initiation ritual. Children who were in at the kill for the first time would have their faces smeared with the severed tail of the fox. It had never happened to me, but I'd known several girls of my age who boasted of being blooded at a blooding. The doctor, showing no interest at all in this scrap of esoterica, asked for another blood pressure check, and again the nurse wrapped the black cuff around my upper arm, inflated it, then watched the needle on the gauge subside as she listened through her stethoscope. This time, the upper figure of the reading was below two hundred, so the pills were kicking in.

I watched Julia, who was keeping the doctor under covert surveillance as she pretended to read her book. It was impossible to tell from her expression just how much anxiety she was feeling at this moment; the best I could do was remember my own surprise at how shaken I had been in 1996, when my father's illness had been diagnosed as fatal. He was seventy-eight then, and I was fifty-four—both of us surely old enough to deal with the experience as grown-ups. But it was with a childish aghastness that I watched him die, the life leaking out of him day by day, then hour by hour, like air from a punctured tire. Looking at Julia now, I worried that she might be struggling with the prospect of her father's death, a subject I was afraid to broach with her in case that thought had not yet cropped up in her mind.

It had momentarily entered mine while we were passing through the Korean section of 99 on our way to the hospital, and in a split second I had dismissed it as absurd and self-dramatizing. For her, though, it might be a reasonable dread. Wanting to reassure her, I asked the doctor what he thought my chances were.

He was checking my peripheral vision, moving his forefinger from one side of my head to the other. "There's often a three-to-five-day window after the stroke when patients recover the use of the leg. Sometimes the arm too. But there are no guarantees."

I liked the sound of the window. In my case it ought to be open at least till Tuesday, and as late as Thursday. If it was prompt in its timing, I should be in my place at Julia's graduation. The doctor moved on to test my capacity to feel sensation in my affected limbs, saying "good" each time I pointed to the spot he'd tapped. Exams of any kind had always aroused my hunger for praise, and this one was no exception: I basked in the glow of being a good student.

When the doctor began to arrange my transfer to the intensive care unit, I encouraged Julia to leave for her mother's house, which was a few miles nearer to the hospital than mine, and where her mother would be still up and about. I told her not to worry; I'd be fine, just fine. With my left arm I embraced her as best I could and watched her go; a black cardigan, blue skirt, and the Birkenstocks of her tribe, weaving between the identical white coats, my own better angel. She was my closest confidante, the only person in Seattle I knew who got my jokes, and her absence made itself felt as a sudden chill in the room.

Too late, I called, "Safe driving!" My voice felt unprecedentedly hoarse, the words like pebbles in my throat.

With my clothes and shoulder bag stowed on the lower deck of the gurney, I was wheeled along a corridor to an open elevator. Somewhere on this journey to the ICU I slid into exhausted semiconsciousness; a netherworld where the institutional fluorescent lighting gave way to the murk of an aquarium in which algae have been left to bloom and multiply for weeks on end. From outside the greenery there came voices quizzing me about my name, the date, my age. I was told to smile, to grasp a latex-gloved forefinger, to follow the movements of a pencil with my eyes. Fighting narcolepsy, I tried to satisfy the inquisitors (or was there only one of them? I wasn't sure).

"Are you right- or left-handed?"

"Left. I'm a southpaw."

"Well, that's lucky."

I sank back through the algae like a slow-swimming tench descending to the muddy bottom of his pond.

Deep sleep was rudely interrupted when I realized that someone was attaching a catheter to my penis.

"Oh, God. Am I being incontinent?"

"That can happen."

"But is it happening now?"

"No. Not yet."

"Then please take that thing off. I can ask for a bedpan if and when I need one."

The catheter went away; a thermometer appeared, and another black cuff was wrapped around my upper arm.

"Just taking your vitals."

I attempted to roll onto my side, but this turned out to be a hopeless ambition. My body was now immovable. If I'd ever really thought of paralysis before, I'd assumed it to be stiff, like rigor mortis, but my right arm and leg weren't stiff at all; in every way but one, they were entirely normal—warm, malleable, sensitive to the touch. Only when I tried to lift them with my left hand did I find that they'd grown incredibly heavy: even my skinny arm had taken on the concentrated weight of a pig of ballast. Both limbs were in good working order, but they'd accidentally fallen out of communication with my brain. It was a temporary glitch. When the promised "window" opened, their blown fuses would be replaced and all would be well. Comforted by this thought, I slithered back into the fishy green phantasmagoria of dreams that were repeatedly disrupted by fresh checks of my vital signs.

These forced reawakenings made me lose all track of time. The watch on my right wrist lay far down in the bed, as inaccessible as if it were in a locked trunk. In the artificial light of the ICU (I could see no windows), there was no clue as to whether it was night or day. Earlier I had been certain of the date, June 11. Now I wasn't so sure. It was probably June 12, but could conceivably be June 13 or be June 11 still. My inability to tell the time worried me as the possible symptom of more serious mental deficiencies. Obviously the stroke had damaged my brain, but just how many neurons had been put out of service was a question I couldn't begin to answer.

When a nurse next came visiting, I asked her the time. It was eight something.

"Sunday morning," I said.

"Yes, would you like some breakfast?"

I had never, as an adult, been able to cry easily, but the simple ordinariness of the word "breakfast" made my eyes well up, and the world swim. Somehow, the stroke seemed to have replenished tear ducts that had lain dry for sixty years like the parched creek beds of a Montana summer suddenly running with water again, and in the next few months I'd find myself starting to blub at the slightest sentimental provocation.

My blood pressure was down to 170 over something, "still quite elevated, but moving in the right direction," and it was gurney time again, as I was shuffled out of intensive care, through the three-dimensional hospital labyrinth of corridors and elevators, to a vacant room, which was, as I remember, windowless, though that detail may be more a measure of my state of mind at the time than an accurate reflection of the room's amenities. At any rate, I could see nothing of the world outside.

I had never in my life been so helpless. With one side of my body now completely paralyzed, I had to be lifted from gurney to bed, from bed to wheelchair, from wheelchair to toilet seat. I could barely tilt my head from the pillow, and to make any substantial movement I had to summon assistance by flipping a switch on the left-hand side of the bed. Also, I was overwhelmed with fatigue. Every few minutes I'd pass out, as if clocked on the skull with a hammer, only to come groggily awake a few moments later.

Yet the mood of irrational well-being which had visited me the night before stayed with me still. I could make light of the paralysis. My life, such as it was, had always taken place primarily inside my head; my body, with its hungers, aches, and upsets, was the mind's inconvenient accessory. So long as my brain was intact (and it remained to be seen if, or how far, that was true), I could get by. But such thinking was silly and alarmist: the window of my recovery was yet open, and I planned to escape clean through it.

A nurse had assisted me into the wheelchair, and I was dozing there when Julia arrived to visit. The oddity of the situation made us both shy. We were deferential newcomers to the conventions of the hospital, like tourists with lowered voices tiptoeing around a foreign cathedral. She had brought with her my shaving kit from the house and a copy of *The New York Times Magazine,* published that day.

It had a piece by me in it and half a dozen photos taken by Julia. In April, we'd driven down to Stanford from Seattle, a thousand-mile ride, so that she could spend a night in a dorm and sample some university classes. My idea was to hug the coasts of Washington, Oregon, and California, savoring the landscape of volcanic upheaval and earthquake fault lines as a rehearsal for the pending temblor that would shake both our lives when Julia went to college.

"How is it, Bird?"

"Good."

"Your photographs?"

She showed me. They were inset in a box on the second page—shots of the road in fir forest and snaking around sea cliffs, the illuminated OPEN sign outside an Oregon café where we'd dined in a rainstorm, the steel tracery of the great four-mile bridge over the Columbia River, a generic California motel. The piece was introduced by a cunning picture taken by a photographer whom we'd met by prior arrangement in Sausalito, just short of the Golden Gate Bridge, and showed Julia and me in the parked car, top down and seen from behind. Julia's face, hair tangled by the wind, was reflected in the rearview mirror, while I was visible as a weathered pink baseball cap busy with the Rand McNally road atlas.

I had called the piece "Letting Go," but the *Times* had retitled it "The Last Father-Daughter Road Trip."

"Look, the *Times* has gone into the prophecy business."

"Oh, of course it won't be the last road trip we take." I was much reassured by the indignation that Julia brought to this statement: her belief in my recovery was essential to my own.

"Does my voice sound odd to you? It sounds old-man croaky to me."

"No. You sound a bit tired, that's all."

I wondered how far her mild and ordinary tone reflected not so much my apparent return to something like normality as her need for a father in acceptable working order. To expect candor from her under these circumstances was asking too much. We were both acting our parts in the old hospital repertory, the recovering patient and encouraging visitor.

Julia left soon after, bound for a graduation party at a friend's house. I'd just relapsed into unconsciousness in the wheelchair when a nurse woke me to ask if I would like a sponge bath. I told her I could handle that myself but would be grateful if she'd wheel me over to the hand-basin and mirror.

"I'll stay in the room, if you don't mind." Not a question. The nurse hovered watchfully over my right shoulder.

With my good hand I reached for my wash bag on the sink counter and fumbled with the zipper, extracting the aerosol of shaving foam with some difficulty.

"I wouldn't do that if I were you, unless you want to go straight back to the emergency room. You're on a blood thinner—don't you have an electric shaver?"

She had a fund of cheerful stories about patients she had known on blood thinners who had nicked their chins with regular razors and bled by the bucketful.

I hadn't seen myself in a mirror since the stroke. The pallor, stubble, crinkled bags under the eyes, unruly tufts of gray hair sticking out over the ears, and general appearance of shrunkenness were only to be expected. What took me seriously aback was the right-hand corner of my mouth. It drooped. The droop was slight, but enough to give the face in the glass a distinct leer and allow a glinting thread of slobber to leak from the sag in the lips.

So this was what Julia had confronted. I saw now the effort it must have taken her to keep up her show of equanimity.

I was wearing boxer shorts and a hospital "gown." The nurse offered help, which I testily declined. Seeing her in the mirror, I tried to stare her down.

"You like your independence, don't you?"

I stared at the reflection of my naked right shoulder. The arm appeared to have fallen out of its socket. The bump of the end of the bone in the upper arm hung an inch or so below the bump of the shoulder blade; I warily touched the space between the two with the tip of my functioning forefinger.

"Subluxation. Very common with strokes. The occupational therapist will help you to fix that."

The nurse's presence was obtrusive and inhibiting. Stripped to the waist, I ached for privacy as I dabbed at my armpits with a wet flannel.

The attempt to give myself a one-handed sponge bath while the nurse watched every movement was laughably ineffectual. I quickly became exhausted with the business.

The gown lay in my lap. I realized that I had no idea of how to put it on again and let the nurse instruct me from a distance.

"Put your left hand through the armhole. No, the other one. Now take hold of the right hand and pull it through. That's it! Now . . ."

Even in the fog of annoyance and fatigue I was aware that I was being a lousy patient and the nurse was being a perfectly good nurse. I apologized to her for being so inept and intractable.

"I understand. A stroke is a life-changing event."

That was a phrase to which I'd soon become inured. It was always delivered in a blandly optimistic tone, as if paralysis and brain trauma carried with them the promise of some glorious self-renewal, like inheriting an ... wn feeling was that, of all life-... to beat.

... the bed. A meal came. Its ...-schools, hospitals, asylums, ... tray as I lay with my head ... from which I was almost ... or vital signs.

... question. The stroke had ... it had just been patiently ... e median age for stroke ... iad been just three days ... or many years I had left ... daily wine drinker and,

... ed, my inhibited reck- ... ke risks without suf- ... e people I liked best ... n in England during ... it) were all smokers, ... in my address book. ... rder, held together ... it couldn't bring ... had sent it to me ... died of smoking

Blessings
ON
ST. PATRICK'S DAY

in January 2001, aged fifty-seven, her lungs wrecked by emphysema. I flew to England for her funeral. In a borrowed car, I drove another close friend to Norwich, where Lorna was to be cremated. We smoked cigarettes all the way; cigarettes over a vinous dinner; cigarettes over the hotel breakfast; cigarettes on the drive to the cemetery. Early that summer, I heard Ian had inoperable cancer. He died in December. He was sixty-three.

It wasn't as if we didn't know what we were cooking up for ourselves. Of course we knew. In the 1950s, long before the cigarette companies were made to print warnings on their products, we already talked of smokes as "cancer sticks." Their danger was part of their allure, just as it was an essential ingredient of our guerrilla resistance to the sanctimonious lectures of parents, teachers, doctors who preached against smoking even as they, or many of them, continued to smoke themselves.

The hospital's unnatural lighting made day and night look interchangeably alike.

Strangers came to the room pushing silver equipment trolleys. Vitals were taken (my blood pressure was still coming down), and one worker replaced another as shifts changed (though I couldn't tell how long these shifts were). I had some difficulty entering her number with my good forefinger but spoke with Julia on my mobile, then slept, and woke to find her in the room.

She'd stopped at a pharmacy and bought an electric shaver for me. More interestingly, she had been back to her school one last time and used the darkroom there to produce half a dozen enormous prints of photos from our trip to the Bay Area. She'd also asked permission at the nurses' station to stick pushpins in the wall of the room, which she was turning into a gallery of images from the journey.

Every photograph was an invitation to memory, and it was reassuring to discover that each unlocked a fluent sequence of associations. The picture of the car parked in front of the motel room, for instance: I couldn't name the settlement on Route 101, but we'd stopped there on the first night of the return leg from Palo Alto to Seattle, with Julia practically levitating with excitement after staying in a dorm and taking a couple of classes at Stanford. That morning I'd dropped her off at the Palo Alto Caltrain station so that she could measure the "real distance" to San Francisco, where she'd arranged to meet a friend from summer camp for lunch, while I followed her on the freeway and lunched alone. The print brought back our tense escape from the city, in heavy Saturday afternoon traffic, as we overtook an immense funeral cortege on I-80, the line of stretch limos with smoked-glass windows flanked by motorcycle outriders, some police and some civilians, followed by a multicolored assortment of private automobiles. Everyone in sight was Black. A biker on a big Harley, with dreadlocks and no helmet, swerved over to yell at me to get the fuck out of the lane we were in; Julia used her iPhone and the *San Francisco Chronicle* site to try to figure out whose important corpse was riding in the hearse—preacher? gangster? politician?—but had no luck.

"What was the name of that place where we stayed the night?"

"I don't know that I ever knew it."

I found that reassuring too.

"The motel clerk was a Pakistani woman," I said. "The promising-looking restaurant was closed, and we ate at the Mexican place."

"I remember." Her mouth was full of pins.

Being able to remember now felt like a privilege: I could too easily imagine how the pictures that Julia was hanging might mean nothing to me at all.

Her graduation ceremony was the next day, but no window had opened for me; half my body was paralyzed, spells of exhausted sleep were intermitted with passages of torpid wakefulness, and I clearly wasn't going anywhere tomorrow. Before the stroke catapulted me into this new terrain of age and decrepitude, I had been gritting my teeth against the tedium—the milling parents, the speeches, the interminable rounds of acts and entertainments put on by the students. I could smell in advance the dusty air of the converted church in which the event would take place, its tinctures of Dior and dry-cleaning fluid: I have spent a good deal of my life avoiding attendance at rituals in churches, and this one was no exception. Yet now I couldn't go, I felt truly sad at the prospect of not being there.

"I'm so sorry, Birdie."

"Of course you can't."

So while Julia went off next morning to Town Hall (formerly one of Mary Baker Eddy's temples, raised against Error) to collect her high school diploma, I was being pushed in a wheelchair down a fresh corridor and into the office of a Romanian doctor. I instantly warmed to her: when she asked me how I felt today, it seemed more like an ordinarily human question than a medical one, and when I answered that I could feel worse, she said, "You're so English!" I heard in her own accent a friendly trace of Englishness, perhaps the echo of an English teacher back in Romania. In my mind, she and I were two Europeans met in a foreign land.

I wanted to question her, but I was stymied: I needed the name of Romania's socialist dictator, along with the name of its capital city, and could recall neither. That eagle's-beak nose above lips like a pair of plumped cushions . . . A clip of smudgy black-and-white film, seen on TV, showing the dictator and his wife under trial in a kangaroo court, then, immediately afterward, their execution by machine-gun fire; two people in overcoats fallen on flagstones. But I had lost his name, and as for the name of the city, all I knew was that it wasn't Belgrade.

The doctor was talking about the neurological rehab ward at Swedish hospital in downtown Seattle. Whenever she used the word "rehabilitation," I just saw mental patients weaving baskets, and eventually admitted what I was thinking.

"I think they've got past that stage," she said.

"You really think it would be useful?"

"Well, they seem to think so. They've accepted you, and they don't accept everybody by any means." She made it sound like a college.

Would I be in a ward or have a room to myself? A room, she said. How long would I be expected to stay? About two weeks, maybe more, maybe less. And Medicare would pay? Yes. Would I be free to discharge myself at any time? Yes.

I remarked that I'd been to an English boarding school, which was said to be an excellent preparation for life in prison. As soon as the sentence left my lips, I wished I could recall it, for it was a stupid thing to say to anyone who had lived under the regime of the dictator whose name escaped me and who had imprisoned many thousands of his subjects. But she was kind enough to laugh anyway.

I told her—facetiously, I thought—how much I'd miss being able to drink wine in the evenings.

"Just about everybody I know in England would be classified here as a functioning alcoholic."

"In Romania too."

"Rehab is meant to be a halfway house between the hospital and the outside world. I don't see why your wine should be a problem—how much would you want to drink?"

"Just a glass with dinner." Best to open with the lowest possible bid.

"I'll give them a call and let you know what they say."

Five minutes later, when the chair had been rolled to the door of my room, she caught up with us. "I spoke with Dr. Clawson. He says fine to the wine."

"Thank you so much. So when do I move?"

"Tomorrow. An ambulance will drive you there."

Elated by the prospect of such a civilized rehabilitation, with friends dropping in for drinks before dinner, I reentered the room. The photographs on the walls momentarily surprised me. One image, of the remains of breakfast at a roadside café, got my memory going: Julia had taken it on our first day, when rain had fallen, with steadily increasing force, from dawn to dusk and long beyond. Twenty minutes after leaving that café we'd quit the freeway for the dripping fir plantations and sodden cattle of western Washington; then crossed the wind-swept Columbia on the four-mile bridge, where the tidal water was the color of milky cocoa. As we drove through the makeshift towns of the Oregon coast, the little car felt like a submersible. By dinner, a full gale was blowing off the ocean, the rain horizontal and stinging. Water cascaded from the choked gutters of Yachats, whose sloping main street flowed like a river in spate. Inside the restaurant (its ceiling hung with inverted umbrellas), the aging hippie with his guitar and fifty-year-old songs had a hard time making himself heard over the snarling ruckus of the surf.

Still staring at the photograph, I remembered that today was my birthday.

Chapter 2

WE WERE AN inseparable couple, my mother and I. Our address was: The White House, Hempton Green, nr. Fakenham, Norfolk. Here we stove in the shells of our breakfast eggs with teaspoons to prevent witches from using them as boats (the eggs came from Mrs. Artherton, who helped my mother in the house and kept chickens at her nearby cottage). Here we listened to the news on the wireless twice and sometimes three times a day. My father was a distant rumor. He was away in the war, and my mother believed that she might hear something of him if she listened closely enough to the news. "Hush! It's time for the news" punctuated our days as reliably as a chiming clock.

First came the pips at one-second intervals, then: "This is the BBC Home Service. Here is the news and this is Alvar Lidell reading it"— a voice like God, from far-off London. My mother frowned as she listened, while I wriggled around to peer inside the set through the ventilation holes in its fiberboard back. The valves glowed and flickered like a miniature city in the darkness, and the whole mysterious apparatus gave off the smell of its own importance: oil, solder, burned dust, electrochemistry at work. It was magnificently incomprehensible. So was the newsreader's voice, issuing from the front of the wireless, to which my mother attended with a face of studious perplexity.

The squirming child was all skin and bone. I had a wasting disease known as celiac, or so my mother had been told. Several times a day I would vomit in the lavatory, with my mother cupping my forehead in the palm of her hand. This illness (and as an adult I was told that it almost certainly wasn't celiac) was worn by me as a sign of great personal distinction. It entitled me to the secret hoard of bananas that were kept in the cool and musty larder off the hall, whose darkness and echoey flagstone floor, a few steps down from ground level, spooked me sufficiently that I never dared to go there alone. The mice, who scurried over the draining boards in the kitchen, made their head-quarters in the larder.

In wartime England, nobody had bananas except me. They were specially imported just for my benefit, my mother said. When they arrived, they were firm and green, but quickly ripened to black in the larder, infecting the whole house with the stink of their decomposi-tion. I liked the taste of sweet, putrescent ooze, and it's hardly surpris-ing that, given such a peculiar diet, I spent much of my time crouched over the toilet bowl, emptying my stomach of these rare luxuries, which, I believed, were flown to Fakenham for me by airplane.

My mother was teaching me to read, for I was her chief distraction from the war. My three brothers would all come later. When she wasn't listening to the wireless or writing her daily letters to my father, she and I were playing alphabet cards—sounding out the letters and mak-ing words. "Cat," "mat," "hat," "sat," "rat," "fat." Pretty soon, I could mouth the words in the headlines of *The Times,* which appeared in our letter box each morning, even when I was clueless of their meanings. This wasn't precocity on my part but a measure of my mother's atten-tion to her child and anxiety for her husband, a product of the special circumstances of war.

It was a job for which she was unusually well qualified. My mother had only a smattering of formal education (the finishing school from which she graduated at sixteen, in Vevey, Switzerland, used books pri-marily as objects to place on students' heads in deportment lessons), but she was an avid reader of Mrs. Gaskell *(Cranford),* Flora Thompson *(Lark Rise to Candleford),* and Stella Gibbons *(Cold Comfort Farm).* At seventeen, she took a correspondence course from the Regent School of Successful Writing ("101 Infallible Plot Situations"), and began to send out stories to women's magazines. *Horner's Weekly* responded with an acceptance letter, and soon she was contributing monthly tales of romance in the countryside, each between ten thousand and fifteen thousand words long at two guineas per thousand words. Years later, my mother would belittle the stories, saying they were no good, and the magazine was "just for servant girls." She didn't publish them in her name but under a pseudonym. The wartime paper shortage killed the magazine (and most of the servant girls joined the war effort as land girls, working the fields in headscarves and breeches).

What survived of these efforts was my mother's Ford Popular, license plate AUP 595, bought from the profits of her writing. It lived as a shrouded ghost, under dust sheets and an old blanket, in the wooden garage in our back garden, until the German surrender, when petrol rationing was reintroduced for private motorists. It was a black saloon, with upholstered seats that smelled of leather and, more faintly, of dog—the last remnants of Sam, a Staffordshire bull terrier, who had been reluctantly given away to a dog-loving wing commander not long after I was born. In my mother's many photos of him, Sam appeared to be a genial and frolicsome sort of dog, but he had acquired a nasty reputation as a canine terrorist. Now I sat where he had used to sit in the front passenger seat of the car, where I channeled his ghost, woof-woofing my way along the Norfolk lanes.

I loved AUP 595. Not the least of its fascinations were the two half-moon holes in its floor, just behind my mother's feet as she worked the accelerator and the clutch. Through these holes I could watch the graveled surface of the road as it sped into a vomit-colored blur, then came into sharp focus again when my mother braked. The movements of the road interested me at least as much as anything I could see through the windows. The holes obviously meant that someone with large feet had owned AUP 595 for a good many years before my mother bought it in 1937 or 1938; I never thought of it as an old car at the time, and have no memory of it ever breaking down.

When my mother had enough petrol coupons, we'd drive to Granny's house in Sheringham, a long ride of nearly twenty miles. The narrow, twisting road ran past Little Snoring and on to Holt, where we often stopped to break the journey and look in shop windows. Then, from a wooded ridge, the land below us was rimmed with the mysterious sea. Here my mother switched the engine off and let AUP 595 coast downhill. For a mile or more, there was just the sound of the wind, the rustle of tires on gravel, the creaking of the elderly chassis as the car submitted to the gravitational pull of Granny's house. My mother had enlisted as an ambulance driver early in the war and never missed an opportunity to save petrol. She allowed the car to come almost to a standstill before switching the ignition back on and letting out the clutch, so that it restarted with a series of bone-shaking jerks and a roar. Or it didn't. When it stalled at the bottom of the hill, my mother would get out and, to "save the battery," effortlessly swing the crank handle.

Granny's house, Notch Hill, St. Austin's Grove, stood several streets short of the sea, up a sloping cul-de-sac. Past the gate, one had to climb a crazy-paving path flanked on either side by a rock garden of lavender and alpine plants. With its small bow-windowed drawing room at the front and whitewashed pebble dash, the house, I see now, was a very modest example of 1930s suburban bijou, but then I thought it grand and magical. Granny in the doorway, looking slightly top-heavy with her bosomy torso balanced on girlishly slender legs, dogs yapping behind her, smelled of eau de cologne and cigarettes. In every room there were open boxes of cork-tipped Craven As, the cigarettes nestling, close-packed, in their pillar box–red containers with the black cat logo. To me, Granny's cigarettes were a sign of extraordinary opulence and luxury in the wartime world of shortages and rations.

On these visits, my mother would accept a cigarette when Granny offered, but anyone could see that she was an amateur smoker, breathing in and puffing out between coughs. Granny, though, was a professional: she could convey deep meditation with a drag, dismiss an argument with an exhalation, draw a protective veil of smoke around herself and deliver an oracular remark from behind it, extinguish a conversation and a cigarette in one gesture. She was a study in the rhetoric of smoking. She also had the fascinating knack of blowing smoke rings, for me only, when she was in the mood.

She had just turned fifty. Every expedition to see her was a treat for me, if a rather scary one, for Granny was the first person I knew to maintain a visible disconnect between what she said and how she really felt. Extravagant daily labor went into her appearance—the graying permed hair, the rouge and powder, the scent, the afternoon rests taken in her darkened bedroom, from which she would emerge freshly dressed and in a new and unpredictable mood, along with her dogs, a pair of miniature Yorkshire terriers named Timmy and Charlie who slept at her feet. Granny was a creature of artifice, and though she was always smiling, one couldn't trust her smiles because there was often something wicked to be glimpsed behind them.

She was a doctor's daughter, and had married a newly qualified doctor in February 1915. My grandfather, called Hamilton Sandison, Ham for short, had read medicine at the University of Edinburgh and graduated just in time to catch the beginning of the First World War. He had served—oddly, it now seems to me—in all three armed services, army, navy, and air force, between 1914 and 1919. Doctoring at the front had broken him and given him an addiction to the bottle, or so Granny would say, and he had died in a motor smash in Maidenhead, Berkshire, in 1923—"suicide" according to Granny, "a dreadful accident," said my mother. She was then four, and my uncle Peter was six. Granny took her children to live in Switzerland, in search of "mountain air" to cure my uncle's incipient tuberculosis. There, she had met a retired lieutenant colonel in the Indian Army named Bertram Price Ellwood, who married her in 1928. Ellwood, twenty-two years older than Granny, was also, as it turned out (at least in Granny's version of things), impotent. On my mother's tenth birthday, in November 1928, the colonel gave her his present in an envelope over the breakfast table: inside was a single sheet of paper inscribed with the words "Man Know Thyself."

In 1934, when my uncle had either outgrown or been cured of his TB, the family came back to England, where they bought a house in the village of Saleway in rural Worcestershire. Appropriately enough, the house was called the Gap, and Granny and her colonel bickered inside it until 1941. Uncle Peter left to read engineering at the University of Birmingham; my mother stayed home writing love stories under the pen name Casey Mundell. When Colonel Ellwood and Granny finally separated, Granny got the house, which she managed to sell quickly and for a good price.

When my parents married in 1941, and later bought the White House in Hempton Green, Granny followed them. Like a secret policeman, she kept a discreet distance, but was always on our trail. Wherever we moved, she would set up house nearby, going from Worcestershire to Norfolk, Norfolk to Merseyside, Merseyside to Sussex, then Sussex to Hampshire, where she died. Only when my parents made their last move, to Leicestershire, did they escape the watchful attention of Granny, their determined shadow. She never learned to drive a car but always knew her taxi drivers by their first names and kept a Bradshaw's Railway Guide beside the telephone in the hall.

Sheringham in the early summer of 1945 was trying to return to normal life as a fishing village and genteel holiday resort. Along the beach, the rusting coils of barbed wire, wooden stakes, and concrete blocks were mostly cleared, and the antitank ditches were being filled in. Snipers' pillboxes and signs warning of unexploded mines remained, and so did the now-fading self-importance that comes to a place taught to think of itself as being on the front line of imminent invasion.

Above the high-tide line, the beach was a broad ridge of hard-to-walk-on pebbles, where a cluster of scruffy boats was drawn up beside the twin huts that said Ladies and Gentlemen (penny in the slot required). The smell of dead crabs and shit-and-disinfectant was powerful. But as the tide went out, it exposed a reach of glistening wet sand and a shallow spur of rock and drying bladder wrack with fascinating pools full of purple and scarlet sea anemones, darting shrimps, and scuttling crablets. There were no crowds here, just a few mothers and children, and the occasional uniformed soldier and his girl.

My mother and I usually came to the beach in the afternoons, when Granny was taking her rest and I had been enjoined to silence. I paddled tremulously in the foamy dribble left by the small waves but loved the rock pools, sticking my forefinger down inside the tentacled anemones and feeling their queer, otherworldly squeeze and suck. In the distance, where the High Street met the beach, a sparse handful of instrumentalists, all elderly, played from a bandstand, their sound carried by the gusty salt breeze, and for a moment one could catch a scatter of cornets above the rhythmical bass grunting of the tuba. The rock pool held a corner of deep water where tufts of overhanging red seaweed cast the bottom into impenetrable shadow, the lair of what I imagined to be an enormous fish. The more I stared into this deep, the more certain I became that there was life and movement there.

In every passing curiosity and flight of fancy, my mother was my ally, at my side and cheering me on. The word "lovely," spoken in her rather high and breathy voice, always sounded as if it were attached to double or triple exclamation marks. Of course I didn't notice that the lavish attention she paid to me was intimately connected to her nervous anxiety about what the BBC News might bring next, or that her air of rapt enthusiasm was at least in part a product of the Good

Manners curriculum at her finishing school. I just basked in the love and admiration that I took as my due.

Walking back to Granny's, we spelled our way through the town. Sheringham was rich in words, on road signs, shops, advertising hoardings. Every four-way crossing said Halt (which I confused with Holt, the place), and nearly every shop said Open or Closed. The High Street was a marvelous jumble of illegible and unpronounceable ciphers mixed in with words I recognized and could say aloud, like "tea," "fish," "Fry's" the cocoa maker, "draper." Each day I added new treasures to my word hoard. My memories begin in 1945, the last year of the war, presumably because as I learned to associate verbal symbols with the things they signified, I found I had the means to codify and store them.

Granny would serve high tea—grilled sardines (from a can) on toast, presented as a delicacy but which made me gag; sandwiches of presliced brown bread, with the faintest smear of margarine, and Shippam's paste; then raspberries picked from the bushes in the back garden. When the meal was over, I was given permission to get down from the table and play with Charlie, my favorite of the two dogs, in whose large eyes, half-curtained by his fine brown hair, I saw receptive sympathy and high intelligence.

It was Craven A time for Granny and my mother, their twin cigarettes supplying the punctuation for grown-up talk. Smoke filled out each pause and gave it substance, visibility, and smell. Granny would blow hers through her nostrils, like a horse on an icy morning; my mother, not inhaling, would release it from her lips in a succession of dainty mouthfuls.

Granny said, "Oh, I meant my Peter, dear, not yours," clarifying the distinction between her son, a lieutenant commander in the navy, and her son-in-law, my father, a major in the Royal Artillery, both equally far from home. I was then far too young to catch the disparaging tone in which Granny would mention my father, but I hear it now. (I was ten years old when she told me confidentially that my father had married my mother "for her money"—an interesting but groundless accusation, and a reminder of Granny's talents as the chief fabricator in the family on which my mother strung her stories for *Horner's Weekly*.)

We drove home from Granny's through the flat fields of Norfolk. The lanes were imprinted with the muddy spoors of the tractors that were displacing horses on the farms. Here and there one could see a solitary horse towing a plow, but the chief interest of the landscape was its display of toylike red and green machines. Horses, in any case, were everywhere, too familiar to be worth noticing. Most mornings I was woken before six by the irregular clock-clocking of hooves on the road outside my window as the milkman's float drew level with our front door; the rag-and-bone man had a horse and cart; farm produce, like the toppling loads of hay and beets, traveled through Hempton drawn by horses. The primary smell of the village was of horse dung, intermingled with the farty stink of Fakenham gas works, whenever there was any, east in the wind.

Just up the road from our house there was a small and poky everything shop which we visited most days. A hundred yards farther on, on the opposite side, were the coiled barbed wire, high chain-link fencing, and Nissen huts of the prisoner-of-war camp. After the surrender, Germans awaiting repatriation crowded into the shop, where they would make a fuss of me and teach me scraps of German like *bitte* and *guten Morgen*. At Christmastime in 1945 they had me singing, "Stille Nacht, heilige Nacht, Alles schläft; einsam wacht."

A few miles away was an American airbase, from which jeeps full of GIs regularly drove past the house. Americans—so much bigger, pinker, and more open-faced than the English or the Germans— swaggered through our world like a motorized plutocracy, burning through their gallons of unrationed petrol and spreading largesse in their wake. One afternoon an open jeep rolled slowly past our dining room window, the soldiers within scattering PX candy ("sweets" to us) on the street where children, some of my age, dived in the dirt for these treasures. I raced for the front door.

"No, dear: I can't let you go out with the village children."

At that instant, the memory cuts out as abruptly as a film tearing inside a projector. It just goes white. Freud says somewhere that we necessarily edit and suppress our memories of early childhood because we would otherwise have to reexperience the gales of lust and rage that then consumed us. This was evidently one of those moments. I can't recall any lust or rage, but my mother's remark about the village children still rankles. It was my first explicit introduction to my parents' world of anxious class divisions and distinctions. In no uncertain terms, it announced that my lot would be to stand behind a wall of separating glass; a spectator, not an actor, forcibly excluded from the enviable society on the street.

My mother made it plain that one should be afraid of the village children, tough and ferocious creatures whose characters had been formed in what she called "knocky-down schools." I would never go, she promised, to a knocky-down school, but to an establishment better designed to nurture tender plants like me. As it turned out, I was sent to a motley collection of schools around the country, some more knocky-down than others: a dame school, a prep school, two state primary schools, a public school (which in England meant a private school), then two state grammar schools. The main conclusion that I drew from this tour of the British educational system was that I was an obtrusively square peg in a succession of round holes. Academically, I learned as little as was conceivably possible for an otherwise bookish child in fourteen years of formal schooling. Humanly, I absorbed rather a lot of truths that I wished I could unlearn, but couldn't. It was, in other words, an averagely conventional education.

Chapter 3

MY GURNEY, LOADED with all my stuff—clothes; laptop; smartphone; Julia's pictures of our California trip, rolled together and secured by a big rubber band; and my new electric shaver—was wheeled up the ramp of the ambulance. From the pillow, in my new, croaky, old man's voice, I told the driver and his paramedic mate that I was sorry they would not be able to use their siren because I was only going to the rehabilitation ward. This awkward pleasantry was important to me: it was meant to announce that things were not as they might seem, that the supine, half-paralyzed figure on the gurney still had his marbles intact and would be back in the world, fully functioning, entirely rehabbed, in a very few days. For a while, as we drew away from the hospital campus and into the tame suburban streets, I quizzed the men about the shifts they worked, where they lived, and their snarled commutes from the southern townships to the city. They politely humored me in this, recognizing my questioning for the plaintive act of self-assertion that it was. We hit the freeway.

I thought of Larkin's poem "Ambulances,"

Closed like confessionals, they thread
Loud noons of cities . . .

and stared through the rear windows of my ambulance at the truck driver just behind us, who was lost in the business of extracting from his nose a booger with his right forefinger. When this mining operation was complete, he flicked finger and thumb together to get rid of the booger, reached down below my sight line, and came up with a cigarette. I saw the winking silver of a Zippo lighter, and watched him exhale.

Seeing someone else smoke made me count the days that I had gone without. Five, was it? No, four. Or was it only three? But if it was four, then Julia's graduation must be today, and surely that was tomorrow? Math had never been my strong subject, and in the ambulance I found myself wrestling with a simultaneous equation that was bafflingly hard to solve. I was frightened by my inability to do the sum, and more frightened by another piece of arithmetic: on Saturday, when the two "bloodings" hemorrhaged in my skull, several billion neurons had spilled out of my brain, but no one could tell me how many had been lost, or which functions had gone with them.

My backward-facing view showed that we had left the freeway and were in the grid of streets where hospitals and medical businesses were clustered, an area known locally as Pill Hill. As we slowed and came to a standstill, I saw a blank wall of institutional redbrick, old, severe, burgundy-colored, that put me in mind of School House, the dormitory in which I was incarcerated from the age of eleven at my boarding school. While being rolled down the ambulance ramp, I caught a glimpse of a neo-Gothic campanile topped by a substantial cross, made of stone or concrete, I couldn't tell which. We entered a new extension to the building that smelled of coffee and steamed milk. Past a Starbucks and the gift shop, we swung right, and the gurney was fed into an elevator. People stepped in and out as we rose slowly through the floors. Left, left, and left again. A corridor yawned, its length punctuated by double swing doors.

At each set of doors, there was a wall dispenser of antiseptic foam and the command to rinse your hands. My two chauffeurs were so habituated to this drill that they went through the motions of ritual purification like a pair of priests performing without a congregation. Out of the window, I spotted another cross, iron this time, and badly frayed by rust and weather, mounted on a gable end.

I asked the ambulance men if this was a Catholic hospital.

"Not so far as I know. Not particularly."

It must have been so once, I thought; and so it was. It used to be known as Providence Hospital, named for the Sisters of Providence, who were based in Montréal and sent to the West as missionaries. In 2000, Swedish Health Services, a secular nonprofit, originally founded by an immigrant Swedish surgeon in Seattle, acquired the hospital from their old rivals, the Catholics. Eleven years later, though I was in no position at the time to know it, Providence was negotiating to repossess Swedish, which had improvidently overspent itself before the Great Recession.

At the end of the corridor I was delivered to the nurses' station in the neurological rehabilitation ward. My first impression of the place was a man of middle age whose shaven skull had a healing incision that looked as if it had been inflicted with an axe. He was standing in pajamas and dressing gown, eating a doughnut and staring a bit vaguely at the TV set on the wall. I saw no nuns.

A nurse called for "Richard" on the sound system, which was of disconcerting, foghorn strength and was the chief wrecker of sleep on my first night in the ward, in a room just across from the nurses' station. Richard, though, would turn out to be a surprisingly urbane figure, neatly self-contained, with an acidic sense of humor, and I liked him at first sight.

He pushed me and my luggage to my room, lifted me off the gurney, and laid me on the bed, an all-bells-and-whistles sort of hospital bed of many levers. He then went off to find me a wheelchair. He came back with what he called the best of a bad lot, whose black vinyl armrests were peeling to expose their stuffing of pale gray artificial sponge. It wasn't too bad; twelve years on it's the same chair I'm sitting in now.

Richard gave me, in his words, The Tour, beginning with the coffee machine and a stale-tasting paper cup of the too-pale liquid, left over from the morning. Beyond the far end of the nurses' station he spotted a moving figure, Dr. Clawson, the doctor in charge of the neurological rehabilitation ward, and called his name. Clawson had the height of a basketball player and was dressed for jogging, all the way down to his multicolored Nike running shoes.

"Yes, you're the wine man," he said as Richard introduced us. "I don't think I've ever been asked that question before."

If "the wine man" was to become my sobriquet in the rehab ward, I'd've much preferred "the writer," a title I might have basked in. "Wine man" smacked of dipsomania.

I told Richard about the Romanian doctor in the other hospital and how she'd called ahead to ask on my behalf if I would be permitted a single glass of red wine at dinnertime each evening.

"You'd be better off buying your wine by the box, not the bottle," Richard said.

"I remember buying wines in boxes. It was a short acquaintance, not a happy one."

"When did you last buy wine in a box?"

"Twenty-five years ago, maybe, or maybe more."

"They've made huge improvements since then, you'd be surprised." He offered to stop by his local wine shop and pick up a new, hugely improved box for me at the end of his afternoon shift: a gesture that was the most quotidian thing that had happened to me since the stroke, and for which I was truly grateful.

He showed me the twin washing and drying machines for the use of patients, along with a cabinet full of various brands of detergent, then asked me if I'd like to see the gym.

"A gym is a gym is a gym. I'd sooner skip it."

"Well, it's down that long passageway there. Anything else?"

"I don't suppose there's a library here?"

"There probably ought to be, but no, you're right."

So we went back to my room, where Richard unloaded my stuff from the gurney and hung most of it in the clothes closet. Julia and a school friend were now lodging in the house, enjoying a spell of unsupervised adulthood, which left me free to ask her to bring over books from my shelves, laundered shirts, and clean socks and underwear, telling her that these requests were in lieu of rent. She was due to visit again this evening, and I'd given her a shopping list, to be bought at American Apparel, for two pairs of sweatpants and four T-shirts, the regular gear for the rehab ward that had been recommended by the Romanian doctor.

Richard took his leave. I must have eaten a tepid supper at around six, before Julia showed up at seven, accompanied by Jean, her mother, with whom I was now on amiable terms, after years of cool, studied politeness. I was glad to see them both. Julia handed me the brown paper American Apparel bag, blazoned in bold black type with the names of fashionable cities around the world where they had stores. Thus: São Paulo, Zurich, Paris, Milan . . . I checked for Seattle, but though I found Boston, New York, Miami, Chicago, New Orleans, and Los Angeles, there was no Seattle on the list. Was the city too provincial, too grungy in its dress code, or what?

As for the contents of the bag, I found them alienating. The color of the sweatpants, dark gray as I'd asked for, was just right, but each pair had an elastic waist and an elastic ankle, without a grown-up button in sight, let alone a zip. I was put in mind of the observation made by Alison Lurie in an essay for *The New York Review of Books,* written a decade or two before this, to the effect that old people in retirement tend to dress like toddlers as if to signal that their second childhood was now in full swing. I also associate T-shirts as suitable clothing for children, with an extra hazard for me, whose arms at their widest point are about three and a half inches in diameter, a relic of my infantile wasting disease. The short arms of T-shirts, ending several inches above the elbow, always look to me as if they were designed for weight lifters sporting gigantic biceps; my matchstick arms aren't nearly fat enough to occupy a T-shirt's plenitude of space with any aplomb at all.

Tiredness was overtaking me. Several times my head drooped involuntarily to my chest before I shook myself to stay awake. I thanked my shoppers for their work, and said that the sweatpants and T-shirts reminded me of the uniform for a new boarding school that was too keen by half on sports.

Julia, having sought permission from the nurses' station, was thumbtacking her prints of our latest road trip to the walls of my new quarters. Jean was filling the air with small talk. I was falling asleep.

June 13, 1996, about 10:00 p.m. My parents' bungalow in Market Harborough.

Monica and I were trying to shift my father's body from the old bedsheet on which he had been sleeping to a freshly laundered replacement, which meant rolling him as gently as possible from the one to the other. Monica stood at the head of the bed, grasping a corner of the sheet, and I stood at the foot, taking my cue from her. My father lay, naked except for an adult diaper, below us, his whole body yellow with jaundice. In life he'd always been a tall, slim man, but now his cancer had emaciated him to the point where one could see every bone in his body beneath the skin.

His diaper, so eerily like the loincloths in the myriad paintings and sculptures representing Jesus Christ on his cross, made me see double—Peter and his sometime creator and savior all at once. The most visible dividing line between them was the bedside table, crowded with medications, most of them painkillers. So while Christ died of the unimaginable torture inflicted by the nails hammered through his limbs into the wooden cross, my father was dying in the last decade of the twentieth century with the help of all the newest anesthetic medicines available for home use under a doctor's supervision. These made him woozy, but he felt little or no physical pain, at least so far as I knew.

As my mother and I, our four hands well apart, began lifting the sheet, Peter spoke:

"I'm going. I'm going." His voice was clear and strong, his tone apologetic and full, to my ear, of a loving farewell.

"You're not going, my darling! You're not! I'm coming to bed very soon." Her voice was equally strong and defiant.

After we'd spread the duvet cover over Peter, and Monica had determined that he was still with us, living and breathing, I returned in my rental car to the pub hotel, six miles from the bungalow, where I was staying; a half-drunk bottle of Famous Grouse whiskey awaited me in my room.

At 6:25 a.m. the phone beside my bed started ringing. Groggily, I picked up the receiver, knowing what was to be said and trying to prepare what I was going to say in response.

In a wobbly voice, my mother choked out the words, "Peter has gone."

Chapter 4

IN JANUARY 2010 I read a piece titled "Night" by the historian Tony Judt in *The New York Review of Books*. In it he describes living, as he then was, with advanced amyotrophic lateral sclerosis, Lou Gehrig's disease, that would kill him within the next few months. "In contrast to almost every other serious or deadly disease, one is . . . left free to contemplate at leisure and in minimal discomfort the catastrophic progress of one's own deterioration."

He articulates in detail the humiliating horrors of his condition. He was already quadriplegic, and soon he would lose his ability to use his mouth to dictate to his former student Eugene Rusyn, then his "long-time colleague" and collaborator. ALS had robbed him of his ability to scratch an itch, and he couldn't so much as turn in his bed without requiring a helper to roll his body over.

From this position of near total immobility, Judt created for himself a "memory chalet," based on the memory palaces created by Renaissance thinkers and explored by Frances Yates and other historians. His chalet was an actual building in the Swiss Alps that his family used to rent in his childhood for skiing holidays, and where in memory Judt could freely roam from room to room, filling the place with his own recollections. By night, when everyone in the New York apartment was asleep, he would steal into his private chalet, assemble his memories, and commit them to short essays, to be recited to Rusyn so that Bob Silvers could publish them in the next issue of *The New York Review of Books*. Not surprisingly, given his own paralysis, many of these pieces were about movement and travel—by steam train, London bus routes, cross-Channel ferries—and his father's passion for cars. I know that feeling: in my own dreams, almost without exception, I am free to wander on foot, sail boats, make road trips, and fly in single-engine float planes.

Judt's parents were unhappily married. His mother was born in the East End of London and worked there as a hairdresser. His father was of a different stamp altogether: born in Belgium to a Polish Jewish family, he had come to England in 1935 as an immigrant.

> In time he learned to speak impeccable English, but underneath he remained a continental: his taste for salads, cheeses, coffee, and wine ran frequently afoul of my mother's characteristically English unconcern for food and drink except as a fueling resource.

Joe Judt's "continental" taste extended to his cars, most of them Citroëns. Tony Judt says that during his childhood his father bought, serially, at least nine cars—all Citroëns except for a Panhard DB, also made in France. These were all high-performance sports models that had raced at Le Mans and were tuned to within an inch of their lives by Judt's father, who took his son racing on Sundays, going as far afield from London as Norfolk and the East Midlands, to participate in club-level, amateur motorsport events. Joe's obsession with fast cars sits oddly beside the fact that his income derived from the proceeds of a hairdressing shop, and also Judt's remark that his family was "very lower middle class," a judgment that would have severely injured Joe's pride because the cars he bought represented the world to which he eagerly aspired and believed he'd been accepted by. Not for nothing did he become the president of the Citroën Car Club.

Here's Judt on his dad's cars:

> There was something slightly embarrassing about our cars. They suggested, in an age of austerity and provincialism, an aggressively exotic and "foreign" quality to the family—causing my mother in particular to feel uneasy. And of course they were (relatively) expensive and thus ostentatious. I recall one occasion in the mid-fifties when we drove across London to visit my maternal grandparents, who lived in a run-down terraced house on a

side street in Bow. Cars in that part of London were still thin on the ground and were most likely to be little black Ford Populars and Morris Minors, testaments to the limited means and conventional tastes of their owners. And here we were, clambering out of a shining white Citroën DS19, like aristocrats come to inspect their lowly tenants. I don't know how my mother felt— I never asked. My father was enjoyably absorbed in the envious attention his new car was attracting. I wanted to disappear down the nearest manhole.

The Memory Chalet, the book, was posthumously published in the fall of 2010 (Judt died in August that year at sixty-two), and it is one of the most engaging memoirs that I have ever read. It takes us everywhere, deep into Judt's boyhood, his infatuation with kibbutz life in Israel, his education in Cambridge, where he went on to become a fellow of King's College, his acquisition of several languages spoken in Eastern Europe and his travels there, his wary descent onto US soil and its splendid universities, his two divorces and three marriages, and more, much more. Truly, the nondescript, rented-by-the-week Swiss chalet, visited only in the dark, turned out to be an extraordinary treasure house.

For the last decade plus, I've looked up to Judt as a mentor and alter ego. He puts to shame my own disablement and reminds me of just how lucky I am to live in writerly solitude on my own terms still. I never met him in the flesh, but his voice, quiet, even-toned, donnish, and as he said of himself, "very English," in his final years hoarse and short of breath (he had to wear an oxygen apparatus, attached to his nostrils and upper lip like an unwieldy mustache), is a regular visitor to my workroom. If I can do this, paralyzed from the neck down with terminal ALS, the voice growls, what's up with you?

Chapter 5

THE WAR RESCUED my father, Peter Raban, from his first job as a probationary teacher at a primary school in the West Midlands and restored him to his proper station as an officer and a gentleman.

He'd hoped to go on to university (which to him meant Oxford or Cambridge) from his boarding school in Worcester, but his dismal Higher School Certificate results nixed that ambition. He went instead to King Alfred's, a teacher-training college in Winchester, Hampshire, where (as he would point out more than fifty years later) he was the only student from a public school, and in June 1938, when he was nineteen going on twenty, he graduated with a certificate that licensed him to teach in state-funded primary schools.

Tall, beanpole-thin, dark-complexioned with a shock of coal-black hair, painfully shy and socially awkward, my father returned home to the tiny village of Hadzor in Worcestershire, just outside Droitwich Spa, to spend the summer hunting for a job within commuting distance of his father's rectory. Sometime in the nineteenth century the Church Commissioners had combined Hadzor and its equally small neighbor Oddingley into a single parish, so that although he had fewer than two hundred parishioners in all, my grandfather had two ancient churches to maintain and at least two Big Houses, Oddingley Grange and Hadzor Hall, whose owners would expect deference from their local clergyman.

My father was eleven or twelve (he was vague about the date) when his mother, Edith, walked out on my grandfather and went to live in her hometown of Oldham in Lancashire—an event that must have generated gossip in the villages and the Big Houses, and must have caused my father both sorrow and deep embarrassment, for Anglican priests and wives were supposed to set an exemplary marital standard for their congregations. She took my father's brother, Nick, with her. I don't remember my father ever speaking of his mother in my lifetime, but he did visit her for short stays in Oldham at Christmas and other holidays while he went on living with his father at the rectory. His Worcester boarding school was only six miles south of Hadzor, within easy walking distance of home.

My father had hoped to find a job in Droitwich or Worcester, but the only position he was offered was at Colley Lane Primary in Cradley Heath, a town in the industrial Black Country west of Birmingham—a twenty-mile train ride from Droitwich that took my father into an alien world for which he was totally unprepared. Benjamin Disraeli had once said of Cradley Heath that it was the "Hell Hole of England," and the town earned a chapter to itself in an 1897 book on women's sweated labor, Robert Harborough Sherard's *The White Slaves of England*. In the nineteenth and early twentieth centuries, the place was known as the world's capital of hand-hammered chain making, and boasted, somewhat weirdly, that the anchor chain of the *Titanic* had been manufactured there. It was an improvised, ad hoc town of steepling factory chimneys, coal mines with gibbet-like scaffolds for their winding gear, and a tangle of streets lined with terraced hovels, many of them with a furnace in the backyard or in a side room, where men and women melted the iron rods that they hammered into chains, rehydrating themselves with beer at threepence a quart. Pay, at best, was twopence halfpenny an hour. Sherard described it as a "terribly ugly and depressing town."

By the time my father arrived in 1938, it had grown uglier still during the Great Depression. Mechanization had all but killed manual chain making, and most of the coal pits had fallen into disuse. Unemployment figures were so high, even in that era of mass unemployment, that questions were asked in Parliament about the crisis in Cradley Heath.

My father had never seen anything like it in his life, and it terrified him. This industrial slum on the farther outskirts of Birmingham was simply beyond his comprehension. At Colley Lane Primary, he lost control of his class. The children never stopped mocking his lah-di-dah accent, and he found their hybrid Black Country dialect perfectly impenetrable. In the staff room, he was little better off. In a letter written to my mother at the end of the war, he would describe himself as "an out-and-out Conservative"; his colleagues at Colley Lane were, with good reason, solid Labour Party supporters, and he made no friends among them. In another 1945 letter, he described his time at the school as a "year of bitterness and hell that I shall never forget."

Between the "peace for our time" euphoria that Neville Chamberlain brought back from Munich in September 1938 and Hitler's invasion of Czechoslovakia in March 1939, the British public reluctantly came to realize that war with Germany would soon break out, and my father jumped at the chance of escape from Colley Lane and the prospect of a new life. At King's School, Worcester, he had been more successful in the Officers' Training Corps than he was in his School Certificate: he had passed the two-part military test called Cert. A, the basic requirement for being considered for a commission. He went about getting one in the old-fashioned way, by visiting the Big House, Oddingley Grange on Trench Lane, whose chatelaine was a Mrs. White, aunt of Lieutenant Colonel Philip Robinson, the commanding officer of the Royal Artillery Sixty-Seventh Field Regiment, Territorial Army (TA). The Territorials, roughly equivalent to the US National Guard and now retitled as the Army Reserve, were a force of volunteer weekend soldiers. Colonel Robinson approved, and a gruff handshake transformed my father into a second lieutenant, though he had to serve his time as a failed schoolteacher until June 1939.

There was a twist to this Big House story. Before it became the Grange, it had been the rectory, and my father had been born in one of its seven ample bedrooms, and had grown up playing in its garden, so his calling on Mrs. White was for him a sort of homecoming. Shortly after World War I, the Church Commissioners had begun selling off vicarages and rectories by the dozen because they were too big, too expensive to heat and light, and required a squad of servants way beyond the means of the average parish clergyman. My grandfather had been moved to a bungalow, grandly renamed the rectory, on the same street as the Grange, where he made do with a daily housemaid who came in from the village.

By the time my father enlisted, the British government was scrambling to put the country on a war footing. In March 1939, the Territorial Army was doubled in size to 340,000 men. In April, conscription was introduced for twenty- and twenty-one-year-old males to go on a six-month military training course, and on the day that Britain declared war on Germany, September 3, the call-up was extended to able-bodied men between the ages of eighteen and forty-one. Tented camps across the country filled up with civilians learning to be soldiers, my father among them.

His best subject at school had been math; he had a knack for carrying sums in his head which made him a natural candidate for the Royal Artillery, and he possessed his own slide rule (when my father came home from the war at the end of 1945, this instrument became for me an object of occult veneration). Calculation of range and trajectory came easily to him as he practiced lobbing eighteen-pound shells from Mark I field guns left over from World War I.

The regiment left Worcester in the summer of 1939 to camp out near Lyndhurst in Hampshire, then moved in the autumn to Aldbourne in Wiltshire, on the edge of Salisbury Plain. Both were conventionally picturesque places: Lyndhurst was in the middle of the New Forest, an area of woods and heathlands whose wild ponies often wandered into the town's streets; Aldbourne was an unspoiled village with the usual accoutrements of church, five pubs, cottages, a green, a duck pond, and a purling stream. It might be nice to think that the War Office picked these locations to accustom the young recruits to being away from home and to provide them with fresh memories of the peaceful and bucolic country they'd be fighting for, but the nearby artillery ranges in both places were the more likely draw.

At Aldbourne the troops learned that in January they would set sail for France, where they'd become part of the British Expeditionary Force (BEF), which had been assembling across the Channel since September's declaration of war against Germany. Because of the imminence of their departure, the Sixty-Seventh Regiment was granted an extended home leave for Christmas. My father and one other officer volunteered to remain in Aldbourne over the holiday to guard the fort while the other soldiers went home. This saved him from the annual embarrassment of having to choose whether to spend Christmas with his mother in Oldham or his father in Hadzor.

He had another, perhaps more powerful and certainly more consequential, reason to stay on in Aldbourne. He'd been invited to a formal dinner dance at a flash hotel in Newbury just fifteen miles from the village. The party was to celebrate the engagement between my mother's brother, Peter Sandison, and Connie Major, both in their final year at the University of Birmingham. My uncle Peter, as he would become, was slated to join the Royal Navy as a lieutenant on his graduation in June. The war and mass enlistment had already caused a shortage of available men, and my father, who was no dancer, was dragged in to play the role of my mother's partner. He drove to Newbury in his full dress uniform, with highly polished Sam Browne belt (the polishing done by Gunner Tench, his batman, or orderly), riding boots, and spurs (he removed the spurs for "the dancing" to avoid inflicting serious injuries around the floor).

The event, as he wrote more than fifty years later, was his introduction to a milieu more "sophisticated" and "cosmopolitan" than anything he had experienced before, and he was more than a little overawed by the company he was keeping at the hotel that evening. He and my mother had met at the Grange, where my mother sometimes went riding with Mrs. White's daughter Barbara, and they had made occasional trips to the pictures in Droitwich and Worcester in my mother's secondhand Humber, but they were still more acquaintances than friends, having never held hands, let alone kissed. (Their first kiss would happen nearly a year after Newbury.) Listening to my mother talking with her brother in their peculiar sibling argot of French and English, the relic of their Swiss childhood, left my father feeling severely outclassed. But my parents-to-be had much in common, still to be unearthed, especially their shared unhappy secret of being children in disintegrating and disintegrated marriages.

On January 11, after my father had made whirlwind visits to his parents at Oldham and Hadzor, he sailed from Southampton aboard one of two requisitioned passenger steamers, escorted by Royal Navy destroyers, on an overnight Channel crossing to Le Havre. It was his first time abroad, and everything about France was novel to his Worcestershire eyes.

This was still the period of the Phony War, when Britain and France waited for the Nazis to mount an invasion by land or sea and their spies were producing a multitude of conflicting intelligence reports. In England, every day brought false alarms, with the urgent high-low-high-low screaming of air raid sirens, shortly followed by the long, sustained note of the all clear. People were enjoined to carry their boxed gas masks with them everywhere, and the dusk-to-dawn blackout was punctiliously enforced by civilian wardens, causing an abrupt rise in traffic fatalities. But the most conspicuous feature of the Phony War was the havoc caused by the "evacuees" from the big cities: several million school-age children, along with pregnant women and mothers with their under-fives, who were bundled onto government-requisitioned trains and sent out into the countryside in the first four days of September 1939. This chaos, born of bureaucratic panic and a gross overestimation of the likely casualties of German bombing raids, was called Operation Pied Piper, and it plays a central part in Evelyn Waugh's fine seriocomic novel of the Phony War, *Put Out More Flags*.

A photograph from the period, taken in Le Mans, nicely catches the mood. Two teams are playing football. One side—clearly the Brits—is clad in stripped-down battledress, and the other—presumably the French—is in dark shorts and white jerseys. The only spectators we can see are a cluster of British soldiers, one of whom stands behind a single anti-aircraft gun mounted on a flimsy-looking tripod. He seems to have his eyes on the game, not the sky. Anything might happen. The Bren gun is there just in case. There's a war on, but nobody on the field appears to really believe it, and the poor gunner must have been the butt of everybody's jokes. The short magazine above the surprisingly narrow barrel looks as if it holds barely enough rounds to bring down a pheasant, let alone a German bomber.

The Sixty-Seventh Field Regiment, and all its trucks, guns, and supplies, disembarked at Le Havre and set up camp at a nearby Normandy village, where they reassembled themselves and their weapons. No doubt they made plans with the French for a series of football matches to strengthen their alliance. My father was not a football man. He had always played rugby at school and despised football as a game suitable only for the working class. He was, however, a competent player of contract bridge and a keen reader of Ely Culbertson's bridge books. A regular four, including my father, whiled away evenings in the officers' mess playing for low stakes (five shillings was a win worth noting in my father's diary, as was a loss of two shillings and sixpence).

The phoniness of the Phony War in Western Europe was due to the extreme reluctance of all sides to become the first to kill civilians on their home grounds (though Germany showed no such compunction when it came to bombing Polish civilians on its eastern front). Enemy shipping, both naval and merchant, was fair game for the British, French, and German air forces and navies, though when the RAF sent flights of bombers over German cities, they dropped many tons of propaganda pamphlets but no bombs. The first British civilian to be killed at home in the war was an Orkney Islander who died in a Luftwaffe raid on the naval base at Scapa Flow on March 16, 1940. Three days later, the RAF retaliated by sending fifty bombers to destroy the German seaplane base at Hörnum in the Frisian Islands, a raid that lasted for seven hours between 8:00 p.m. and 3:00 a.m. on the night of March 19–20. An officer at the briefing described the atmosphere as "charged with anticipation and excitement at the prospect that we were going to drop bombs instead of those 'bloody leaflets.'" The press called the attack a triumph (VAST DAMAGE IN RAF RAID was the headline in the Australian paper the *Argus*), but an aerial reconnaissance the next day showed the base had escaped with hardly a scratch. The Air Ministry announced that their photos of Hörnum after the raid were of too poor quality to be released.

My father was a member of A Troop, 265 Battery. His troop commander was Captain Jimmy Styles. The usual complement of officers in a Royal Artillery troop at that time was a captain and two subalterns, but nowhere in my father's papers can I find mention of the second subaltern, and it may be that Styles eventually went into battle with just one, very green, second lieutenant.

In Normandy, A Troop went out on training exercises (my father, fast becoming proficient in military terminology and slang, always called them "schemes"), was treated to lectures on gas warfare, and did regular gas drills—an indication of just how closely the Second World War was expected to follow the pattern of the First, and of how misguided that assumption would turn out to be. It took the British far too long to learn that blitzkrieg, or lightning war, was an entirely different war from the long, slow war of attrition they had fought between 1914 and 1918. The sixty-six thousand casualties that the BEF would suffer between May 10 and June 25, 1940, were a measure of their disastrous failure to grasp what it was that they were facing.

One may presume that the bridge four steadily improved their game as they got to know one another's bidding habits and foibles. Monica wrote at least two letters to my father at this time, but there was no particular intimacy in them because she was just taking part in a War Office campaign to encourage women in England to write to servicemen overseas in order to let them know they were not forgotten at home. My mother was a fluent and enthusiastic writer of letters and probably sent dozens to male acquaintances across the length and breadth of France.

Warfare and tourism are less often linked than they should be. For my father, as for so many of his fellow soldiers, this was his first chance to experience the continuous cascade of new sensations that drenches the stranger when he sets foot in a foreign land: the exotic morning smell of freshly baked bread from the boulangerie as it mingles with the fierce tang of unfiltered Gauloises and Gitanes; the surprising styles of architecture, shop fronts, and street furniture; the costumes of the people; the nonstop mental arithmetic as one translates prices in francs into pounds, shillings, and pence—everything, in its strangeness, insists on attention being paid all at once. The soldier is a tourist, not just in every moment he has to himself but in all the other moments when he's meant to be concentrating on something else. How many have died because they became distracted by an oddly colored bird, a zigzag molding around the doorway of a nearby church, a woman wearing a burka, the calligraphy of a foreign road sign?

The main concentration of troops was in northeastern France toward the Belgian border—the same area that the British, French, and Germans had turned into a welter of mud and blood in the dreadful 1914–18 war. So the Sixty-Seventh Regiment set out for battlegrounds that were grimly vivid in the memories and nightmares of the older men.

In an unending slow military convoy, the trucks carrying soldiers and towing field guns, policed by motorcycle outriders (of whom I believe my father was one), wound through the lanes of agricultural France. The soldiers looked out on a land far less crowded than their own; its fields and woods bigger, its villages smaller, its châteaux familiar from the labels on wine bottles, its workers quaint in their berets. Army trucks are made for singing songs and telling dirty jokes and stories. From the trucks came ragged choruses of voices going through the repertoire of songs from the previous war: "Mademoiselle from Armentières," "When This Lousy War Is Over," "We Are Fred Karno's Army," "Oh! It's a Lovely War." The doubling in size of the TA in March '39 with unemployment numbers still painfully high made even the allowance paid for weekend soldiering an attractive proposition, and many of the singers were in their late teens, their faces pitted with adolescent acne.

The view from the back of each jolting truck held the eye because of its inalienable Frenchness—rectangular blue letter boxes instead of the red pillar boxes of England; pissoirs that exposed the trousers and shoes of the men peeing in them; a dead-straight road refining to a point in the far distance and lined with hundred-foot poplars just coming into leaf.

The man-boys know they are immortal; death has no place on their agenda, even though the guns, mounted on limbers that their trucks are towing, all have their barrels trained warningly on the truck behind. Testosterone is a wonderful thing. After weeks of aimless waiting, the soldiers are at last on the move, heading toward their big adventure.

When darkness fell, the convoy slowed to a crawl, each truck relying on a single headlamp, hooded, veiled, and tilted sharply down. The drivers craned forward, noses to the windscreens, as they tried to make out the road ahead and the black, blocky outline of the gun and limber immediately in front.

Crossing the river Somme, the convoy entered the territory of mass graves commemorating the fallen of the First World War in the gently rolling countryside of the old western front. The Imperial War Graves Commission, begun in 1917 and now known as the Commonwealth War Graves Commission, is and was a lavishly funded institution that during and after the Great War was able to enlist the writer Rudyard Kipling and architects like Sir Edwin Lutyens and Sir Reginald Blomfield, along with a roll call of 1920s sculptors. Each cemetery—and there are a great number of them in northern France and Belgium—has one or two, and some have both, prominent memorials, Blomfield's Cross of Sacrifice and Lutyens's determinedly nonreligious and abstract Stone of Remembrance. These stand at the east end of the cemetery, landmarks above a sea of identical pale tombstones that all face east as the Allied soldiers faced the Germans on the western front.

Siegfried Sassoon, the war poet and versatile writer in other forms, who fought in the trenches in France as an infantry officer in the Royal Welch Fusiliers and in 1916 won the Military Cross for "conspicuous gallantry," took an acid view of the work of the War Graves Commission. Ypres in Belgium (known by soldiers as "Wipers") was the site of a many-times-contested salient. Here Sir Reginald Blomfield designed a massive triumphal arch-cum-cenotaph known as the Menin Gate, which was completed in 1927. Wikipedia describes the "barrel-vaulted passage for traffic" called the Hall of Memory as having the engraved names of 54,395 soldiers "who died in the Salient but whose bodies have never been identified or found." Shortly after the opening of this grandiose memorial, widely thought to be Blomfield's masterpiece, Sassoon wrote an angry poem, "On Passing the New Menin Gate," describing it as "a pile of peace-complacent stone":

Well might the Dead who struggled in the slime
Rise and deride this sepulchre of crime.

The young British soldiers of 1940 had far better reason to go to war with Germany than their fathers had in 1914—curbing the egomaniac dictator's ambition to overwhelm the rest of Europe was a more plausible cause than intervening in Russia's quarrel with Austria over the murder of the archduke in Sarajevo by a Serbian assassin. Yet some at least of the defiantly cheery songbirds in the convoy must have felt a twinge of foreboding as their trucks passed the enormous war cemeteries. Here we go again—another four years in the trenches on the western front? What no one could have imagined was how quickly and humiliatingly they were going to be outmaneuvered, outpaced, and defeated by the Germans.

The phony land war in Western Europe abruptly became real on April 9, 1940, when Hitler simultaneously invaded Denmark and Norway. War in Denmark lasted just six hours, with German forces arriving by parachute, in tanks and armored cars, and on bicycles. Denmark, thought of by Germans as a country of fellow Aryans, was very lightly occupied and largely left to govern itself thereafter. Norway was a different matter. Here Germany met with fierce resistance from Norwegian, French, and British armies, navies, and air forces, and the fighting went on for two months until Norway eventually surrendered to the Nazis on June 9. It took a short while for Vidkun Quisling, the collaborationist, to seize power, but his surname lives on, in lowercase, as a synonym for "traitor."

My father's convoy found its destination at the drab coal-mining village of Évin-Malmaison just north of Douai and about twenty miles from the Belgian border. There were no signs yet of German troops moving west, though they were expected any day now. The Sixty-Seventh Field Regiment continued to mount daily gas drills, and was ordered to rehearse a new task: digging and building gun pits.

One advantage of a regiment of weekend soldiers is that the great majority of them have expertise in their weekday professions. So, when builders, ditchdiggers, bricklayers, and other workers in the construction industry were invited to step forward, an entire skilled labor force emerged from the ranks. The army manual on gun pits was passed around, and the men set to work. When Major General Watson, the commander of the Royal Artillery, saw what the Sixty-Seventh Regiment was doing, he summoned the colonels of all other artillery regiments so that they could observe how the job should be properly done—at least so says the regimental history.

The armies massing on the Belgian border became a sea of slightly different shades of khaki (French uniforms were greener than British ones), and they brought a huge temporary boom to the local economy. Everything that could be eaten, drunk, smoked, or sent home as souvenirs vanished from the tables of restaurants and the shelves of shops. The soldiers, in the hyper-acquisitive mood that arises from boredom and nervous anxiety, shopped extravagantly. The Anglo-French football games persisted, and so did the rubbers of bridge in the British officers' messes. The second bottle of wine, the third double Scotch, became the daily habit. All this paralyzed inactivity made the ennui thicken like curdling milk in the French air.

All artillery units in the BEF were ordered back to the Somme for practice on the ranges there, probably because doing something was better than doing nothing at all. Their gunnery practice lasted less than two days; on May 10 they were hastily recalled to the border as news broke that Germany was invading the Netherlands, Luxembourg, and Belgium. The Royal Artillery scrambled to rejoin the flood of troops pouring across the Belgian border, and raced to take up its preplanned defensive positions east of Brussels along the river Dyle.

According to my father's notes made more than fifty years later, the elderly eighteen-pounders (measured by the weight of their shells) had a range of only nine thousand yards, just over five miles, which meant that the enemy had to be too close for comfort before they became a reachable target. Having hastily settled their guns into position on the evening of May 12, A Troop wouldn't actually fire them until May 15, leaving them too-ample time to digest the shocking news that Germany had hoodwinked them, and they had been caught in a trap set by Hitler and his generals.

The Allies believed that in defending the river Dyle they were protecting western Belgium from the main thrust of the German advance, which they saw as another iteration of Germany's invasion of Belgium in the early days of the First World War. This was exactly what Hitler meant them to think. In fact, the westerly advance of the Nazi troops was conducted by Army Group B (with its twenty-six infantry and three armored divisions), while the much larger Army Group A (thirty-eight infantry and seven armored divisions) was secretly heading south into France through the Ardennes Forest, at unprecedented speed.

General Gamelin, now commander in chief of the French armies, though he would be relieved of his command later in the month, had once called the Ardennes "Europe's best tank obstacle," and a prewar French survey of the forest had found that, should Germany try to force their way through the Ardennes, it would take them at least five days. The terrain was too rough, too steep, too thickly wooded to allow faster progress. But the German generals, warning their troops that they would have to forgo sleep for at least three nights running, had issued everyone with Pervitin tablets, a powerful methamphetamine and an early form of crystal meth. High and wide awake, the tank drivers crashed through the forest, hidden from aerial surveillance by the canopy of fresh leaves. Blitzkrieg required its fighters to be on meth, as Norman Ohler has shown in his book *Blitzed: Drugs in the Third Reich*. When on May 12 the seven panzer divisions emerged from the trees near Sedan on the river Meuse, they took the French utterly by surprise. Sedan was thinly defended, mostly by Army Reservists, and the river was crossed on the thirteenth. Beyond it lay many miles of undefended farmland. The tanks, fueled as much on Pervitin as gasoline, sped on, leaving the marching infantry far behind.

The aim of this "sickle cut" (Churchill's phrase for it, later translated into German as *Sichelschnitt*) was to slice the Allied forces in two, to occupy the Channel ports, surround the armies now in Belgium, and drive them into the sea. General Erwin Rommel, who led the speediest of the tank divisions, was said to take Pervitin as if it were his daily bread. Ohler writes: "He had no apparent sense of danger—a typical symptom of excessive methamphetamine consumption."

The British, getting by on tea and Wild Woodbines (or in my father's case St. Bruno Flake pipe tobacco), were a poor match for the Germans on their army-issue uppers. At Leefdaal, the two gun batteries and the regimental HQ at last came under intense German shellfire on May 14; Stukas dive-bombed the British artillery and strafed them with machine guns. On the fifteenth, the German troops came close enough for the batteries' World War I guns to fire at them, which they did in barrages of one hundred shells per gun before they were ordered to retreat to Auderghem on the southeastern outskirts of Brussels, where they were again in action until nine in the morning of the sixteenth, when they had to retreat again to the western side of the Brussels-Charleroi Canal. Here they were heavily bombed yet again, and it was midnight when the order came to retreat to Aspelare, a hamlet a few miles due west of Brussels. According to the brief regimental history published in 1964, the regiment's centenary year, "it was a nightmare move; all the Division was using the same road and traffic conditions were appalling. Exhausted drivers were continually falling asleep over the wheels of their trucks, helping to spread the confusion." It seems likely that the anonymous author of the history was present at the humiliating defeat he describes. His wild misspellings of nearly every place-name in the account (Yvonne Mal Maison for Evin-Malmaison, for instance) suggest a state of battle-weary confusion. The regiment was dead on its feet after more than three days of continuous fighting and retreating, shell-shocked by the noise of both their own and their enemies' artillery, and terrorized by the Stuka dive-bombers' sirens that wailed as they dived and were designed to spread panic far beyond their immediate targets. The Germans were euphoric and alert on crystal meth; the British, French, and Belgians were stupefied zombies.

Somewhere between Leefdaal and Aspelare my father's troop com-mander, Captain Jimmy Styles, was killed. That and the fact that it was "near Brussels" are all that my father mentions in his skimpy notes made in 1995, less than a year before his death, and by the end of the sentence he's arrived at Dunkirk. There's no mention of how my father got along with Styles, no mention of how he was killed, or how long he took to die. Did A Troop dig a grave for his remains? Were other men killed or wounded in the attack? I think that when my father looked back on that long sequence of sleepless nights and days, all he could see was a distressing, phantasmagoric blur in which one fact was plain—not so much Jimmy Styles's death, but how it had fallen to my father to keep the survivors in the troop alive.

Chapter 6

LIKE SO MANY of his generation, my father was taciturn about the war after his return home in 1945. Throughout my childhood and adolescence, I never heard him speak of it, and I was in my mid-twenties before he began to unbutton himself on the subject, mostly in lighthearted stories about, for instance, how he'd returned to his billet in northern Italy after a bibulous New Year's party at a neighboring officers' mess, and fallen through the glass of somebody's snow-covered greenhouse, his floppy drunkenness saving him from injury. But I watched as the lineup of histories of World War II grew longer and longer on his bookshelves. The war was a private matter, a secret to be kept between his older and his younger selves. The sheer incommunicability of actual warfare kept him silent. Writing after the First World War, Siegfried Sassoon was eloquent on how his time on leave in England made him boil with anger because, although the English Channel is barely twenty miles across at its narrowest point, the gulf between the meaning of war to a soldier in the trenches and the meaning of war to the English noncombatants, with their complacent talk of heroes and patriotism and *pro patria mori,* was oceanically unbridgeable even when the sound of the guns across the Channel became audible through Kent and Sussex windows. The flight to Dunkirk must have seemed like that to my father: inexplicable, unspeakable, a lonely, private nightmare.

Luckily there was another second lieutenant, also a Territorial, serving in a Worcestershire regiment infantry battalion, whose very lively thirty-thousand-word memoir, written in 1946, of the retreat from Brussels to Dunkirk bristles with closely observed contingent detail. E. J. Haywood, an intelligence officer answerable to the brigadier in whose car he traveled, was just sufficiently detached from his regiment to take a broad view of the retreat. The brigadier is called "the Brig" throughout; the general commanding the division is known as "Bulgy" and another junior officer as "Puffer." When Haywood refers to a fellow subaltern as "Crumpets," I can hear his English boarding school accent and catch his confident self-possession. He speaks both French and German well enough to make himself understood to the natives and captured invaders, and has about him a lightly worn, unselfconscious patriotism and pride in his regiment. He is also modestly knowledgeable about French wines, and he smokes a pipe. Except in that last, shared characteristic, he and my father seem like polar opposites: the one socially at ease, with sophisticated tastes; the other shy and fearful of saying or doing the wrong thing.

In his memoir, Haywood conjures the state of the roads leading south and west from Brussels in mid-May as one catastrophic traffic jam, with three fleeing armies and their vehicles having to struggle for space with an equal number of civilian refugees headed in the same direction, in hooting cars, on bicycles, with horse-drawn carts laden with piles of hastily packed possessions, topped, as often as not, with a shawled grandparent too sick or lame to walk. Others trundled pushcarts, prams, and wheelbarrows before them. Everyone in their mid to late twenties or older had firsthand memories of the earlier war in Flanders and its dreadful noise and destruction. Since 1918, the land had been patiently restored to a peaceful quilt of farms and repaired villages, punctuated by vast, well-tended military cemeteries. Now the whole horror appeared to be happening all over again.

Haywood writes:

Once that morning I saw German aircraft attacking refugees. A few planes flew up and down the road dropping bombs at will. They then returned, one after the other, flying low over the heads of their screaming victims, spraying them with machine-gun bullets. Our car was in the thick of it, but Jim yelled at the driver to keep going, and we were lucky. We saw people hit or blown to pieces; carts and cars burning or shattered; small children crouching in the ditches in a nightmare of terror; farm horses threshing in agony and making the road slippery with blood. I bounced about in the car, scared and angry, and, in futile rage, leaned out of the window and fired my revolver at the aircraft. It was the only time I ever fired it, and I wasted six bullets. Jim did not turn round, but shouted, "Use a r-rifle, you b-b-bloody fool!" However, by the time I had got the driver's rifle poking through the window, the raid was over. We could do nothing for the civilians. Our job was to get to Goyck without loss of time. Again there was that sickening feeling of "letting down" civilians we had come so far to protect.

Wherever he could, Haywood begged the refugees to go home for their own safety, not just to ease the traffic flow for the soldiers. Few listened to his urgently repeated call, "Ne bougez pas!" When so vast a number of people are going with the herd, who dares to resist the impulse to join them? From cottages and farmhouses came families desperate to put the war at their backs, leaving their homes to be looted—mostly for food and drink—by soldiers and civilians alike.

Haywood describes one such deserted farmhouse, where he, the Brig, and their staff of twenty billeted themselves for the night:

> The adjoining farm was deserted, so we collected eggs and also killed a few hens. There were queer noises coming from an outhouse, so, pistol in hand, I opened the door to investigate. Out came tumbling, squawking hens and grunting pigs, followed by some angry, but dignified ducks waddling into the sunshine and quacking furiously. I found three sheep tied up and bleating. I set them free and they quickly scampered outside. They all had a much better chance of survival in the open.

He was evidently born and bred in the English countryside, for he identifies a peculiar sound associated with the retreat: the disconsolate mooing of cows, their udders painfully distended because they hadn't been milked in days.

The infantry brigade to which Haywood was attached had to march everywhere they went, often for twelve hours and more at a stretch, while the Brig's car kept on falling back to pick up stragglers and look for lost soldiers sleeping in ditches. Frequently the Brig marched in step with his men to bolster their morale. The retreat soon fell into a pattern: each day would be spent trying to hold off the German advance westward with artillery and rifle fire; each night they'd fall back to take up new positions on the west bank of the next river. So the Senne was crossed, then the Dendre, then the Escaut, as the Franco-Belgian upper reaches of the Scheldt are called.

The Escaut is a major river that flows broad and deep from south to north, and it was hoped by the Allies that here the Germans would be not just temporarily deterred but stopped in their tracks. But this plan was jinxed by poor communications between the separate armies that too often depended on easily cut telephone landlines. Upstream of the British and Belgian positions, the French busied themselves with engineering an "inundation" that would place a lake between their own troops and the Germans. The predictable effect of the French dam was that hour by hour the river shrank between its banks, and with every lowering of the water the Escaut became less and less an obstacle to the German tank divisions. After four days of heavy fighting, the Allies had to abandon the river.

The troops were now flat-out exhausted, hungry (on half rations, then on whatever they could scavenge), dirty, and smelling rank as skunks. On narrow roads clogged with marching infantry, vehicular traffic, and hundreds of thousands of panicking refugees, the retreating armies, harassed by German shellfire and regular attacks from the air, were lucky if they could achieve walking pace for more than a few minutes at a time. The din of honking horns only underscored its own futility.

The Pervitin-fueled German Army Group A continued its advance into French territory, only temporarily slowed by an Anglo-French counterattack at Arras on May 21. On May 22, the Channel port of Boulogne was cut off from the rest of the BEF, and Calais was similarly encircled the next day. On May 24, just before noon, with German tanks less than twenty miles from Dunkirk, acting on the advice of Colonel-General Gerd von Rundstedt, the commanding officer of Army Group A, said that the tanks must stop where they were. This "halt order" has been a subject of dispute ever since it was issued.

British Nazi sympathizers, like the novelist and journalist Henry Williamson, the author of *Tarka the Otter*, claimed that Hitler was showing friendship to his British "cousins" by deliberately allowing their army to escape. Two facts stand in the way of this compassionate-führer theory. First, Dunkirk's immediate hinterland was bad tank country: a boggy low-lying plain, riddled with canals, dikes, and ditches, to which the French had added yet another "inundation" by opening some of the dikes, thereby forcing many of the fleeing Allied troops to wade through waist-deep water. Second, Hitler had been persuaded by Göring, his Reichsminister of aviation, that Dunkirk would be best left as a wide-open target for the Luftwaffe with its bombs and machine guns. This would also serve to remind Hitler's competing generals who their real commander in chief was. As General Guderian, co-architect of blitzkrieg as the new method of warfare, wrote of seeing the halt order, "We were utterly speechless"—which was at least half the point. The order was rescinded two days after it was issued, but those forty-eight hours were an unexpected gift to the Allies, who used them to shore up Dunkirk's defenses and assemble their impromptu fleet of ships and small boats to rescue the troops.

I've lost my father in the long confusion of the retreat to Dunkirk. He next breaks cover, in his own account, on June 1, on Dunkirk's perimeter canal, where he and his troop were reunited with Major A. O. McCarthy, known as Little Mac, a Regular Army officer who was the battery commander. A Troop's guns were set up on the inside bank of the canal, from where they fired their last barrage until their supply of ammunition was exhausted. The troop then "spiked" the guns, rendering them unusable by the enemy, and left them where they stood, before clambering into and hanging on to the sides of the one remaining 8-cwt truck that was in working order for the short ride to what little was left of the town.

Bad weather on May 30 and 31 had largely grounded the Luftwaffe, but June 1 was a day of clear blue skies, and an air raid had just started when the truck arrived in the already bombed-out city. A Troop immediately took shelter in a basement. The remainder of the regiment were already on the beach, from where they would eventually be rescued by HMS *Worcester*.

Photos taken in May 1940 show Dunkirk as a smoldering wreck: buildings ripped right open, fires blazing, an enormous plume of thick black smoke rising from the bombed oil refinery, the only thing left apparently intact the freestanding Gothic bell tower of St. Eloi

Church; at 190 feet it was—and is—a landmark visible from many miles around and across the soggy plains of the northern Pas-de-Calais. The Dunkirk beaches had turned into a vast garbage dump of military vehicles and artillery pieces—tanks, trucks, cars, most of them set on fire by their last occupants. Rifles and Bren guns were stacked in heaps, rucksacks scattered everywhere along the sands. The sea itself broke sluggishly and with difficulty under the weight of the enormous oil slick released by more than a hundred sunken ships, many of whose masts and funnels showed above the water. In that water, marbled with all the colors of the rainbow, floated the distended corpses of men and horses. The horses were another throwback to World War I: the French still used them for military transport. The air itself was foul, stinking of piss, shit, burning oil, and the unattended dead. Meanwhile the troops waded in orderly columns up to their shoulders in the noxious sea, patiently waiting—often for hours on end—to be rescued. When Dunkirk survivors spoke of their experience long after the event, the most frequent word they used was "hell," hell on earth, a living hell. They were hardly exaggerating.

My father and his troop were extraordinarily lucky, at least in his own abbreviated notes. As soon as the Luftwaffe raid was over, Little Mac, who clearly knew his way around, told them to move at the double to a destroyer at the end of the narrow eastern breakwater (or mole). HMS *Esk* was about to cast off to answer a Mayday call from a requisitioned passenger ship, the *Scotia,* which had been bombed in the raid and was sinking fast near No. 6 buoy in the harbor approach channel with roughly two thousand French soldiers aboard. Since the *Esk* had only just arrived in Dunkirk during the raid, A Troop may have been the first and last British soldiers to embark on her.

The *Esk*'s rescue of the *Scotia* is well told by David Divine in *The Nine Days of Dunkirk,* first published in 1959. "She [the *Scotia*] embarked about 2,000 French troops. As she reached No. 6 buoy on the return voyage she was attacked by three formations of enemy aircraft in groups of four. The ship was hit abaft the engine-room on the starboard side and on the poop deck, and in the final attack one bomb went down the after-funnel. *Scotia* was heavily damaged and began to sink by the stern, heeling steadily over to starboard." Divine then hands over the narrative to a written report by Captain Hughes, the master of the *Scotia:*

Commander Couch of HMS *Esk* had received our SOS. He was lying at Dunkirk at the time; he came at full speed to the rescue. By now the boat deck starboard side was in the water and the vessel was still going over. He very skillfully put the bow of his ship close to the forecastle head, taking off a large number of troops and picking up hundreds out of the sea. Backing his ship out again, he came amidships on the starboard side, his stem being now against the boat deck, and continued to pick up survivors.

The *Scotia* had by now gone over until her forward funnel and mast were in the water. Two enemy bombers again approached us dropping four bombs and machine-gunning those swimming and clinging to wreckage. The *Esk* kept firing and drove the enemy away. Commander Couch again skillfully maneuvered his ship around to the port side, the *Scotia* having gone over until the port bilge keel was out of the water. Hundreds of the soldiers were huddled on the bilge and some of them swam to the *Esk*, while others were pulled up by ropes and rafts.

Divine's book is unusually interesting because he made three cross-Channel trips in a "stolen" twin-screw Thames motor cruiser, "about 30-foot in length," named *White Wing*, to pick up BEF survivors from Dunkirk, yet was quick to scotch the sentimental myth of the "little ships." This popular story told of how Britons spontaneously came together, ditching all distinctions of wealth, rank, and social class, and took to their boats—fishermen, bank clerks, and patrician yachtsmen alike racing across the English Channel to Dunkirk in order to save their stranded army. The "Dunkirk spirit" became a favorite trope for Conservative politicians from Churchill to Mrs. Thatcher to the 2017 film by Christopher Nolan, but it twists the truth. Divine could have cast himself as an exemplary hero in this myth, but instead he insists that the mass evacuation, known as Operation Dynamo, was in fact a hugely complex, if continuously improvised, naval exercise. There are several photographs showing how most of the so-called little ships reached Dunkirk: in rafts of several dozens at a time, all of them empty, many without their owners' knowledge or permission, being towed by oceangoing tugs. They were essentially stolen from their moorings. The primary use of small boats in the evacuation was to ferry men in the shallows to the big, deep-drafted ships waiting just offshore, and a very large number of boats were lost to the sea because the soldiers who manned them were all desperate to escape, and set the craft adrift as soon as the last man had climbed aboard the rescue ship. Used once, lost forever.

The salvage of French troops from the sinking *Scotia* by a British destroyer came at a moment when everyone was blaming everyone else. The French blamed the British for again proving themselves to be perfidious Albion. The British blamed the French for their poor morale and readiness to surrender to the Germans. British soldiers unjustly blamed the RAF for failing to protect them from the Luftwaffe: in one incident, a British Army officer rescued a pilot who had parachuted to safety from his stricken Spitfire; the officer made him quickly change his RAF uniform for army battledress to save him from being beaten up, or worse, by his fellow countrymen. Even aboard the *Scotia,* Captain Hughes (who spoke no French) had to borrow a revolver (from a French officer) to restore order to his shipload of evacuees, but the *Esk/Scotia* episode was a seemingly rare case of international accord among the fractious and quarrelsome Allies.

My brother William tells me that our father once told him of the "ingratitude" shown by a French officer after he'd helped the officer climb over the *Esk*'s rail from the scrambling net on the ship's side. The frozen, waterlogged Frenchman, far from saying a word of thanks for my father's assistance, let loose a tirade against the English, shouting that they were interested only in rescuing themselves while leaving the French to defend the Dunkirk perimeter and be taken prisoner by the Germans.

On the short voyage back to the English coast, the returning soldiers were sternly lectured on the need to keep silent about what they had seen in Dunkirk, for fear of the damage it could do to civilian morale at home. That silence enabled the "little ships" myth to triumph over the story of what had actually happened, which in itself was mythical enough. Nearly 340,000 soldiers were rescued from Dunkirk and its beaches. The troops themselves knew that they had been conclusively defeated by the far superior tactics of the Germans, and expected to be met at home with relieved but glum faces, as befitted a failed army. Their actual reception astonished them. Eloquent photographs show waving flags and cheering people crowding the road bridges over the Dover–London line as trains packed with Dunkirk survivors pass under the arches. Dazed, sleepless, filthy, but happy soldiers wave back from the train windows. The myth was working its magic.

Churchill, who had succeeded Chamberlain as prime minister on May 10—the same day the Phony War ended and Hitler invaded the Low Countries—called Dunkirk "a miracle of deliverance" in his speech to Parliament on June 4, the last day of the evacuation, but acknowledged that the defeat of the BEF was a "colossal military disaster" and that "wars are not won by evacuations." Churchill's "miracle" (*Wunder* in German) was the same word used by the Nazis to describe their lightning conquest of France, which formally surrendered on June 22.

The *Esk*, after rescuing close to a thousand French troops from the *Scotia*, with HMS *Worcester* assisting, sailed, unmolested by the Luftwaffe, to Dover, from where my father and Little Mac caught the train to Victoria Station in London. As officers they were required by military regulations to travel first-class, while other ranks were ordered into third-class compartments to avoid any undesirable "fraternization" between officers and their men. (Second class had been abolished in the nineteenth century, but the numerical space, or no-man's-land, between one and three helped, I suppose, to emphasize the gulf between the classes.) So the return to England from Dunkirk signaled—lest anyone had failed to notice—a return to strict social conformity.

Trying to keep track of my father and his troop as they move through this momentous sequence of events is like trying to keep one's eyes on a single small fish in a vast migrating shoal of pilchards. Now you see it, now you don't, and you never will again. Other people were watching him far more closely than I possibly can, and they noticed that he was cool under fire, shouldered responsibility when responsibility was thrust upon him, spoke like a gentleman, and could play a decent hand at bridge. He was earmarked for early promotion.

Chapter 7

"Do you want to go potty now?"

I felt my cheek muscles tightening and an upwelling surge of temper beginning to break inside my head. I was outraged by the nurse's stupid condescension. The Romanian doctor at the Swedish hospital in Edmonds had promised me a halfway house between hospital care and home; this was more like being sentenced to go back to my bloody infancy.

Trying to keep my voice on an even keel, I said that nobody had spoken to me like that since I was two years old. The pasted-on professional smile of the nurse didn't budge.

"Do you know what the word 'infantilization' means?"

"What does it mean?" She was humoring me as one might humor a potentially dangerous lunatic. Closer to my own age than any of the staff I'd spotted in the neurological rehab ward so far, she had silver-gray hair trimmed in a tight helmet around an elvish face. Her name tag said PAT. I gave her a pedantic two-sentence lecturette on how people speaking in baby talk to other adults made those adults feel like babies, and how, as a freshly minted sixty-nine-year-old, I was not prepared to be treated as a baby.

"I've been saying that all my life and no one's ever complained before."

"Well I'm complaining now, so please just think about it, and try to understand what I've been saying."

Pat gave an offended shrug and left my room with her nose in the air, pushing her steel trolley with its clinical equipment of drips, blood pressure cuffs, thermometers, rubber gloves, and hand towels. I heard the trolley go on down the corridor, rattling with her annoyance.

As soon as she'd gone, I began to regret my outburst. I'd made an enemy of a nurse, which wasn't a smart move. I also remembered my last disagreement with someone on this subject. It was back in 1981. I was going over the copyedited text of the American edition of a book set in the United States. On one page I had written the word "lavatory," for which the copy editor had substituted "toilet." She had also written an explanatory note in the margin, saying that "lavatory" would stand out unnecessarily for American readers, and that both words were equally euphemistic.

I had always assumed, without thinking, that to say "lavatory" was to call a spade a spade while "toilet" was a coy euphemism deployed by the lower-middle classes. In this I was following Nancy Mitford's article in *Encounter* magazine in 1954, where she laid out a glossary of "U" and "Non-U" (the *U* standing for upper-class) terms, the words "lavatory" and "toilet" conspicuously among them. I had been taught by my mother in my infancy to say "lavatory" (though by no means were we remotely upper class) and despised "toilet" as unpardonably infra dig. (While I am on the subject of Latin, "lavatory" comes from *lavatorium,* meaning a basin for washing one's hands and face, so it is every bit as much a euphemism as "toilet," and a prime example of English snobbism.) Below the copy editor's marginal note I wrote "Thank you!" as I let her substitution stand.

In my rant to Pat about "go potty," had I just stumbled into the linguistic minefield that awaits Brits and Americans whenever they cross into each other's territory? I still don't know for sure, and still think that "go potty" is an insufferable and infantilizing phrase, but I'm aware that, after living for more than a quarter century in the United States, I still sometimes find American English a bewildering language, and myself a foreigner here. I made up my mind that when I next crossed paths with Pat, I'd do my best to make amends for my display of temper, but would continue to insist that speaking baby talk to a newly disabled adult stranger is to kick him where it really hurts when he's already down and nearly out for the count.

I was in a state of colossal lethargy: it seemed that I had never been so tired in my entire life, and I kept on slipping in and out of consciousness. There was a large wall clock in my room, and the time it showed surprised me whenever I looked at it. I had no sooner gone to sleep than I was woken up by a cheery-sounding nurse saying, "Just need to take your vitals." Vitals? The word seemed to mock my deathly fatigue. But after she left, I couldn't get back to sleep.

Wearily, I clicked the light switch on the bedside table with my left hand, and retrieved my Kindle. I remembered that I had long promised myself to read Tony Judt's *Postwar: A History of Europe since 1945*—a long book that covered my own lifetime and a good test of my working brain cells after the stroke. Prodding at the dense miniature keyboard of the Kindle, which was propped against my knee under the thin hospital bedclothes, I had difficulty picking out Judt's name, but succeeded after several botched shots at it.

On my first night in the rehab ward, I began to read *Postwar:*

I first decided to write this book while changing trains at the Westbahnhof, Vienna's main railway terminus. It was December 1989, a propitious moment. I had just returned from Prague, where the playwrights and historians of Václav Havel's *Civic Forum* were dislodging a Communist police state and tumbling forty years of "real existing Socialism" into the dustbin of history.

Typical Judt. He loved trains and railway stations for their ability to swiftly connect disparate communities and countries, and his nostalgia, especially for the expansive train lines of his youth, bears out my theory that any technology invented a century or more before our own birth becomes more a thing of nature than of culture. *Vide* windmills (picturesque) versus wind turbines (NIMBY). Drifting back into sleep again, I thought of Philip Larkin's phrase "the reek of buttoned carriage-cloth" in his train poem, "The Whitsun Weddings," and was woken by yet another demand for my vitals, shortly followed by the arrival of a heavyset male nurse's assistant, whom I asked to help me to the bathroom.

"You wet?"

"No, I'm not 'wet,' but I need to use the bathroom."

Wordless, he plucked me out of the bed and sat me in the wheelchair. In the "bathroom," which had only a shower, plus the toilet and handbasin, he lifted me up again, told me to pull down my boxer shorts, then deposited me on the toilet seat and stood by, waiting. The phrase "assisted living" came tauntingly to mind, sounding like the two most ominous words in the language.

"D'you mind waiting outside for a few minutes?"

He left me to myself and welcome solitude. When I'd finished, I called him back.

"You wiped yourself?"

"Of course I have. And pulled the plug, before you ask."

We went through the humiliating routine in reverse, stopping at the big basin in the main room while I washed my hands. Back in bed, I reached for Tony Judt.

My next visitor was Richard, who carried two cups of coffee, one for me and one for himself. "Happy Bloomsday!" he said.

"Bloomsday! June the sixteenth . . . How did you come to know that?"

"I was an English major."

"Where?"

"University of Michigan."

"I've been there, it's a nice campus. I did a conference paper there once."

"I figured you'd be the only patient here who'd get the reference."

He explained that the director of something or other, who had a private office on the ward, knew my books and had told the staff that I was a writer. After the "go potty" nurse and the taciturn weight lifter, Richard's presence in my room made my spirits rise as I felt that the neurological rehab ward might indeed become the promised halfway house. We spoke about James Joyce for a bit, then Richard asked me how I'd slept. I tried to make a comic catalogue of my night: the unending traffic of gurneys and trolleys past my door, the color-coded hospital alerts from all the floors in the building issuing from the loudspeaker at the nurses' station, the sleep-wrecking demands for vitals, everything blurring into everything else. It was, I said, a night to remember.

"Titanic," he said and promised to find me a quieter room later in the day. Lying on the bed, I squirmed myself into my new hospital uniform, a black T-shirt and beige elasticized sweatpants—an effort that left me wanting to sleep again. I needed Richard's help to sit upright and get my useless right foot into its loose-fitting deck shoe; assisted

living again, but this time without humiliation because the assistant was already seeming like a friend.

I brightened further when Richard said I had an appointment with the ward psychologist in fifteen minutes; he'd look in again then and show me where her office was. I wheeled myself over to the mirror above the basin and tried to get rid of the bristles on my face and neck with the new electric razor that Julia had brought me from Bartell Drugs. I usually liked shaving and its soapy rituals—working up the lather and making a smooth clear-cut with a new blade. But this felt like trying to lay waste a cornfield with a blunted scythe, missing more stalks than one could sever. The razor whirred and whirred, but the skin still felt rough after its passage.

I had a lot to talk about with the psychologist. I assumed that she'd seen the photographs from my brain scan and could explain which areas of the brain had died in the double hemorrhage on the left-hand side of my skull. I didn't think my vocabulary and basic thought processes, or my memory, had been severely affected, but I worried about my new helplessness with numbers. Oh, I could recite to myself the multiplication tables (eight eights are sixty-four, nine eights are seventy-two, ten eights are . . .), but I was remembering the words and the rhythms of the tables like memorized poems, not as numbers in their own right. Ever since the stroke the simplest sum of addition, subtraction, multiplication, or division had turned into a disheartening puzzle, and rendered me fogbound. When I listened to my voicemail or read the online *New York Times* on my laptop, everything numerical, from phone numbers to percentages, exited my head as soon as heard or glimpsed. Were the hemorrhages going to leave me permanently in this state?

Richard tapped on my door, and said it was time for my "tests," to which I looked forward with the proper anxiety of someone heading for a stiff examination. Inside the barely furnished psychologist's office, I was faced by a rather stout, fair-haired, fortyish woman with yet another professional smile in which I detected no sign of real warmth. I asked her if she'd had a chance to look at the results of my brain scan in the other Swedish hospital at Edmonds. No, she said: because the Edmonds hospital was a recent acquisition, Swedish still had problems integrating their communications systems, blah, blah. So gone was the chance to talk about the what and where of my left-brain "deficits."

"Speech is unimpaired, cognition seems good," the psychologist said. "What about your memory?"

"Well, I have memories only because I remember them—some vivid, some not so. I mean, how could I remember them if I have forgotten them?"

The muscles that sustained her smile relaxed, and the corners of her mouth sank downward, into an expression of generalized discontent with the world. She was evidently not in the least entertained by what I had tried to convey as a playful question. She busied herself with leafing through a pile of pages on her desk, muttering things like "Oh, far too easy for you!" and "No, you'd hate this one" before she settled on a single piece of paper near the bottom of the pile and said, "It's a very simple story, but you'd be surprised how interesting the answers can be."

The psychologist began to read the story to me. She had a pleasant reading voice, not the upsy-downsy voice of an adult reading to a child, and not overstressed as if half the text were printed in italics. The story, such as it was, concerned a woman (elderly, I thought, and possibly in the early stages of Alzheimer's) who went shopping in a nearby super-market. Once inside the store, I tried to put the Frances Yates memory method to work by imagining myself in the local branch of Metropolitan Market on Queen Anne Hill. We started in the vegetable section, moved to dairy products, then to canned foods, and so on, adding purchases to our basket as we went. When we reached the checkout, we discovered that we'd left our purse behind or had it stolen, so we returned home empty-handed, and that was pretty much it—it was as dull a story as any I had heard. When the psychologist asked me to list the items in the woman's basket, I retraced my steps through the aisles of Metro Market and named in order all the objects that the woman had taken from the shelves.

"Very good," said the psychologist, about whose professional abilities I was harboring grave doubts.

Still, seen from her point of view, I was an old man, past retirement age, and lucky to be alive. I might as well be sitting in my wheelchair in a sunlit park somewhere, and talking to the pigeons as the old are wont to do. The psychologist's boxes had all been checked, and our fifteen-minute interview was at an end.

Outside, I looked for Richard, but he was nowhere to be seen. So I steered myself with my left hand and left foot on a distinctly wobbly course back to my room, where I found an occupational therapist waiting for me. She was standing beside a whiteboard on the wall with a bunch of categories, some in the form of impenetrable acronyms, permanently printed on it in block capitals. All the spaces attached to them had been wiped clean.

"First things first," the therapist said. "Now, what is your goal?"

One thought came to mind. My primary goal was to get to the bathroom unassisted, and return to the bed on my own. But this seemed at once to be both too modest and too immodest to fill the space beside "GOAL" for all to see.

"I don't think I really have a goal, at least not a specific one."

"Oh, you can do better than that. Everyone has to have a goal."

"How about to walk again?"

She wrote "TO WALK" on the board. "Now we have something to aim at. Your physical therapist will help you with that."

Here she exposed the (to me) very odd American system: the separation of powers between occupational and physical therapists, who divided the human body into two parts, above-the-waist and below-the-waist. OTs worked on the former, PTs on the latter. Since the source of the problem lay in the brain and its eighty-six billion neurons, my first thought was that the therapists were muddling up cause and effect, like plumbers trying to fix a burst pipe by messing around with the faucet.

The OT touched my right shoulder. "Sublux," she said, and told me I must remember to rest my elbow on the arm of the wheelchair to encourage the humerus to fit back into the shoulder socket, saying that the subluxation should heal itself. She then took my wrist and asked if I could make a fist. I couldn't. But I could feel my thumb and fingers trying to move, and had the strong sensation of actual movement until I looked at my hand and saw it was completely motionless. The therapist said this was a good sign and we could work on it together. Evidently the brain was still in some sort of contact with the finger and thumb muscles. Next she suggested that I bend my arm from the elbow. With terrific effort I was able to lift it clear of the armrest and awaited her applause.

"No, you see all the movement is coming from the shoulder, not the elbow. I didn't think you'd be able to do that, but I just thought it was worth asking."

She took the limp arm and bent it until the hand touched the shoulder, then repeated the action ten or a dozen times, and I realized that my analogy with plumbers and burst pipes was wrong. The therapist was trying to catch the attention of the brain, reminding it of what it could do so effortlessly and without conscious thought until last Saturday. Unfortunately, the brain didn't seem to be listening. Or the relevant neurons had been killed stone-dead.

Forty-five minutes of occupational therapy left me in a state of heavy-lidded torpor, but also encouraged by a sense of real progress in the gradual recovery of my right arm. Cheered by this, I reimmersed myself in Judt's *Postwar*, where he was painting a picture of a Europe devastated by Allied and German bombing, from Coventry to Minsk and Kiev, Le Havre to Dresden and Warsaw, a vast landscape of wreckage and ruins, a literal Waste Land, when a nurse interrupted my reading to bring me lunch.

"It's been waiting for you at the nurses' station, so I thought I'd better bring you your order."

"My order?"

"Yes, you made it out last night, remember?"

I had no such memory. Looking at the unappetizing creation, its limp lettuce, bits of raw carrot, and what looked like slices of black pudding, I thought, Oh God, this must be the onset of stroke-induced amnesia, but said, "Of course, sorry, I should've picked it up myself."

"Not to worry, you're welcome," the nurse said as she left my room.

But I worried like hell before I could persuade myself that I had a dim recollection of ticking items on an unpromising menu.

The lunch, when I began to eat it, was unmistakably institutional in its character, but it was a good deal better than the food on which I lived at boarding school (my father's old school, of course), when I was incarcerated there from 1953 to 1958. At least those dates were still sharp in my memory, unlike the menu from which I'd ordered last night.

Richard showed up again: he'd found me another room, and could move me there before my next appointment, with a physical therapist. The room was not far down the corridor, which turned out to be a cul-de-sac that ended in a snug enclosed balcony with chairs and a table; a good place for reading, I thought. The room itself seemed larger than the one I'd left. There was a ratty 1950s armchair with a footrest, and beyond that a window with a strange, idiosyncratic glimpse of the city. Views in Seattle from any sixth floor usually include mountains or water, fresh or salt, but the scene from this window was of a flat landscape, occupied by nondescript timber-built housing, empty crosswalks, trafficless streets with, down on the left, a big wooden shed that may have housed some kind of light industry. Nothing to draw the eye—not even a church or a school or a parade of shops. This view was worth having for its prominent absences. I couldn't get my bearings because there was nothing at all that I could recognize and use to orient myself, and this blankness gave the view an air of mild mystery.

Richard came back carrying the stack of Julia's photographs.

"Not even a church," I said.

"I hate churches."

"I rather do, too, but what's your reason?"

"Oh, when I was a student I got involved in Scientology."

"I hope your English major cured you of that."

"Kind of, sort of, but I got in trouble with them."

"How so?"

"Long story, but I'll tell you sometime."

Identities of strangers were blurring into one another on this hectic day of appointments, when the physical therapist paid me a call. Her name was Kelli, and from the moment she walked into my room she roused my attention. She looked like a living advertisement for her craft: tallish, clean-limbed, fresh-faced, with fair hair falling to her shoulders, she had a smile that seemed entirely spontaneous—the first such smile I'd encountered since my arrival in the rehab ward, where all smiles appeared to be obligatory accessories. I told her that I hoped she'd be able to teach me how to walk again. She said she'd certainly try. I said that if she did, I'd feel like Lazarus, raised from the dead. She laughed—a light, tinkling, musical laugh that pleased me no end.

Kelli took command of my wheelchair, saying that this time she'd push me to the gym because I didn't know where or how far I'd have to go, but in future she'd expect me to wheel myself for the sake of the exercise. I said I'd cut a deal with her: if she got me halfway there, I'd do the rest. Again I was treated to her musical laugh.

The corridor was long, with periodic swing doors and handwashing facilities on the wall. Through the continuous row of windows on its left-hand side, I at last picked out a landmark I could recognize—the Smith Tower, Seattle's oldest skyscraper, and, a mile or so beyond it, and more or less in line, the Space Needle. The white tower was topped with a faux campanile, like a dunce's cap, copied from the Metropolitan Life Insurance Company Tower in New York, which was, in its turn, a copy of the campanile of San Marco in Venice. Seattle promoters liked to boast that the Smith Tower was the tallest building west of New York, then Ohio, then Chicago, then the Mississippi, then Kansas City, then the Rocky Mountains, and so on until it was dwarfed by neighboring towers in downtown Seattle. It was built in 1914, had 34 stories, and was 462 feet high—a shrimp by the standards of the later twentieth century, let alone the twenty-first, but still an arrestingly conspicuous height, and now I could see where I was.

The gym. I hadn't actually used a gym since I was at boarding school, and hadn't entered one since Julia played basketball in the one at her middle school when she was a seventh grader. This gym smelled different from both. It smelled of old people, their unmistakable sweet-and-sour decomposition, ineffectually masked by the various scents and colognes they used to disguise their own sweat from themselves.

The rehab gym was filled with unfamiliar equipment: stand-alone flights of steps that went four up and then four down; a full-size mock-up of a car with open doors but no front end; parallel bars for apprentice walkers; giant mattress-like things, clad in navy-blue vinyl, that brought to my mind the Great Bed of Ware in the Victoria and Albert Museum. It was to one of these that Kelli pushed me, then made the thing descend to the same level as the seat of my wheelchair.

"You haven't made a transit before?"

I hadn't.

She flipped up the arm of my chair so that the Bed of Ware and I were as closely contiguous as possible, then told me to place my left hand a little way forward of my body and well inside the edge of the vinyl. Using my good arm and leg, I had to raise myself almost to a standing position, then swivel my body to sit down on the Great Bed. It was more of a struggle than I expected. For a good while, I jiggled up and down in the chair without achieving the lift I needed.

"Don't worry about falling. I'm here to catch you."

I quite liked the idea of being caught by Kelli, but on perhaps the twelfth attempt I managed to haul myself upward and swing my body around before I plunked down safely on the bed.

"That looked good for a first transit."

Always a glutton for compliments, I basked in her praise and looked around the gym at my fellow patients, some in pajamas and bathrobes, others in sweatpants and T-shirts. Nearly everyone looked older than me and at a far more advanced stage of rehabilitation, and each patient was attended by a therapist who looked young, trim, impersonal, like a curator of these relics. Well, I was now a museum piece myself, and I wanted to sing along with Marie Lloyd, the great Cockney music hall star, in 1922, the year of her death, "I'm one of the ruins that Cromwell knocked about a bit." I first heard the song, as recorded by Lloyd's daughter, in 1953 when Tony, my father's much younger half brother, just seven months senior to me and the only child of my grandfather's third marriage, played the song to me on his windup gramophone. The shellac record, a badly scratched 78, made Lloyd's voice sound as thin and distant as that of a sheeted ghost, under the ancient apple tree where we sat amid a great profusion of mint that had run wild in the back garden of Tony's parents' thatched retirement cottage in Old Alresford, Hampshire.

Kelli told me to lie down on my back as she hoisted my dead leg onto the vinyl. She bent it at the knee, making an angle of about 150 degrees between the calf and thigh, and asked me to try flattening it against the pressure of her hand on the sole of my shoe. I tried. Not much happened. I quoted Beckett to her: "Try again. Fail again. Fail better." She laughed and said, "Say that again?" I did so, confessing that the words weren't mine but had been stolen from *Worstward Ho.* I said I thought it should be the official motto for physical therapists everywhere, which triggered another bell-like laugh.

Laughing (her) and failing (me), we went on trying, with Kelli assuring me that each time I tried to push she could feel it clearly on the palm of her hand.

After forty-five minutes of exercise in the gym I was dog-tired and heavy-lidded, oscillating between sleep and wakefulness as Kelli wheeled me back to my room, where I dipped into *Postwar,* nodded off, and as quickly surfaced again with a project in mind. I wanted to make a transfer on my own, from the wheelchair to the bed. The bed, made by Hill-Rom, as it said, was fully articulated with an array of buttons to push on its port side. I pressed them one after another, making the bed wheeze and groan as it shifted its shape. The action took me back to the summer of 1997, Sea-Tac Airport on British Airways 048, waiting for the last passengers to come aboard before Julia and I faced the long nonstop red-eye flight to Heathrow. We'd been mercifully promoted to club class from economy, and seats in club ingeniously converted into beds and would project footrests at the press of the right button. I had the window seat and faced the tail plane, Julia the aisle seat facing the cockpit. A screen divided us.

Four-year-olds love to find themselves in charge of new, powerful pieces of technology, and Julia had turned her seat into a perpetual-motion machine that writhed and ducked, making her head appear above the screen for a moment, then disappear the next. She was rapt in a private adventure. I caught the disapproving eye of a flight attendant, and leaned over the screen to tell Julia to stop immediately lest we be blackballed from club and herded back to cattle class for the next nine hours.

In the hospital room, I carefully lowered the bed to the exact level of my wheelchair seat, flipped back the left-hand armrest, put my left fist on the bed, and levered myself into a shaky, near upright position, where I was attacked by a fit of pure funk. Paralyzed by fear of falling, I sank back into the safe terrain of the chair, false teeth chattering with nerves. I needed Kelli to help me do this trick—her encouragement and, more than that, her laughter.

Chapter 8

AT VICTORIA STATION, my father and Little Mac were told to take a cab to Waterloo. From there, another train would take them to Wokingham, where there was a camp for soldiers who'd found themselves displaced from their regiments during the Dunkirk evacuation. The enterprising major didn't take to Wokingham, and after sampling dinner in a local hotel with my father, he proposed that they should reestablish themselves in central London, to be "closer to the War Office." Next morning they entrained again, checked into a hotel near Piccadilly Circus, and set out to explore the available nightlife of restaurants, clubs, and theaters. My father, still wet around the ears on such matters, must have tagged along with his senior officer, wide-eyed at the major's urbanity and readiness to chalk up alarming sums to military expenses. They took it in turns to badger the War Office over the phone, and it was only after several days of lingering in the London fleshpots and being all-too-vulnerable pedestrians in the blackout that they were told that the Sixty-Seventh Field Regiment was being reassembled in Leeds, Yorkshire, which in itself says something about the mood of the country in early June 1940.

Worcestershire was home for the regiment, but the War Office was understandably anxious that the troops returning from Dunkirk, regarding themselves as a conclusively defeated army, might just go home and back to their farms and offices if the WO didn't make it absolutely clear to them that the war was still very much on. Leeds was only about 120 miles from Worcester, but these were long English miles, and Leeds meant the industrial North, a foreign land for most of the soldiers posted there.

Churchill's parliamentary speech on June 4 (the same speech in which he called Dunkirk "a miracle of deliverance") primed Britain for an imminent German invasion, but did so with such relish for antique, romantic, and extravagant language that he managed to clothe the year 1940, which until now had been a succession of military disasters, in the ancient trappings of King Arthur and the Knights of the Round Table and, for good measure, the medieval Crusades. In Churchill's words, the half-starved Britons of the 1940s were about to effect a historical renaissance of gallantry, heroism, and valor not seen since time immemorial.

> Even though large tracts of Europe and many old and famous states have fallen or may fall into the grip of the Gestapo and all the odious apparatus of Nazi rule, we shall not flag or fail. We shall go on to the end, we shall fight in France, we shall fight on the seas and oceans, we shall fight with growing confidence and growing strength in the air, we shall defend our island, whatever the cost may be, we shall fight on the beaches, we shall fight on the landing grounds, we shall fight in the fields and in the streets, we shall fight in the hills; we shall never surrender.

Up until now, the war had been largely fought with World War I–era tanks, guns, and transport, nearly all of which had been left behind at Dunkirk, turning that city into a great garbage dump of sabotaged matériel. Now, the steel mills and factories, working around the clock, were hungry for every scrap of metal that was going: wrought-iron fences around people's houses and gardens, the silver paper in cigarette packs (Granny made fat globes of these scraps of foil as her contribution to the war effort), old cars, old bikes, old everything. Unemployment, the great misery of the 1930s, disappeared as new guns, new planes, new trucks and tanks rolled off the assembly lines, many of them now manned by women.

My father and the major took the train from Kings Cross to Leeds, where they rejoined their depleted regiment (the casualties in the BEF in May–June 1940 ran to 16.6 percent, only a whisker short of the

17 percent of British soldiers in the infamously bloody First World War).

Leeds turned out to be an unexpectedly civilized and civilizing posting for my father, and a great relief from the brutalities of warfare and defeat. He was billeted with an amiable "young middle-aged couple" whose house was in Roundhay, a genteel, long-standing suburb to the north of the city. The couple introduced him to the splendors of Roundhay Park, originally an eleventh-century hunting ground, with its woodlands, lakes, lawns, and gardens, along with an early nineteenth-century folly and neoclassical Regency mansion. Troops were still trickling into Leeds from the various ports and assembly stations to which their rescue ships had taken them when the city's substantial Jewish community put on a slap-up variety show at the Grand Theatre to welcome home the survivors of Dunkirk. The music hall and radio stars were enticed up from London, and all drinks were on the house. In the 1990s, my father still recalled that evening fondly, though he also remembered being mildly scandalized by the novelty of attending such a show on a Sunday evening against his inbred Anglican scruples.

The best thing about Leeds and Roundhay for my father was the proximity—ten miles by bus—to the prosperous spa town of Harrogate, where the D'Oyly Carte Opera Company was staging a summer season repertoire of Gilbert and Sullivan's Savoy operas at the Grand Opera House. My father had listened to the operas on gramophone records and the wireless but had never watched a live performance of any kind of opera before. At Harrogate, sitting up in the gods (the cheapest seats), he was enchanted, and he repeatedly took the bus to see as many operas in the repertoire as he could. His next chance for operagoing wouldn't happen until British and American troops entered Rome in the summer of 1944, when my father would become an instant fan of Verdi, Rossini, Donizetti, and Bellini.

Although he continued to stay on as the officer commanding A Troop, his duties in Leeds seem to have been light, leaving him ample time for (mostly solitary) recreations. For much of the time his mind appears to have been elsewhere, as when he drove his army motorcycle to regimental headquarters in the city center on the right (i.e., wrong) side of the road, forgetting he was not in France. Not until the regiment was fully assembled, with its losses in Belgium and France replaced by new recruits who were in training when the BEF was being put to flight, were the soldiers at last granted a ten-day spell of home leave.

My father's brother Nick, now a sergeant in the Royal Engineers, who would soon earn his own commission, had been serving in western France when the Nazis sliced the expeditionary force in two with their blitzkrieg "sickle cut." Nick was one of the many evacuees who were rescued from the Bay of Biscay port of Saint-Nazaire on June 16–18.

Nick and Peter's safe return from France made for a family celebration at the rectory in Hadzor, where my grandfather had just joined the Home Guard as a private. He'd been commissioned as a second lieutenant in both the Boer War and World War I, and would go on to gain his third commission as the local intelligence officer, though I doubt if many German spies were likely to be found lurking in the woods around Hadzor.

Through the summer of 1940 the friendship between my father and my mother steadily consolidated. They met at the regular Sunday night dinners given by Mrs. White at Oddingley Grange to her genteel neighbors, and Mrs. White was, I think, a tactful but determined matchmaker in her widowhood. Granny and her colonel were still living unhappily together at the Gap, but no doubt kept up a united front whenever they left the house, for appearances counted much more to them than the long squabble of reality. Whatever scraps of leave my father wangled out of his commanding officer—a couple of nights between his various "schemes" and courses, along with his regular duty defending England's east coast against invasion, predicted to happen on every successive full moon—he spent them staying at the rectory and walking out with Monica.

They went to the pictures at cinemas in Droitwich and Worcester with my mother driving her elderly Humber (soon to be replaced by her Ford Popular, AUP 595); they took long walks on the eastern bank of the River Severn with Monica's dog, Sam, the Staffordshire bull terrier. Sam had to be kept on a permanent short leash: though friendly and playful with humans, he detested members of his own species, and, faced by another dog, he reacted instinctively by flying for its throat.

Peter and Monica had reached the stage of mailing book parcels to each other because a shared book was a safely neutral subject of conversation. In this spirit, Monica sent Peter a copy of Maupassant's *Boule de Suif and Other Stories*. The title story is set in the Franco-Prussian War of 1870–71, aboard a horse-drawn coach traveling from Rouen to Dieppe through a persistent snowstorm that has closed the usual inns and restaurants along the way. Of the ten passengers, who represent a well-chosen cross section of Normandy society, only Boule de Suif (Ball of Fat), a sex worker, has had the foresight to bring her own food and wine, a meal she graciously shares with her fellow travelers. The going is slow, and after fourteen hours on the road the coach is still barely twenty miles from Rouen. In the dead of night it stops at Tôtes, a small town under Prussian occupation where the officer inspecting the travelers' papers at the only hotel takes a fancy to Boule de Suif, who detests the sight of him, the war, and his presence in her country. The Prussian officer says that the coach will not leave Tôtes until she sleeps with him. Her fellow passengers implore her to comply (for isn't fornication her daily livelihood?). She holds out for two days, then, on the third night, she gives in, with shame and revulsion, for the sake of her companions. On the fourth day, the officer allows the coach to complete its journey to Dieppe. This time it's Boule de Suif who's forgotten to bring food. The other people, for whom she has sacrificed herself, won't look at her, let alone share their provisions with her. She sits alone in a corner of the coach, hiding bitter tears from her tormentors, while one of them first whistles and then sings "La Marseillaise."

My father, missing the point, said of the story that he found it "a bit racy."

My mother would also sometimes miss the point. When my father sent her a copy of *Disenchantment* by C. E. Montague, he was, I think, trusting her with a book of great importance to him, and was understandably disappointed by her response. Montague's disenchantment was with the Great War, for which he'd volunteered in 1914, aged forty-seven, in spite of his former pacifism, and dyed his hair (he'd gone white in his twenties) to fool the medical board. He had served in the trenches as a private and sergeant in the Royal Fusiliers before his promotion to lieutenant, then captain, in military intelligence, and finished the war guiding VIP visitors, from Prime Minister Lloyd George to George Bernard Shaw and H. G. Wells, around the battlefields. He'd seen the war from many angles, some privileged and others not at all, and his leisurely and humane book of essays, first published in 1922, adds up to a broad indictment of British politicians, generals, staff officers (living comfortably in their headquarters far behind the front lines), army chaplains, and the jingoistic press, who had kept the war going, and by their stupidity and incompetence had wasted a million British lives.

In less than a month of active combat with the Germans, my father had fought on the same terrain that Montague had occupied in World War I, and his retreat across Belgium, river to river to river, from the Dyle to the Escaut, was a speeded-up version of the same trench warfare described in *Disenchantment,* except that in 1940 the British were the losing side. When my mother failed to mention his latest gift, he wrote to her: "It has occurred to me that Montague's book must have bored you immensely—why he should write such amazing prose about the Army, I cannot imagine!"

Monica wrote back: "You didn't expect me to be interested in the book *Disenchantment*—as a matter of fact I was, particularly as I've never read anything else but fiction concerning the last war." And that's it. In the next sentence she gets onto safer ground, writing about a novel by Maxim Gorky that they'd both enjoyed, and sending him a copy of *Revue,* another novel, by the literary chatterbox Beverley Nichols.

"Amazing prose," coming from my father, is an astonishingly warm commendation, and Montague's writing clearly touched him deeply, if rather surprisingly. Montague was a committed Liberal in his politics, and both protégé and son-in-law of his employer, C. P. Scott, who was the editor of *The Manchester Guardian* for fifty-seven years from 1872 to 1929 and owner of the paper from 1907 to his death in 1932. Before he volunteered in 1914, Montague was the chief drama critic and senior leader writer for the paper, which my father would dismiss in the 1940s and '50s as "that liberal rag." Where he found common ground with Montague in 1940 was Montague's belief in the natural "chivalry" of the ordinary soldier in the First World War. Again and again in *Disenchantment* he found examples of chivalry among privates, NCOs, and junior officers. There was the young private who escorted a German prisoner down a British trench after a fierce fight between the two; when asked why he hadn't finished the German off with his rifle, he replied that the man hadn't been looking at him at that moment, so he couldn't. Or the soldiers billeted on poor families in Cologne, who went hungry because they fed their rations to the starving German children. Or two drunk Scotsmen from a Highland regiment trying to console a Cologne burgher over the German defeat, long after the night curfew had sounded: "Och, dinna tak' it to hairrt, mon. I tell ye that your lads were grond."

I like my father the more for finding a superior but kindred spirit in Montague's book, which must have puzzled and irritated him in many places. My father was far from being a liberal, whether spelled with a small or big *L*. His narrow upbringing and education had led him to an affection for members of the village working class—sexton-gravediggers, carpenters, plowmen, family servants, and the like—but urban industrial workers inspired in him a mixture of fear and contempt, only exacerbated by his short and miserable experience of Cradley Heath. I'd love to know what he thought of Montague's temporary abandonment of Christianity in favor of chivalry. But I see exactly what he admired in Montague: the complexity of mind (gained, my father would have thought, at Balliol College, Oxford, from where Montague began publishing reviews in *The Manchester Guardian* as an undergraduate); the natural candor; the judicious character of his well-turned and balanced sentences; his readiness to include the reader in his own civilized and erudite company by, for instance, quoting Latin verse without thinking to accompany it with an English translation.

It was in 1957, I think, when I brought back to my father's vicarage a dog-eared copy of a Pelican reprint of another book by Montague, *A Writer's Notes on His Trade,* bought for a few pennies, to add to my collection of all the books I could find by writers about writing. My father immediately spotted the name of the author and said, "Now, he really was a good writer," a compliment he'd never have paid to D. H. Lawrence, James Joyce, Ernest Hemingway, or anyone else whose books I treasured and kept in my bedroom (some in false dust jackets), all of whom roused his haughty disapproval. His praise for Montague so prejudiced me against the book I was holding that I vowed never to read it—but, like most of my promises, it was one not strictly kept, and a chapter title from *A Writer's Notes* still rings in my head as a motto—"Easy Reading, Hard Writing"—though I haven't set eyes on the book for sixty years.

Chapter 9

————————

MY PARENTS' SLOW courtship, conducted mainly by post, muddled along against the aerial backdrop of the Battle of Britain. Peter returned to his regiment in Leeds, while Monica volunteered for a series of jobs: as a nurse, as an ambulance driver, as a French translator. Britain, especially in its bombed cities, was in a mood of hypomania compounded of sleeplessness, adrenaline, moment-to-moment anxiety about the expected German invasion, and the elation of simple neighborliness. More than thirty years after war's end, in the winter of 1977, when I was living with my girlfriend on a terraced street in Putney, West London, I was shoveling snow away from our front door and pavement, and doing the same for a next-door neighbor, a woman in her eighties. Hearing the rasp of the shovel on her doorstep, she came out and beamed at the snowbound street, saying, "Isn't this nice? It's just like the Blitz!"—an era that for her had fermented into a cask of happy memories. She told me that she'd then lived in the East End close to the London docks, which the Heinkel incendiary bombers had nightly turned into a wilderness of fire and explosions that blew whole streets to bits while their residents, if they were lucky, took refuge on the platforms of the nearest Underground station.

Birmingham, about twenty miles away from Droitwich, was bombed in August 1940, but that was at a sufficiently far distance that my father could write of it as little more than a spectacle worth noting. Leeds would not be bombed until March 1941, when my father was long gone from the city. As soon as the regiment was reequipped

with new trucks and guns (twenty-five-pounders this time), it traveled east in convoy, from Leeds to Louth in Lincolnshire, where it joined the too-thinly-scattered line of defenses along the North Sea coast. The most likely spot for German soldiers to set foot on English soil was St. Margaret's Bay which faced across the Dover Strait close to its narrowest point, but the east coast was also believed to be vulnerable.

But before any landings could take place, Hermann Göring's Luftwaffe had to empty the British skies of RAF planes, which proved a lot harder to do than the unfailingly boastful Göring had promised. First, the British fighters, Hurricanes and Spitfires, were lighter and more nimble and adroit than their German counterparts, the Junkerses, Stukas, and Messerschmitts needed to escort the fleets of lumbering Nazi bombers; secondly, they were flying over home terrain, so they could land and refuel quickly and often, while the Germans were severely limited by their range and would have to return to France to take on more fuel. It was said that Hitler once asked Göring what he needed to win the Battle of Britain; Göring's supposed reply was "a squadron of Spitfires." British casualties between July 10 and October 31, 1940 (the usual parameters of the Battle of Britain), were heavy: more than 40,000 civilians died in the bombings; 1,495 aircrew members were lost, including 449 young fighter pilots, whose average age dropped from twenty-five to twenty during those four months. But the Germans consistently lost even more planes and more pilots, and Hitler first postponed and then abandoned Operation Sea Lion, the planned amphibious invasion of Britain that had been scheduled for September 1940. By September 20, Churchill, described by Evelyn Waugh as "a master of sham-Augustan prose," told Parliament: "Never in the field of human conflict was so much owed by so many to so few."

Meanwhile, back in ordinary life, my father bought a secondhand car—a 1932 Austin 10, for which he paid ten pounds. By registering the Austin as a vehicle for military use, he'd hoped to travel freely between Lincolnshire and Worcestershire and evade petrol rationing. As it turned out, the car was so chronically unreliable that every lengthy road trip had to be made by train.

My parents' correspondence began to accelerate in September— the first, hesitant installments that would grow to a mighty archive. By now, they opened with "My dear Monica/Peter" and ended with "Yours," which eventually shifted to "Yours affly.," and "Affly. yours."

My mother sent bright, self-consciously humorous reports from the domestic front, about her dog, her mother, the servant problem, and her first experiments with cooking (not apparently on the syllabus at her finishing school) when the Ellwood household was between cooks, along with comments on books they'd read and tender concerns for Peter's welfare.

Written from the Gap on October 11:

Remember that maid I told you we were going to have?—Well, we had her—for five days! She was stark staring mad, both lewd and lunatic, a loathsome mixture, and although I can only tell you some of her eccentricities—believe me, there were others!!! Just to give you an idea of what we had to deal with. She was slightly pear-shaped, swivel-eyed, with a chalky white, carrot nose sticking out of a chalky white face, false teeth which always seemed to stay in a tumbler and never on her gums, and one of those depressing lipless mouths which seem to go hand-in-hand with toothlessness. On top of all this, 50 years sat very heavy on her, and she had a nice little knack of saying long words, of which she got in all the letters, but neatly rearranged them to suit herself. Probationer nurses became "Proberation nurses." "Delomished," another of her words, is so descriptive that I'll leave you to guess it for yourself, with the hint that it applies to houses, just to help you on. As often as not I was "Miss Acinom" instead of Miss Monica. Being undecided as to whether her last place was a Vicarage or a Rectory, she compromised cleverly and called it The Victory.

Our nice, respectable old gardener, Barley, held a fatal fascination for her. In the five days she was with us she pursued him, tracked him down, and proposed to him!—After that he was frightened even to come in for his "elevenses." She also, apparently had designs on Father. "They wouldn't never leave me alone in the 'ouse with 'im, would they?" she said wistfully to our charlady—"they" being Mummy and myself—"Because they'd know I'd get off with him!" she completed, evidently sure that she was irresistible!

Father, I think, as well as Barley, trembled when she turned er gimlet eye on him (and of course it was never more than one eye at a time).

She also showed signs of violence, and although she finally went quietly, we were beginning to think in terms of straitjackets and ambulances.

The passage is so much of its period that it sits on the page like the fly in amber. For the English middle class, their servants had to work overtime as convenient comic turns, complete with funny grammar, dropped *h*'s, mispronunciations, and all the rest of the evidence of their illiteracy, as if servants were another species. (P. G. Wodehouse refreshes this convention by inverting the roles of master and servant; Jeeves is the all-knowing sage, Bertie Wooster the brainless buffoon.) The maid is nameless throughout, which helps to emphasize her generic character, and, though every servant story tends to hyperbole and embroidery, my mother's story seems more extravagantly embroidered than most: I can more or less believe in "proberation" and "delomished," but not in "Acinom" or "victory," which smell of the fiction writer at work. That the misfortunate woman of the story should have been taken on by Colonel Ellwood's household at all is a measure of how domestic service as an occupation was being wiped out in wartime Britain as "maids" of all kinds were finding alternative employment in armaments factories and agriculture. The Ellwoods were scraping the very bottom of the barrel.

My father also had a servant problem. His new batman, Gunner Ransome, needed to be found a good billet in Louth.

I'm afraid to say that the people here are very interested in seeing just how much money they can obtain by billeting refugees from London—prices for even a single room are exorbitant. Whilst trying to billet my batman (Ransome) yesterday, at one house I was received with all due honour and made to sit in the very best armchair. However when the conversation turned to more mundane matters: i.e. the income to be obtained from this transaction, I rather foolishly blurted out that the Army paid the huge sum of 2d [around two cents] per night per man (admittedly it is pretty shocking!)

the atmosphere became somewhat heavy and I was slung out
as quickly as any form of politeness would allow!! I managed
eventually to find a house where the people weren't quite
so intent upon making their fortune at the country's or my
expense.

He found a billet for himself a few miles south of Louth—"to everyone's disgust as it is the only one with either electric light or hot water
in the house!" which doesn't say much for the infrastructure of Louth
and environs in 1940. In any case, less than a month later the regiment
shifted its headquarters to Sleaford, thirty-seven miles southwest of
Louth, where Peter got his best billet yet. "We are having a grand time
at present," he wrote from the Longmynd, Grantham Road, Sleaford,
a large bungalow rented by another second lieutenant and his wife,
Jake and Valerie Gilbart-Smith, who sublet their two spare bedrooms
to Peter and his friend Martin Daly, a would-be classical pianist who
"ruined Mozart" on the house's piano. This nest of junior officers
seems to have been a happy household for them all.

Full moon followed full moon, with still no sign of the threatened
German invasion. On June 13, 1940, the BBC broadcast a national
order that church and chapel bells were not to be rung on Sundays, or
any other day, so that they could be used instead to signal the arrival
of invaders by pealing emergency carillons across the land. Once,
my father came within a whisker of phoning the vicar of St. Denys's
Church in Sleaford to tell him to set his bell ringers loose when, during a night exercise, a newly commissioned subaltern failed to preface
his signals with the word "EXERCISE." Contacted by radio, the subaltern continued to insist that invading troops were coming ashore
in clear view—or so at least my father understood the man to say.
For the next two minutes, A Troop was in a panic of indecision, for
no one could see any sign at all of an enemy landing; then the voice
of the commander of the troop involved came over the radio to say
that the whole thing was a feckless false alarm—so the vicar was left to
sleep on.

For the coastal artillery there was really nothing to do at this stage
of the war, but the army's staff officers were determined to keep every
unit in a state of endless improvised busyness, sending officers and sol-

diers on courses along with sometimes bizarre "schemes." My father's troop practiced being a "mobile unit" by trekking around Lincolnshire with an inch-to-the-mile Ordnance Survey map, from one set of coordinates to another. The regiment was sent from Sleaford to Otterburn in Northumberland—a round trip of about five hundred miles on dodgy roads and in strict convoy—in order to fire a maximum of twelve shells per gun on the artillery range there; this in freezing weather.

On a schedule so crowded with shenanigans, it was hard to get any leave at all. ("We are entitled to 48 hours a fortnight but never get it, though not for the want of trying.") Peter applied to his battery major for permission to spend Christmas Day, 1940, at Hadzor. Request denied: he would be needed at Sleaford on December 25, but was told he could take the twenty-first through the twenty-third (Saturday to Monday) off. Aching to see Monica again (they hadn't met in person since September, though their letters had grown warmer and increasingly frequent over the autumn), Peter dwelled obsessively on this forthcoming weekend, buying her a Christmas present—a jeweled and enameled Royal Artillery brooch that represented a field gun surmounted by a short flying pennant saying "Ubique" ("Everywhere") and topped with a crown; below the gun, a longer pennant with the words "Quo fas et gloria ducunt" ("Where right and glory lead"). The gun's wheel was inset with tiny diamonds.

I remember that brooch. My mother wore it daily until my father came home from the war in December 1945. Unless I took great care, the brooch would scratch my face like a vicious cat.

My mother's present for my father was rather less memorable. It was a pair of socks.

She met Peter at the station, and they set off for a hectic weekend together—dancing at Droitwich, Sunday dinner at the Grange with Mrs. White and her daughter, then, on Monday, a long walk beside the River Severn. Peter had meant to propose marriage to Monica then, but was too shy, tongue-tied, and poker-faced to make the change of gear from riverside small talk, and they returned to the car with the question left unasked.

That evening they went to another dance at Droitwich's cathedral-like brine baths (the baths presumably closed for the winter and boarded over to make a dance floor). On the way back to Hadzor, Monica heard the creak of Peter's Sam Browne belt, and taunted him by saying that the leather belt concealed a leather heart. When she dropped him off, both stepped out of the car to exchange their presents and best wishes for Christmas at the rectory gate. In a feat of extraordinary courage (for my father's sexual experience at that moment was very, very close to zero), Peter put his arms around her and kissed her on the lips; she responded with a warmth that he could hardly credit. It was an epic kiss.

My father passed the next day alone in a succession of empty first-class railway compartments, in which the momentous event of the previous night wholly preoccupied him as he returned to Lincolnshire and the billet he shared with the Mozart murderer and the Gilbart-Smiths. Upon his arrival, he wrote to Monica:

> Darling,
> I still cannot believe that last night was more than a dream—actually the fulfilment of what had been before but a very optimistic hope on my part. Thank you, dear, for the many pleasant memories on which I shall thrive until our next meeting (I hope all this is not too complicated but my command of the language is not sufficient for me to express myself clearly without descending to banalities!)
> Perhaps it is enough to say that the journey back consisted of a three-hours wait at Birmingham and various other delays so that I landed in Lincoln at 6 a.m. and only arrived here at 10 a.m. Despite all this, the time passed very quickly—I didn't attempt to get any sleep. New Street Station was completely "blacked out"—to such an extent that two people at least suffered the indignity and shock of falling onto the lines— a nightly occurrence apparently. Otherwise the night was very quiet.

Etc., etc. He signs off, "With all my love, Yours, Peter."

The arrival of his letter was a little delayed by the heavy traffic of Christmas mail, but when it came on December 27, Monica swiftly wrote back:

My dearest Peter,

    This morning I got your letter, mine is only a question mark.

    I didn't wonder until I got it, but you don't say whether you care?

    You see I've been kissed before as you kissed me. I loved him and thought he loved me—and so he did, but not romantically!

More etceteras. She signs herself with a businesslike "Yours, Monica." Reassurance was immediately offered by Peter, but the most important thing was that he was granted a week's home leave by the battery major, from January 1 to 8, Wednesday to Wednesday, a whole ocean of time to spend in Monica's neighborhood.

On January 4, a Saturday, they took another riverside walk, on which Peter's shyness overcame him yet again. When they got back to the car it refused to start—a challenge for my father, who was becoming an expert at repairing recalcitrant army trucks. He traced the problem with AUP 595 to a failed coil in the ignition system, so the two of them took a bus into Worcester, where he found a Ford garage and bought a new coil. Hey presto! The car started at the first turn of the switch. Wearing his kudos as a mechanic lightly, Peter managed, at long last, to propose, and Monica eagerly accepted. The only question now was whether to postpone their marriage till the end of the war, as Peter thought best because he could not bear to imagine Monica as a widow in her twenties, or to marry as soon as possible, as Monica insisted.

Now that they were officially affianced, Monica and Peter's letters became an intimate cascade of writing once, twice, sometimes three times a day, and expensive, difficult-to-arrange, long-distance phone calls between the Gap and the Longmynd were made, some lasting a full hour, in spite of the interference of both electronic gremlins and dominatrix-style telephone operators. For the next five years their marriage would necessarily be mostly a long-distance affair in which they would collaborate to produce an ideal fiction that closely resembles an epistolary novel. My mother was already an enthusiastic writer of stories; my father, who at boarding school had labored every weekend to produce the compulsory letter home, was surprised to discover in himself the joy that comes with escaping the immediate present and losing oneself in an alternative world of words. The inevitable result was that when my father eventually returned from the war, they would both have to struggle to reconcile their glorious epistolary story with the day-by-day reality of ordinary married life.

In its January 28 issue, *The Queen,* the fortnightly "society" magazine, published a studio portrait photograph of Monica, with a caption announcing her engagement. In the same week, Peter's name appeared in the *Droitwich Advertiser,* in an announcement that he had been caught parking without lights. Colonel Ellwood paid a visit to my grandfather, the rector, and elicited from him the fact that Peter's salary as a schoolteacher had been £160 a year, which made the colonel sniff (as my mother wrote to Peter, "Pa is being rather stepfather-ish, but it all slides off me and I give even better than I get"). The rector announced that a March wedding date would be impossible, for it would fall in the fasting season of Lent. Later, he would delve into the small print of canon law and find that servicemen liable to be sent abroad could be granted exemption from this rule. Granny said that engaged couples should meet as often as possible before their marriage, and planned to chaperone Monica on a two-week stay in Sleaford, where Granny sent off for "tariffs" from the two most respectable hotels in town. Peter inspected them, found them wanting, and booked mother and daughter into rooms at an upscale lodging house called Eastholme on Eastgate (all meals included).

On February 3, he sent his daily letter to Monica, in which the last sentence of the sixth paragraph reads: "A far worse catastrophe has happened to the country today as there is a new Captain in the Army . . . that counteracts a lot of the War Effort in other quarters." Monica didn't get it. She wrote back: "A little bit of news in your first letter was obscurely worded, that I didn't know whether it was sad or glad news, whether you wanted sympathy or congratulations—DO tell me, WHO is the new Captain the Army has got?" This wouldn't by any means be the last time that Peter would have to explain to her his faux-modest, circumlocutory shafts of irony.

My father had skipped the rank of full lieutenant, going from one to three pips on his epaulets, which won him a lot of chaff from some disgruntled lieutenants.

The marriage banns ("If any of you know cause, or just impediment, why these two persons should not be joined together in holy

Matrimony, ye are to declare it") were read in St. John the Baptist's Church in Hadzor, St. James's at Oddingley, and St. Denys's in Sleaford, and wedding presents and congratulatory letters and telegrams began to pile up at the Gap.

At Sleaford, Peter's mail included a check for three guineas, sent by the couple who'd supplied him with his billet when he attended a signals course in Huddersfield in November 1940. They had admired the photo of Monica that lived on his bedside table and had egged him on to make his proposal sooner rather than later—welcome advice from two people he had learned to trust during his stay in Yorkshire.

The wedding date, which had been sliding back and forth over the calendar for several weeks now, was finally set for Tuesday, March 18. It was no coincidence that the regiment was due to leave Sleaford at eight that morning for a major field exercise, leaving the coast clear for the bashful, newly promoted captain and his bride.

Monica, Granny, and Sam the Staffordshire bull terrier had set off from the Gap on February 21 and driven to Sleaford in AUP 595, following road directions supplied by Peter. On March 18 they were still lodging with Mrs. Piper in her rooms in Eastholme, and Monica had been introduced to all the members of A Troop and had become a regular visitor to the officers' mess and the billet at the Longmynd.

On his early arrival at St. Denys's (an abbreviated version of Dionysius), my father was appalled to see that the entire regiment was still in Sleaford's old market square across from the church because the buses hadn't yet arrived. Everything happening three or more hours late seems to have been par for Britain in wartime. My father and his brother Nick (who had the ring) let themselves into the church as inconspicuously as they could by using the south door, just around the corner from the square.

St. Denys's is an imposing building—a twelfth-century Gothic church with one of the tallest "broach spires" in the land, built on the site of an earlier Anglo-Saxon church of the same name—and it must have loomed over the tiny congregation on this Tuesday morning like a great cathedral. Colonel Ellwood had come by train, and was gruffly complaining about the tedium of the journey. My father's mother, Edith, was there, and so was Nick, Peter's best man, wearing plain battledress with his three sergeant's stripes on his upper arms, in sharp contrast to the bridegroom's military finery with its Sam Browne belt and three glittering pips on his epaulets to mark his newly minted captaincy. My grandfather, Edith's ex-husband, H. P., would conduct the service. There was Granny, of course, with my uncle Peter Sandison, now a lieutenant in the Royal Navy's engineering division and still recovering from a bout of measles for which he'd been hospitalized in Belfast in Northern Ireland, and his wife, Connie, who was visibly pregnant. Miss Hawxby, known as Hawkie, who had been my father's favorite teacher at his prep school, also attended. If there was a theme to this gathering, it might have been "Beware, marriage may not last."

Lent, the war, and the ordinary weekday combined to make the service more than usually austere: no flowers in the church, an organist but no choir. My grandfather knew by heart the form of solemnization of holy matrimony in the Book of Common Prayer with its dark warnings against sexual incontinence and its repetitive stress on the subjection of the wife to her husband.

At the end of the service, accompanied by the organ, the two newlyweds walked down the aisle to the west door, to be pictured by their wedding photographer as they stood in the doorway alongside Nick with his sergeant's stripes, arm in arm with a woman I can't identify, possibly his and my father's half sister Eileen. Nick appears to be the only happy camper in the photo; he's smirking, and, a head shorter than my father, he looks the younger of the two, though in fact he was two years older. My parents aren't beaming with happiness as they should be; they look like a pair of hunted animals—more precisely, they have exactly the same expression on their faces that my daughter Julia's dog wears when she stands, ears swept back, brow deeply furrowed, in reluctant submission, waiting for her collar to be put on in preparation for the short car ride home, an ordeal she loathes.

The Sixty-Seventh Field Regiment was still in the market square waiting for its buses to show up. The men loafed, bored, cold, running out of cigarettes, wanting anything in the way of diversion, when out of the blue stepped the captain and his bride, as a reward for their irksome patience all morning. Here, at last, was some entertainment worth having. They burst out clapping, blew rude raspberries, voiced jeering cheers, and kept up running commentaries on what was happening on the church doorstep. Immediately behind the photographer, not in the picture, is a happy raucous crowd of ironic well-wishers—exactly what my father had most feared.

Peter had been given just forty-eight hours of leave for his wedding and honeymoon. After a restaurant lunch with their invited guests, he and Monica drove seventeen miles northeast to the Petwood Hotel— a vast, grandiose 1905 fantasia of "Tudor-Jacobean" black-and-white architecture with countless gables, tall brick chimneys, leaded windows, oak-paneled rooms, carved-oak staircases, fireplaces, doors, and Grecian pillars. This no-expenses-spared masterpiece of Edwardian kitsch, standing in forty-two acres of woods and gardens, had been commissioned as her country retreat by the sole heiress to the Maple department store and furniture fortune. Its great merit as the site of a very short honeymoon indeed was its startling unforgettability, more like a US tycoon's mansion on Long Island or the Hudson River than anything to be seen in England. Over the course of the war Peter and Monica would vest their marital epiphany in the word "Petwood," as when Peter wrote from North Africa in October 1943, "I know at least that the Petwood is a certainty, just so soon as we can, to celebrate our real honeymoon, not just a paltry 48 hours!" though when he wrote that sentence the Petwood had been requisitioned by the RAF and was serving as the headquarters for the "Dambusters" squadron. After the German surrender, it reverted to being a hotel, as it still is now.

Chapter 10

From 9:00 to 9:45 a.m. Kelli and I were in the main gym, practicing transits and working to restore the use of my right leg. I felt painfully tired and disoriented after another night of sleep irregularly disrupted by demands to check my vitals. As I told Kelli, everyone had heard of the Chinese water torture, but few had experienced its even more intolerable rival, the Swedish vitals torture, at which, gratifyingly, she laughed, before saying that I should talk to Dr. Clawson about it. In my experience of the rehab ward so far, Clawson was the civilized and tolerant grown-up in charge of the place, and I thanked Kelli for her advice.

She also told me that she'd be leaving Seattle this time next week to join her extended family on a ten-day cruise around the Caribbean, flying to Miami and sailing from Fort Lauderdale. My first, ungenerous thought was What will I do without you? But what I said was "Have you read David Foster Wallace's piece about doing just that . . . cruise ship, Fort Lauderdale, Caribbean islands, everything?"

She hadn't.

Wallace had occupied a dubious place in my reading life for several years. I had first tangled with his work when I packed his novel *Infinite Jest* on the bookshelves of the boat I sailed from Seattle to Juneau, Alaska, and found it tedious and brilliant in equal parts, with riffs of hilariously exact observation succeeded by pages and pages of self-concerned exposition and commentary along with reams of footnotes. I blamed my unenthusiasm for the book on the circumstances in which I read it, mostly stormbound in dodgy anchorages with anxious trips upstairs with a hand-bearing compass every fifteen minutes to make sure the anchor was holding. One month before my stroke felled me I had reviewed *The Pale King,* his posthumous, unfinished novel about boredom and repetition, which was set in the headquarters of the IRS in Peoria, Illinois, and was in itself triumphantly boring and repetitious. But his essay on his seven-day cruise from Fort Lauderdale, "A Supposedly Fun Thing I'll Never Do Again," seemed to me a small masterpiece, perfectly executed: funny, lethally accurate in its skewering of the cruise ship industry, and a sublime self-portrait of Wallace himself as a walking, talking psychiatrist's waiting room of allergies and phobias.

Enthusing about it to Kelli, I told her that I had a copy of the piece on my laptop and could send it to her by email if she gave me her address. She asked me if I'd ever been on a cruise ship, and I replied, Sort of. Fifteen years before, I'd crossed the Atlantic from New York to Southampton in the *QE2.* Cunard had offered me, Jean, and Julia a first-class cabin, meals, and honorarium in return for a couple of talks on the sea in literature. I'd jumped at the chance, but the crossing turned out to be the five most tedious days I'd ever spent at sea. The fog set in off Coney Island and, thinning and thickening all the while, lasted until the morning of the fifth day, when a broad shaft of sunshine lit up the Brittany coast and the Isle of Ushant on the starboard bow, the land looking freshly washed and rinsed and shining brilliantly, as it so often does when one happens on it after a long bout of fog at sea.

Aside from that, there were few highlights to the voyage. I felt deeply disinclined to visit the deluxe shopping mall or play bingo in the main amphitheater (let alone listen to horticultural talks by some famous TV gardener, which filled that space to overflowing); I dreaded the pretentious dinners (tuxedos, black ties, and gowns expected, though not worn by everyone) and the stilted conversations with our tablemates. But I enjoyed escorting Julia, then three and a half, to the ship's crèche in the stern each morning, where, as often as not, I'd see Rod Stewart sitting astride an oversize beach ball, looking sullen, hungover, and out of sorts with his wife. I knew the man was Rod Stewart only because Jean, who grew up in New York, possessed an infallible radar that picked up celebrities of any kind a mile off, and pointed Stewart out on our first evening aboard. The Stewarts and their two young children occupied a suite on the topmost passenger deck, traveling in a class stratospherically higher than first.

Mostly I remember sitting by a window in our cabin or one of the bars, book on my knee and staring into the impenetrable gray. Often, the sea itself was lost to sight because it was so far down from the deck that it was hidden beneath the fog. I took comfort from Coleridge's first sea voyage, when he sailed from Yarmouth to Hamburg in 1798 just weeks after he had finished writing *The Rime of the Ancient Mariner*. The poem was richly fueled by his reading of voyages, from Hakluyt's voluminous seventeenth-century collections to more recent ones by Captain James Cook and others, including the account of Cook's first voyage to the Pacific by the naturalist Joseph Banks, who sailed with Cook aboard the *Endeavour*. Coleridge, now author of the greatest seagoing poem in English, at last finding himself afloat on the real sea, was profoundly disappointed by the experience:

> At four o'clock I observed a wild duck swimming on the waves, a single solitary wild duck. It is not easy to conceive, how interesting a thing it looked in that round objectless desert of waters. I had associated such a feeling of immensity with the ocean, that I felt exceedingly disappointed, when I was out of sight of all land, at the narrowness and nearness, as it were, of the circle of the horizon. So little are images capable of satisfying the obscure feelings connected with words.

For me, as I told Kelli, there wasn't even one single solitary duck.

She laughed as she wheeled me out of the main gym, past the open door of a smaller adjacent gym area. I caught a whiff of the increasingly familiar scent of elderly people at their exercises, but there was another, more pungent and intimate aroma mixed in with it.

"What's that smell?"

"I'm not smelling anything," Kelli said.

But I was. It was the ugly stench of unwashed loins, and as it continued unabated on our progress down the corridor, I realized, with deep self-disgust, that it was coming from my own body. My first instinct was to put myself as far away as I could get from Kelli. I said I'd push myself—I needed the exercise—and, gripping the pushrim of the left-hand wheel and furiously levering the floor with my left foot, I did my best (which wasn't nearly good enough) to leave her well behind.

What the hell had I been thinking of? Wittering away to Kelli about cruise ships, David Foster Wallace, and Samuel Taylor Coleridge, how had I managed not to notice my own repulsive odor? I wasn't just an old man now, I was a smelly old man, and, worse, a smelly old European man at a time when Americans liked to single out the whole subcontinent for its lax personal hygiene. I, who normally took a daily bath, liking to read books while up to my neck in suds and hot water, stank like a skunk. Eugh!

We reached the door to my room. Kelli reminded me that I'd asked for her email address. I handed her my ring-bound notebook and a pen. This time around, I couldn't wait for her to be gone.

The larger washbasin was in the main part of the room—too vulnerable to unannounced intrusions by the nurses. But there was a small handbasin just inside the bathroom, whose door, unsurprisingly, had no lock and opened outward, making it impossible to block from the inside, so I had to keep my ears cocked for unwanted visitors. I rid myself of my black T-shirt and struggled with sweatpants and underwear to untrap them from under my ass and get them down around my ankles. Using soap from the wall dispenser, I sloshed—but "slosh" isn't the right word, given the very meager amount of water you can cup in the palm of one hand. I needed a sponge or a flannel, but neither was provided. Slapping at my various parts and pits with a wet and soapy hand, I felt like a flagellant monk mortifying his sinful flesh. Water pooled on the bathroom floor around my wheelchair.

After toweling myself down, I wheeled myself back to the bed, to which I managed a shaky transfer and was able to arch my body, using the left leg alone, and pull up my pants. One last effortful transfer back to the wheelchair, and I felt as smug as George W. Bush looked and sounded when he proclaimed victory in Iraq in 2003, standing in front of an enormous banner reading "Mission Accomplished" aboard the USS *Abraham Lincoln*. In my case, the feeling was no less premature than the president's.

Chapter 11

JUNE 1941. THE fear of invasion was losing its edge, with people growing inured to the constant warnings on the BBC and the placards in every train compartment. Rumormongering had become a national sport, with everyone, including Granny, claiming to be in possession of military secrets otherwise unknown to the world whenever she returned from her hairdresser. Rationing had brought the black market into full bloom, with spivs and wide boys everywhere, doing well out of the war. But rationing also put Britons on a healthy diet and made them fitter than ever before, or since. (It would be after the war that food shortages would lead to conditions of near-starvation.) All across the nation, in cities and the countryside alike, allotments, tended by single gardeners and middle-aged couples, provided fresh vegetables and fruits. In the future, the period between Dunkirk and Pearl Harbor would be sentimentally remembered as the time when the United Kingdom stood proudly defiant and alone.

In 2016, shortly before the "Brexit" referendum took place to determine whether Britain should leave or remain in the European Union, the former Conservative cabinet minister Michael Heseltine, born in 1933, summoned his boyhood memories of the solitude of the British.

> We were sovereign. We were alone. Our convoys sank in the Atlantic. Our finances bled. Our overseas armies faced isolation. That was real sovereignty and we were powerless until America entered the war. . . .

Every time I hear those who proclaim the desirability of independence and national sovereignty, I shudder with the memory
of 1940.

But what is chiefly memorable about this passage is what it for-
gets: the Canadian naval ships that helped escort the convoys, the
Gurkhas from Nepal exercising in the English countryside, the Aus-
tralians, New Zealanders, South Africans, Rhodesians; the foodstuffs
arriving from Britain's tropical possessions (many of Heseltine's convoys still got through the wolf packs of German U-boats more or less
unscathed, thanks to their vigilant escorts and their well-aimed depth
charges). Throughout the Second World War, the remnants of empire
(all colored salmon pink in my early school atlases) were still largely
intact and were a vital source of everything from manpower and food
to military matériel. There's an obvious place for postcolonial guilt,
but this kind of self-imposed amnesia doesn't help at all.

In addition, and not from the empire, there were Polish pilots and
their planes, along with Norwegian and Dutch naval ships, the Free
French, and other refugees from countries recently occupied by Germany. England had never been so diverse in its military population as
in 1940–41, and when 1942 dawned, it would become spectacularly
more so with the arrival of American troops.

On June 1, 1941, the last British and Commonwealth surviving
troops left Crete after their humiliating defeat on the island. On the
home front, Colonel Ellwood left the Gap in Saleway and went to live
with his sister, who was married to yet another Anglican clergyman.
Granny took refuge with the parents of her recently married daughter-
in-law, Connie, in Sutton Coldfield, a town not quite yet the suburb
of Birmingham that it was soon to become. In Oldham, my father's
mother, Edith, was suffering from varicose veins. Her doctor suggested
a surgical procedure so minor that it wouldn't be necessary for her to
leave her terraced house and go to the hospital. On June 26, her doctor
attended her at 162 Coppice Street and began the operation. At some
point he left the room, and when he returned he found her and her
bed soaked in blood. An ambulance was called, and she was rushed to
Oldham Royal Infirmary, where my father's mother was pronounced
dead on arrival. She was either forty-seven or forty-eight.

My father's 1995 notes say that he was recalled from an exercise to be told the news, and that he and Monica drove across the country to attend his mother's funeral, which was held at a cemetery, not a church.

Here, for me, a puzzle begins. Peter's letters to Monica, though full of easy, casual references to my grandfather (H. P., short for his two given names, Harry and Priaulx), never ever allude to his mother, Edith. Her sudden and early death must have shocked my father at the very least, but a few days after her funeral he was sent off on another exercise in Otterburn, Northumberland, taking with him my mother's dog, Sam, from where he wrote a jaunty letter about the success of B Troop on the artillery range and a lengthy two paragraphs on Sam's adventures there. My mother's letters from Sutton Coldfield (she was taking advantage of the Otterburn exercise to go by train, FIRST CLASS, her capitals, to visit her newly deserted mother) make no mention of Edith either. Ordinary life seems to have resumed without a hint of grief.

My father was an alumnus of the old school of stiff upper lip. Strangle emotions at birth. Betray your feelings at your peril. Grin and bear it. My mother's gibe at him when she playfully accused him of having a "leather heart"—made of the same material as his Sam Browne belt—was well aimed. Perhaps he saw his grief over his mother's death as a test of his manliness, and he was doing his best to keep it properly bottled up.

But I doubt that. His mother had absented herself from his life when he was at most twelve years old, taking with her his older brother, Nick, who lived in the Oldham house during his apprenticeship with Ferranti, the electronic engineering giant that still has a base in Oldham. So the greater grief may well have been suffered when my father was on the brink of adolescence, and in 1941 he was disinclined to let his mother's going interfere with the overwhelming joys of his three-month-old marriage. Her death enters his letters on only two businesslike occasions: her "small legacy," which enabled him to buy the White House, Hempton Green, for £770, and the division of her furniture between himself and Nick.

There's also the question of how the brutalizing experience of war came into play. After Dunkirk, my father was necessarily hardened to seeing friends, acquaintances, and total strangers die suddenly and turn to cadavers. Soldiers rapidly grow indifferent to the sight of strewn bodies, as so many have attested. Did my father manage to file in his mind the death of his mother as another war casualty, akin to the many civilians who were being slaughtered by the German bombing of Britain's industrial cities?

Chapter 12

I HAD SOMEHOW lost my eyeglasses, cheap twenty-dollar things bought over the counter at the drugstore, but I couldn't read Tony Judt or the *New York Times* online edition without them. I'd scoured my room. No sign. Kelli searched the gym for me, and reported back that they hadn't been handed in. She suggested the gift shop down in the lobby, which I had noticed when I was first wheeled in on the gurney.

I got my wallet out of my jacket in the closet and set off for the shop, but was intercepted at the nurses' station.

"Where you going?"

"Just to the gift shop, I know my way."

"I can find a nurse or therapist who can help you."

Mildly irritated, I said, "But I need no help, thanks."

Kelli happened to be passing. "I can take him down."

As we entered the elevator, Kelli was joined by a friend, and as we descended, I said to them both that there was something distinctly Kafkaesque about this journey. I hadn't known that I was a prisoner in the rehab ward until that moment.

"Not a prisoner!" Kelli said, laughing.

"Well, quite evidently, I'm hardly free, which equates in my mind to at least a mild form of imprisonment."

Worse was to come in the gift shop, where I found my nose barely above the level of the counter, a position that gave me a child's perspective on the grown-ups chatting above my head. But they had several different pairs of +2 glasses. The sales clerk asked my prison escorts, "Would he like these, do you think?"

The question took me straight back to a BBC radio program that I used to occasionally listen to in the car when I lived in England. *Does He Take Sugar?* was a program for the disabled whose title, I saw now, brilliantly encapsulated the depersonalization, infantilization, and condescension shown by the nondisabled world toward the disabled. I was surprised to encounter this attitude in, of all places, a hospital. You'd have thought they would've known better.

"I'm your customer, so would you mind talking to me directly, please?"

The clerk at least had the grace to say sorry, and our transaction went ahead. On the way back to the rehab ward, I told Kelli and her friend about *Does He Take Sugar?* and how well that title fitted our experience in the gift shop.

"I liked your restraint," Kelli said. "I saw her blush, and I hope she'll think twice before saying that again."

I wondered what was the primary cause of the clerk's behavior: Was it simply the presence of my two minders, so clearly in charge of their disabled patient? Was it my height, reduced to that of a child? Was it the wheelchair, signaling my general disability and dependence? All three seemed plausible and I had control of none of them, except perhaps the use of my voice to assert from the beginning that I still had my marbles. In future, I decided, I'd try to speak up without asperity, and stake my claim from the outset of every such encounter.

Returned to my room, I found two parcels addressed to me. After clawing ineffectually at their packaging with my working hand, I retrieved my Leatherman penknife from the pocket of my trousers that were hanging in the closet. One contained a hinged hamper of fresh fruit and other boxed and bottled delicacies from Oregon; the other was a half case of Oregon pinot noir; both ordered by my friend Paul Theroux, to whom I'd talked on the phone only yesterday, from his summer quarters on Cape Cod. Sure that such a quantity of wine would be considered contraband here, I hid it as best I could behind the clothes in the closet, and forwent lunch to nibble around the edges of the cornucopia of food.

That evening I used the push-button mic by the bed to ask for help using the bathroom, and was glad when Robert came to my room. It was impossible to take a dislike to Robert; his air of unruffled cheeriness, his instinctive helpfulness, his seemingly total lack of self-consciousness, made him a paragon of his kind. One would hear him coming up the corridor, calling on each room, "Knock, knock! Who's there? It's only me!" by which time he'd be inside and dishing out a fresh hospital "gown" for the evening. Each night I idly wondered how many people had died in the gown I was now wearing, and imagined patients piling up in whole generations. But cheerful Robert seemed to give little thought to the vortex of departures I contemplated.

He lived in Tacoma, where the cost of living was lower and so were the union-negotiated wages for hospital workers, and commuted daily to Seattle along thirty-plus busy highway miles, a journey about which I never heard him complain.

He lifted me easily from the wheelchair to the toilet seat, then left the bathroom and waited outside, where I could hear him humming. As soon as I'd finished, I called his name through the door and he lifted me back into the chair. I wheeled myself over to the small sink in the corner where I had earlier made my ablutions. The next thing I knew I was lying in bed surrounded by watchful faces that I didn't recognize. They looked like a sparse audience at a book-tour reading. Some grinned at me as I looked them over.

Robert was there beside the bed. "I bet you don't remember any-thing," he said. I certainly had no recollection of passing out, and no interval of time divided the washbasin from the audience of strangers, whom I was beginning to resent. "I think the show's over now," I told the audience, and to Robert only, "How long was I out?"

"Not long—fifteen minutes? Twenty? Just enough time to put out an alert and get people from other floors up to your room."

"Thank you, Robert."

"Oh, don't thank me, I just put you back in bed. You didn't even fall out of your chair." Then he remarked, "People always like alerts, it breaks the routine."

After breakfast next morning, Dr. Clawson came to my room and said he'd seen the report on my blackout. He carried out a brief, non-intrusive medical inspection, asked a few questions, diagnosed dehy-dration (despite my having swigged down three mugs of coffee already that morning), and put me on a drip for the next few hours. He said he'd canceled all my therapy sessions for that day, and that I should concentrate on getting rest.

"Talking of rest . . ." I said, and told my tale of nightlong torture by the "just getting your vitals" brigade. As I told him, I'd been reading up on strokes, and physical exhaustion was a major complaint among the memoirists. I never slept so badly in my life as I did in the rehab ward. Once woken for my vitals, I found it very hard and sometimes impossible to get back to sleep, and spent my days in a groggy, somnambulatory state. I presumed that this was the basic cause of my blackout last night.

Clawson was sympathetic. He prescribed 2.5 milligrams of Valium, to be taken after each peremptory awakening, and said that in the next two or three days he'd be able to post a notice on my door saying that I was not be disturbed between 11:00 p.m. and 8:00 a.m., so long as I didn't put on a repeat performance of blacking out between now and then. That seemed like a promise of deliverance, and I said how grateful I was to hear it.

Sitting in bed hooked up to a saline drip, I had a day before me with all appointments canceled—no therapists, occupational or physical. I thought I ought to use the time in a general assessment of my position in the hospital. Swedish was, like a jail or an old-fashioned boarding school, a "total institution," as Erving Goffman described it in his 1961 book, *Asylums*. Patients were "inmates"; those who worked in the hospital, from cleaners, nurses, and doctors to the upper echelons of business management, were "staff," privileged to return daily to the outside world as shift succeeded shift—a freedom denied to those who were temporarily incarcerated twenty-four seven.

The rehab ward was a special case: patients' stays were usually measured in weeks, not days—my own stay would end up lasting for the best part of six weeks, three times longer than the Romanian doctor had guessed—time enough to take measure of exactly how the hospital hierarchy functioned with all its rules, conventions, and protocols, many of them designed as "assaults upon the self," in Goffman's phrase. In addition, rehab patients were neither properly fish nor fowl: some were there to adjust to their new and permanent disability; others to rid themselves of disability with the help of therapists. As hospital inmates, we all lacked the drama of the lifesaving operation and the compassion elicited from nurses and surgeons that saving lives brings.

At four sessions of therapy a day, each lasting just forty-five minutes, I couldn't help but feel we were the slackers in the hospital system (even though I felt exhausted much of the time, thanks to my chronic insomnia). At any rate, it seemed to me that we as rehab patients were pretty much at the bottom of the hierarchical heap.

It wasn't until long after my stay at Swedish Health Services that a London friend recommended *The Man Who Lost His Language,* Sheila Hale's wonderfully lucid account of how the National Health Service in Britain had treated her husband, Professor Sir John Hale, the eminent Renaissance historian and chairman of the board of trustees at the National Gallery. On July 30, 1992, when he was, like me, sixty-eight going on sixty-nine, so just the right age and a smoker to boot, he suffered a massive stroke in the left hemisphere of his brain, which robbed him of all his once-eloquent language except for one phrase, "da woahs." No one, including Lady Hale, knew what "da woahs" was meant to signify (wars? walls? words?), but Sir John endlessly repeated it as a question, an assertion, an interjection, or a sign of agreement until the end of his life, seven years later.

He had no private health insurance because he believed in spending money on pictures, books, houses, and any aesthetic object that caught his eye, trusting the National Health Service to care for him in the unlikely event of some medical catastrophe. When his stroke came, he was taken by ambulance to a hospital in the outer London suburbs; an institution that (at least to Lady Hale's expatriate American eye) appeared filthy and neglected, infected by almost ubiquitous low morale among its staff. His titles meant nothing to anybody, nor did his numerous television appearances. Professor Sir John Hale was dumped in a public ward full of other sick men, and was barely even noticed by the staff when he arrived, though he was eventually put on a saline drip for rehydration and intravenously medicated for his high blood pressure.

A certain Dr. X is the archvillain of the first part of the book. Sheila Hale finds his name on a grubby card above her husband's bed. Dr. X is formally assigned as the physician in charge of John Hale's case. The man turns out to be nearly impossible to meet and talk to, but Sheila Hale is indefatigable in her pursuit, and Dr. X eventually turns up, apparently practicing his golf swing while they talk. Having looked at Hale's CT scan (taken ten days after the stroke; in other words, far too late), he pronounces the case to be hopeless, refuses to grant Hale admission to the rehabilitation unit ("It would be a waste of limited resources"), and tells Lady Hale to put her husband in a home ("You're still relatively young. You don't want to spend the rest of your life tied to an infarct"). She asks him: "What if we could somehow raise some money? Would that buy him treatment?" Dr. X replies: "I've seen patients carried out of here on stretchers and flown to America. It doesn't work. Nothing does. Your husband is not going to walk out of this hospital. Take my advice. Put him in a home."

Nearly twenty years can be a long period in medicine, and prospects for stroke patients greatly improved between 1992 and 2011 in both Britain and the United States, not least because of improved understanding of the brain's "plasticity" and ability to repair itself. In my own case, for instance, when I was first admitted to the emergency room at Swedish's hospital in Edmonds, a doctor asked me whether I was right- or left-handed, and when I said left, he said, "That's lucky"—a remark I took to be verging on the fatuous. But since then I've read that a considerable portion of left-handed people (some say as many as half) have their verbal and cognitive facilities located in the right hemisphere of the brain, which would explain my relative ease in talking, thinking, and remembering, despite my hemiplegia; so perhaps the doctor was not being half as fatuous as I thought at the time. But the Dr. Xs are still with us, as I found later in my spell in the rehab ward.

As it turned out, John Hale, hugely helped by his resourceful and intellectually curious journalist wife, made a remarkable recovery in all ways but one. He had always enjoyed walking, and it was not long before he could limp, with a stick, to the local shops and enjoy a stroll along the path that followed the Thames, which lay at the bottom of his garden. He was an avid reader, and he soon returned to that habit, taking in biographies, scholarly books on art history, and, finally, fiction. He aced the SATs (Standard Aptitude Tests, taken by students in the United States to measure their fitness for university admission and recommended to Sir John as a way of improving and testing his language abilities), with their multiple-choice answers. At parties, fellow guests would come away from talking with him under the impression that his conversation was as lively and witty as ever, even though he had said little more than "da woahs" in different tones of expression. After the stroke he was no less gregarious than before.

The couple took many vacations abroad—to Rome and Venice and New York, among other destinations—where they roamed the art galleries, with John standing rapt before a single canvas for half an hour, glorying in its mastery, just as he'd done before the stroke. The first time he spontaneously wrote a word was during one such visit: after looking at a reproduction of *Woman with a Lute,* he carefully spelled out V-E-R-M-E-E-R, which then seemed to be a triumph. He went on to compose simple notes to friends, some of them reproduced in Sheila's book, which have the ingenuous charm of children's thank-you letters—and which were, like them, frequently written with some third-party suggestions.

When I compared it with the hell that John Hale had to endure at the hands of the British NHS, I would look back from a distance at my stay in Swedish with gratitude and relief. I had a room to myself with an en suite bathroom. I never needed to argue with a roommate about the volume or channel on the TV that was mounted high on the wall opposite my bed and was rarely turned on. The hospital was never noticeably understaffed. I liked all but one of my therapists, occupational and physical, and worked hard to please them. Most of the time, I had the luxury of privacy, with ample space to read. (In addition to Judt, I read Jill Bolte Taylor, whose best-selling memoir, *My Stroke of Insight,* I found to be an unsatisfactory blend of neuroscience, woo-woo, and outdated locationism; Jean-Dominique Bauby's *The Diving Bell and the Butterfly,* a book I thought implausible on more levels than I could count; and *My Year Off* by Robert McCrum, the British publisher, author, and literary columnist, whose stroke came at him out of the blue when he was forty-two and just married. It's a measure of how I needed McCrum's memoir that of the three books listed here, *My Year Off* is much the most dog-eared, dirty, its pages crinkled with damp, its binding coming apart. There's not a word of woo-woo in it, and its English tone of matter-of-fact irony and ordinary modesty make it the most companionable first-person stroke account that I've read.)

The relatively comfortable life I led in Swedish didn't mean my life was mentally confined to the hospital. I followed the news in the online editions of *The New York Times* and *The Guardian* as best I could, planting myself deep in the crowds gathered in Cairo's Tahrir

Square, where by June and July the elation of the "Arab Spring" was souring fast. The demonstrators who had rejoiced over the fall of President Mubarak on Friday, February 11, and conditionally welcomed the provisional government of the Egyptian Army were angry with what they now called the "military junta." Rarely has any spring transitioned into autumn and winter quite so speedily without a hint of summer.

But by far my best and most immediate contact with the external world was Julia, who found time to visit me nearly every day and had re-pinned her big, blowup prints of our drive from Seattle to Stanford on the walls of my new room, where they were enjoying the compliments of the hospital staff. She had taken a summer job with an agency called the Fund for the Public Interest, for which she and a partner would be dropped off at a road junction in a neighborhood and enjoined to collect signatures and donations for a "liberal" cause. Offered the choice between fundraising for a modest extension to Mount Rainier National Park or calling for the abolition of corn subsidies for corporate farms in the Columbia Valley (subsidies originally intended for small farmers by the Roosevelt administration during the Great Depression), Julia opted for the easier sell of the national park, because on any clear day you could see Mount Rainier and its glaciers from Seattle and environs, while the Columbia Valley, hidden behind the Cascade Mountain Range, was out of sight and out of mind.

The terms of the job were less draconian than they sounded. Gumshoeing from street to street, winkling out suburban liberal donors from their shells, the fund's employees were expected to raise an average of at least $140 a day over any three consecutive days, working a six-day week from noon to 10:00 p.m. Anyone who fell below the quota was threatened with the sack, though Julia knew of nobody to whom this had happened during her employment with the agency, had several times failed to reach the quota herself, and, before I left the hospital, was promoted to trainee manager.

She was naively surprised by the anger she provoked among householders. This being America, one man ordered her off his property shouting "I have a gun!" from behind his front door. Other doors were slammed in her face without a word from the slammer. Only rarely was she allowed even to begin her pitch for the park. After the far-flung workday ended, the fundraisers repaired to a bar to swap horror stories, with the older ones buying Julia's beers.

I couldn't get enough of this job. I needed details of every neighborhood she visited, every dollar she had raised and from whom, every
rebuff she had met, every story she had heard in the bar—requirements
that must have sorely taxed Julia's patience, but were necessities for my
vicarious life outside the rehab ward.

Chapter 13

My parents were trying for a baby, whom they named Jonathan Mark Nancy Virginia well in advance of my actual conception. According to the rumor mill, my father's regiment was about to be deployed abroad at any moment, so time wasn't on their side. From Sutton Coldfield, where she was staying with Granny in rented "rooms," Monica wrote to my father, still on an exercise in Northumberland with Sam in tow: "I've started another monthly (ridiculous after only two weeks!) and am rather disappointed as I felt beautifully sick yesterday, from early morning till lunchtime."

That was on July 10. On August 30, after more than a month back in Sleaford, they took the train down to London, where they splurged on a second, Saturday-night-and-Sunday-morning honeymoon, staying at the Dorchester Hotel and going to the theater to see Noël Coward's new play, *Blithe Spirit,* saving their tickets and the bill from the Dorchester as precious souvenirs. Total outlay: five pounds, three shillings, and threepence, as my father took pains to record. On the Sunday morning they went their separate ways—Monica back to Sleaford and Peter to the Royal School of Artillery at Larkhill, where he had to attend a fortnight's troop commanders' training course. Since he'd been an official troop commander for the past eight months, and, unofficially, led his troop from the moment when Jimmy Styles was killed at Brussels, Peter was disinclined to take the course too seriously. The report he received at the end of the fortnight read: "Given time, he will make a good troop commander."

For the course's first week he had a double room to himself at the officers' mess, but when Monica rejoined him at the weekend they decamped to the comfort of the George Hotel, Amesbury, where they could devote themselves for the next week to arduous and satisfying philoprogenitive work. My own bet is that I was conceived in a bedroom at the George sometime in the second week of September 1941.

In November, the regiment was ordered to move about seventy miles southeastward, from Sleaford, Lincolnshire, to Raynham Hall in Norfolk, the ancestral home of the Townshend family and a grand example of Jacobean and Georgian domestic architecture, long said to have been designed by Inigo Jones (1573–1652) with later additions and embellishments by William Kent (1685–1748). In the autumn of 1941, the broad avenue of ancient limes that leads from the front of the house down to the eighteenth-century artificial lake was under occupation by the army: its immaculate lawns trampled into mud, Nissen huts everywhere, bales of barbed wire still waiting to be unrolled, dugout latrines, field guns, cigarette butts, checkpoints, and all the rest of the unlovely landscape architecture of war.

My father, as a "son of the cloth," was able to take advantage of his connections to the national freemasonry of Church of England clergymen whose vicarages and rectories were too big for them to heat or light; he billeted himself and Monica with the Reverend and Mrs. Kingsford-Smith in their rooms at the South Raynham vicarage, an easy walk or bike ride from William Kent's violated landscape gardening.

Norfolk's chalky flatlands and its relative proximity to occupied Holland and Germany made it a natural candidate for airfields. There were RAF bases at West Raynham, Great Massingham, and Sculthorpe, all within a very few miles of Fakenham, the nearest real town, whose population swelled with off-duty airmen from all over the English-speaking world, as well as from a Free French squadron and a good number of Polish aircrews. So, for the duration, rural Norfolk turned into a surprisingly cosmopolitan place, especially after the arrival in 1942 of the USAAF with their Flying Fortress heavy bombers. (The name "Flying Fortress"—because it bristled with machine guns—was coined by a journalist at *The Seattle Times* when the first B-17 was rolled out at Boeing Field at a 1935 press showing, and the Boeing Corporation immediately trademarked the phrase for its own exclusive use; I hope the journalist, one David Smith, was adequately remunerated.)

It was in Fakenham that my mother found a Dr. Norman who confirmed that she was pregnant and that mother and fetus were both doing well. She was given a due date in early June 1942. Meanwhile Granny (now reinstalled at Mrs. Piper's lodging house, Eastholme, in Sleaford, where she and Monica had stayed in the days before the wedding) continued to collect vital snippets of military intelligence.

Now that Monica was officially pregnant, it seems that Granny's efforts as an intelligence gatherer were redoubled because she was determined to assert her presence as a major player in the relationship between her daughter and her son-in-law. Every tidbit of gossip about my father's regiment that she managed to overhear on her shopping expeditions was reported back to my mother with, no doubt, some colorful embroidery of Granny's own.

She would certainly have been pleased to learn in March 1942 that my parents were moving to more settled quarters, just north of Fakenham, near the village of Little Snoring; a large modernized cottage (as well as hot and cold running water and electricity, it boasted a telephone) on the estate of Thorpland Hall, not as imposing as Raynham Hall, but older, built in the 1500s and renovated in the early, pre-Victorian nineteenth century. The pretty rented cottage, two hundred yards south of the hall, was my parents' first proper home, though its three upstairs bedrooms meant that Granny right away earmarked one for herself.

Apart from the intermittent thunder of bombers overhead, Thorpland Cottage felt far away from the war, a peaceful spot surrounded by woods, fields, and farms, with the River Stiffkey, a trouty chalk stream, flowing westward at the back of the hall, whose owners, Major and Mrs. Savory, were my parents' landlords. The one disadvantage of the cottage was its distance, about seven or eight miles, from Raynham: officers were expected to live in their mess in Raynham Hall unless they and their wives were billeted "within a stone's throw" of the hall, so Peter had to make do with visits to the cottage at weekends and free half days, getting there on his bike or by jeep.

My mother was now entering her third trimester, and it was at about this time that my father began to subscribe to the quarterly magazine *The Countryman*—a subscription that crystallized an important aspect of his character, persona, and political ethos. *The Countryman* had debuted in April 1927, when back-to-the-land movements were in their heyday on both sides of the Atlantic—most of them with ties to the political far right, like Hilaire Belloc and G. K. Chesterton's Distributist League (which owed a good deal to Mussolini's Italian fascism and many of whose members were hobbyists and cranks) and, in the United States, the Southern Agrarians (a nest of explicit racists and white supremacists, including several renowned writers of the time like Allen Tate, Robert Penn Warren, and John Crowe Ransom, who championed the slave-owning Old South).

At first blush, *The Countryman* looks as if it might well belong with the Chesterbellocs of the world. It was edited by J. W. Robertson Scott from his manor house in deepest Oxfordshire, and the front cover of its first issue announced SOME CONTRIBUTORS, listing six names, all men and all with titles, who between them held a peerage, three Right Honourables, and four knights. But if one Googles the names, one sees that all but two of them were notable experts on agriculture, and Robertson Scott himself was a Quaker and a pacifist who skipped the First World War and went to Japan to research and write his well-regarded book on Japanese agriculture (his other books include studies of farming in China, England, and the Netherlands). He abhorred blood sports, but made an exception for trout fishing (at least *The Countryman* sometimes ran reviews of books by fly-fishers). In 1947, he would be appointed a Companion of Honour by Clement Attlee's Labour government for services to agriculture and rural life—a rare distinction in Britain, where such companionships are limited to only sixty-five living persons.

The Countryman was an extraordinarily eclectic magazine for which the term "sui generis" might have been invented. Two random essay titles from the midcentury period: "A New Defence Against Rats" and "The Private Life of the Earwig." Field Marshal Earl Wavell, lately the viceroy of India, best captured the magazine's contents in a doggerel poem that he submitted in 1948:

> The ethics of "bundling," the methods of trundling
> A wheelbarrow, trolley or pram,
> Dogs, badgers and sheep, a girl chimney-sweep,
> The way to make strawberry jam;
> Dunmow and its flitches, the trial of witches,

The somnambulation of wigeon,
You'll find them all here, with discourses on beer,
And maternal lactation in pigeon.

The Countryman, alongside *Farmers Weekly,* sent on to him by Monica in monthly bundles, followed my father through the war, from North Africa to Italy and Palestine. It was, as Robertson Scott proudly stated on the cover, of NO PARTY, but it represented the world that my father instinctively understood, the tangible English countryside with all its smells and sights and creatures and customary habits. When he came back from the war, on the four days of the year when the magazine arrived with the post, he'd neglect *The Times* on the breakfast table and carry *The Countryman* upstairs to the lavatory, whose door would then stay locked for an age as he caught up with the news from farms and hedgerows.

If *The Countryman* had a fault, it was one of its era: genteel condescension to those of the laboring class, whose words of rural wisdom were printed complete with dropped *h*'s and copious phonetic misspellings as if they belonged to another species, like elves or pixies ("Yew ha' tew winter 'em and summer 'em 'fore yew git tew know 'em"). The advertisements for farm and garden machinery and cruises round the Mediterranean and the West Indies clearly announced *The Countryman*'s intended readership of gentleman farmers who owned their own land and well-off retirees living in handsomely restored cottages in the country. For soldiers serving abroad, the magazine brought alive the villages, hills, and dales that they were fighting for, in every minute particular.

Chapter 14

——————————

"I THINK YOU'D find Simon interesting," Kelli said, and I did. Simon was an occupational therapist who worked with outpatients in another gym on the ground floor, but Kelli talked him into visiting me in the rehab ward. He showed up at my room carrying a large rectangular looking glass and a primitive-looking electrical gadget—a battered black plastic box with two wires coming out of it, each attached to an electrode at its end. As Kelli had told me, Simon was the only person at Swedish who practiced "electro-stim," and he looked the part, a lean and wiry man in his thirties who might have been electrically stimulated himself, a patient of his own medicine. He spoke very fast: sentences, many unfinished, flew from his mouth at escape velocity, and I caught his Canadian accent with its softly hooting vowels, a relic of the many Scottish immigrants who had settled western Canada.

Simon was an excitable enthusiast of, and insatiable reader of books by, the ever-increasing tribe of popular brain scientists like Norman Doidge *(The Brain That Changes Itself)*, V. S. Ramachandran *(The Tell-Tale Brain)*, David Eagleman *(Incognito: The Secret Lives of the Brain)*, and, not to forget their godfather, and the most eloquent, modest, and humane of them all, Oliver Sacks. He rattled off these titles and author names, and told me that I shouldn't miss a website of podcasts in which neuroscientists discussed their discipline in easily comprehensible terms. "You'll find out a lot about strokes there," he said as I scribbled, trying to keep up with his uber-rapid articulation.

He then gave me a practical demonstration of his electro-stim device, placing one electrode on my upper right arm and the other a few inches below the elbow, attaching them there with sticky tape. Nothing happened, no shock, no zap, no tingle, even when Simon turned the voltage up to maximum. He had to reposition the electrodes several times to elicit any response from my arm until I felt a sudden involuntary contraction of the muscles around my elbow.

"We're trying to wake the brain up."

"Or raise it from the dead," I said.

"Are you a Christian?"

"No, but I used to be in my infancy. I grew up in an Anglican vicarage."

Simon continued to operate his machine: off, pause, on. Whenever the slight jolt came, the elbow didn't exactly move, but, to a believing eye, it definitely twitched, although the brain showed no sign of awakening.

"The test is if I take off the electrodes and you can still make the movements, if only for a minute or two."

I failed the test.

Simon's next trick involved the looking glass. He positioned it upright, nestling against my right shoulder, its base on the tabletop, so that what I could see was my good left arm and its reflection.

"Now bend your elbow . . ."

When I did so I had the momentary illusion of both arms restored to normalcy, but it lasted for only a fraction of a second as my left hand joined its mirror image on the table. I tried to explain to Simon how very nearly I had come to being deceived, and how I thought this therapy might work for me in time, if only I could concentrate on what I saw and relax my attention to what I knew was real.

"Are you a pot smoker?"

Only for politeness's sake, I said. Cannabis had given me hallucinations on too many occasions; something I put down to my being a regular tobacco smoker. I knew all too well how to inhale, and in the past I'd managed to overdose myself before the slow-acting drug began to take effect. I'd never taken LSD, but I recognized other people's accounts of bad trips on acid from my own experiences on pot.

"Pity," Simon said. "I've noticed that habitual pot smokers respond best to the mirror treatment."

I saw exactly why that should be so. Cannabis certainly relaxed my own hold on rationality and might well enable me to believe in the visible reflection and ignore the reality of the paralyzed arm hidden behind the looking glass.

Our forty-five minutes were up, and I think we'd both had fun. Neither of Simon's therapies had actually worked, but these, as he said, were early days. After he'd gone, I downloaded to my Kindle a small digital pile of books he'd recommended. Leafing through them, I picked up a tone common to them all, a kind of mechanistic triumphalism. The brain, a three-pound lump of gray and white matter whose predominant consistency has been likened to soft tofu and blancmange, has now been mapped and named to the present limits of dissection, microscopy, and magnetic resonance imaging, but much of it remains impenetrably mysterious. Then there's the question of the neuroscientists' vocabulary, with neurons "fired," brains "wired," "circuits" formed and broken, along with such details as "servo-loops," "autopilots," and other bits of (mostly electronic) technology. For the reader, it's a bumpy metaphorical ride: in the course of a single page one may find oneself inside an internal combustion engine, a home computer, a navigational system, before one feels that one is drowning in a gooey mixture of soft tofu and blancmange.

Until his death in 2015, it was evidently de rigueur to send page proofs of any new book on neurology to Oliver Sacks, who was certainly generous with his blurbs, for it's a rare book about the brain that doesn't carry the Sacks seal of approval. But his name on the jacket invites negative comparisons between his radiant simplicity and sense of wonder, and the raging technophilia of the neurologists who came after him. All of Sacks's patients are unique human beings, brought to life on the page with affection and respect. The doctor moves among them as an instinctive democrat, vulnerable, as they are, to the unexpected quiddities of the brain. In his books, Sacks dresses in mufti and never wears a white coat.

Chapter 15

AT THORPLAND COTTAGE, my mother engaged the services of a "monthly nurse" at four and a half guineas a week. Nurse Moore came with a sheaf of tributes to her skills in midwifery, and took up residence at the end of May in the last vacant upstairs bedroom while Granny slept in the other. My father and his regiment were away at the Welsh village of Sennybridge for exercises on the artillery range there, from May 20 to June 5; then he was off again to Glenridding, on the shores of Ullswater in the Lake District, for a regimental instructors' course on gas warfare, from June 7 to 20. Major Savory of the grange visited Monica in the cottage and huffed over these postings, saying he would never have allowed a young officer under his command to leave his wife in my mother's imminently expecting position.

From Wales, my father wrote to say that if "JMNV" hadn't arrived by June 7, he'd ask his own major if he could send another captain to the Army School of Gas in his stead; then, in the next clause, he trampled over that suggestion by saying how very improbable it would be for such leave to be granted. Knowing as I do now my father's temperament, I doubt if he ever spoke to the major about the matter. Childbirth was women's business, and Peter would be a supernumerary dogsbody at the cottage, with both his mother-in-law and Nurse Moore ordering him about. Better to keep well out of things, in Wales and the Lake District, though he affected a suitably disgruntled tone when he described his activities in both.

Meanwhile the Savorys left the hall for a ten-day holiday, telling Monica that she should freely make use of both their chauffeur and their gardener while they were away.

Salter, the chauffeur, was needed to pick up the nurse, who lived seventeen miles away, and Nurse Moore herself stipulated that Monica should ride in the car, on as bumpy a route as possible, as "a nice shaking up of me will probably shake him down"—"him," for once, not "it," I notice.

Nurse Moore had other requirements as well: "With everything so ready, including me! whom Nurse insisted on shaving down below this morning, I feel badly about keeping you all waiting. I do feel the preliminaries to a birth are most indelicate. Luckily I find that my little bit of nursing—seeing others all sizes and sexes, in every stage of nudity, is the best help in not minding too much oneself."

That was on Friday, May 29. On Sunday, my mother wrote: "I don't think JMHPNV"—she had added the *H* for her father, Hamilton, and the *P* for Priaulx from her father-in-law's name—"shows the right spirit of modern independence, rather than try to stand on his own feet, he prefers to stand on his head a bit longer! I tried skipping with a bit of the clothes line yesterday morning, and two good walks, and . . . had a good hot bath—NO RESULTS! WHAT A CHILD!"

Nurse Moore tried dosing her with castor oil. Again, no dice. "A bomb woke me up with a start last night, and I thought 'Ah! That should do it!' But it didn't." German Junkerses and Messerschmitts, flying home after raiding English cities, made a habit of dropping any remaining bombs at random before they reached the North Sea, so that loud explosions in the night were familiar sounds in the East Anglian countryside.

Granny was making her own contribution to the cottage drama by falling into a prolonged period of general indisposition: "Mummy isn't feeling awfully well," wrote my mother to my father, and Granny's ailments caused abrupt cancellations of proposed expeditions to Fakenham by the three women. For a day, she held the household in suspense by issuing hourly bulletins on her health: she wasn't up to watching Howard Hawks's superior propaganda movie, *Sergeant York*, with Gary Cooper as the eponymous hero (1941), then she was, then she wasn't, then, finally, she went. This spell of depression happened to

coincide not only with my own birth but with the completion of the
sale of the Gap for £2,500 (a sum, my father said, which was at least
twice what the house was actually worth but did reflect the en masse
flight from Birmingham, then being heavily bombed, of middle-class
families who could afford the stiff prices required for becoming daily
commuters).

The regiment with its trucks and guns returned to Raynham on
Friday, June 5, and Peter was able to snatch a foreshortened weekend at the cottage before he entrained for Penrith and Ullswater—
a tiresome journey with a string of changes and missed connections at
Peterborough, Rugby, and Crewe. It was a feature of wartime that the
trains were apt, without warning or explanation, to come to a shuddering halt in the middle of nowhere and remain there, sometimes
for hours, sometimes minutes, no one could tell. The air in their carriages steadily thickened to a dense blue gray as passengers resorted to
tobacco to soothe their impatience.

On the Monday morning, Monica wrote to Peter and fondly
remembered how they'd managed to escape the cottage, Granny, and
the nurse, and find snug refuge in a nearby meadow of tall grass.

> Oh! It will be lovely to have you back! And we did have a lovely
> weekend, didn't we? I'll always remember lying deep in the grass
> with you in our field of clover. Will it all be stubble next time
> we go there?—might be if they're cutting the hay already in
> some parts, but let's hope it will still be long and wavy, green as
> the sea, with a pink cloud of clover above. And that I may lay
> in your arms in the midst of it, with Jonathan Nancy no longer
> "entre nous" but safe in his or her cot at home.

I think this is the first time that I'm mentioned as an obstacle between
them—a trope that will eventually become a persistent theme.

Dr. Norman looked in to check on the progress of the pregnancy,
said all was fine, and recommended that the nurse give Monica a large
dose of castor oil the next day, a "hot enema," and a "boiling-hot" bath
to make "things as uncomfortable as possible for JMNV in the hope
of shifting him. I can see I shall have a jolly morning too!!!!" None
of these prescriptions had any tangible effects on me or my position,

wedged in above the cervix, waiting for it to dilate and grant admission to the birth canal.

My mother fretted over the cost of paying Nurse Moore, who was now in her second week in the cottage. Four and a half guineas was as near as makes no difference to my father's salary as a junior captain, and the two weeks now threatened to become three. She was also having to cope with Granny's ever-deepening depression.

On June 11, late at night, Monica wrote:

I'm awfully worried about Nurse and expense but today, at least, this evening, I was, and am really glad to have her here. Poor Mummy's period has culminated in a mood of most bitter depression. Nothing whatever to do with anything I've said or done, it's just settled on her like a black cloud. When she's like that I don't feel it's her at all. When I said goodnight to her, she talked about gas ovens and having no future. I know it's just her time of life that makes her say those things and that the mood will pass off in a day or two, but it's most upsetting.

On June 14 I finally made my appearance in the cottage. At 1:20 a.m. Monica scribbled a note to Peter saying that her labor pains had begun in earnest. "Well, my Darling, things are looking brighter, aren't they? We could both hear each other on the telephone which was a lovely change! Our baby looks like coming at last! Nick's getting a commission! And Mummy is herself again—here's hoping I'll have better news for you still, even."

By 6:00 a.m. her pains were so "horrid" and "nasty" that she took to Nurse Moore's room and lay down on the bed there. "After observing me for about 10 minutes she decided she'd better get moving and thereafter everybody, including me, were very busy."

I am described as

a lovely looking chap with a round head, very broad shoulders, broad hips and large hands and feet. His eyes at present are dark blue and his hair, dark brown (both of course may change), his ears are very close to his head, and his expression is one of unvarying dignity!

He's got a lovely complexion and no birthmarks, though the

forceps have made a pink mark on his temple (poor little fellow, I expect they gave him a headache) but that will be gone in a day or two, probably before you see him. He's got side-whiskers and looks as though he could do with a haircut already! Oh, my Darling, isn't it heaven to have a son!

Chapter 16

SIMON AND I were faffing about with his electro-stim machine in a small, self-contained room in the gym complex at the end of the long corridor. It was tricked out with bits of household furniture—tables, chairs, a walk-in closet, a chest of drawers. We were sitting at a table which Simon had positioned so that there was a six-inch gap between it and the twin knobs of the closet, and my job was to reach forward across the table with my right hand and pull one of the closet's doors ajar. No one else was in the room.

Making conversation, I remarked on how heartened I'd been three years before, when Washington State passed its Death with Dignity law, which allowed physicians to prescribe lethal drugs for adult residents of the state with a terminal illness so long as the patient had been given six months or less to live. I said that the widespread taboo on suicide was a religious superstition because it hinged on the assumption that only a merciful God could take away life, making every suicide a calculated insult to God's grace. I argued that any adult nonbeliever should have the right to choose death over life when life became too fraught with pain or disabilities to bear.

I described to Simon how Julia and I had visited my mother in the last stages of Alzheimer's, just a few weeks before she died (of natural causes) one month short of her ninety-first birthday. Her final years had been passed in misery and terror as unhappy widowhood gave way to a vegetative state in which memory had gone and she couldn't recognize members of her family and was prone to inexplicable fits of panic like a deranged lettuce in a high wind. In my last memory of her, she is out of her nursing home for the day and in the big back garden of the bungalow that she and Peter bought for their retirement in Market Harborough. Peter died in 1996; Monica hung on till October 2009, thirteen years, divided equally between chronic grief and the great fog. In the garden, she is walking, very slowly and unsteadily, badly crippled with arthritis, supported by a daughter-in-law, and crooning in a singsong voice an interminable nonsense string of disconnected phrases from French and English nursery rhymes. Occasionally she would escape from the nursing home through a hole in the hedge, and be found wandering in the village of Sibbertoft, out of her mind.

The Death with Dignity legislation would have been no help to her. First, the "of sound mind" clause would have ruled her out, and, more importantly, she was a believer who at least hoped against hope that heaven was a real place where she and Peter would be reunited, and she would not have jeopardized that hope by committing the ultimate sin of self-murder. (In the year before he died, Peter admitted to me that he had long ago lost faith in the supernatural claims of Christianity, then said, "But don't tell Monica.")

Caught up in telling my story, I failed to notice Simon's face, which had paled and was now wearing an expression of grave severity. He said: "I don't mind you talking to me like that, but you have to remember that this is a hospital, where everyone's instinct is to save life. I warn you, don't ever say those things to Dr. Clawson, or the nurses, or the other therapists. They'd put you on suicide watch. You'd hate that— you with your obsession with privacy. They'd check up on you every hour, or less . . ."

"I've never felt less suicidal in my entire life." This was true: a mood of high elation is sometimes a side effect of strokes, and when I talked to distant friends on the phone, they all seemed surprised by my good humor in the rehab ward. The elation hasn't completely abandoned me even now, more than twelve years later.

"I just think it's important to remember that we do have a choice here," I told Simon, who was now repositioning the electrodes on my arm.

Better to die when still in possession of one's marbles than to live, as my mother had done at the end, without a functioning brain. I remembered muttering to my brother Colin in the Market Harborough garden, "This is why we need to go on smoking." Colin quit for good a very few weeks later; I persisted, not unmindful of a warning I'd heard years before from a doctor on BBC radio: "Smoking is slow-motion suicide." But these were thoughts I could no longer share with Simon.

I'd put my foot in it again, with another member of the hospital staff. My loose talk about physician-assisted suicide and the right to choose had obviously landed Simon in a troublesome position: he had said, "I don't mind you talking to me like that"—but did that mean he would keep what I had told him to himself, or would he feel obliged to report the conversation to Dr. Clawson? I thought the latter more likely, and wondered what I could do if and when the "suicide watch" came into effect: Was I free to discharge myself, as the Romanian doctor at Swedish in Edmonds had promised? And, thinking more largely, now that Swedish was reverting to being a Roman Catholic asset as a result of its affiliation with (or takeover by) Providence, would it forbid any contentious procedure of "choice"—not only assisted suicide but also abortion—from being performed on its premises?

Meanwhile, I repeatedly tried and repeatedly failed to seize hold of the knob on the closet door, both with and without electrical stimulation.

Chapter 17

AFTER GRANNY'S PHONE calls from Thorpland Cottage to one and all, after the toasts in the Cumberland officers' mess, after the notice under Births in *The Daily Telegraph* and the blizzard of congratulatory telegrams to Monica, Peter, still attending his gas course, wrote:

> I can hardly wait for Saturday to hear the full details and see this bumptious Jonathan for myself—temperamental is he? That will have to come to a stop: he's had his own way far too much already!!

Facetious of course, but accidentally prescient of the future relationship between father and son.

Until my arrival, Monica's pregnancy had been the dominant factor in both my parents' lives, and it temporarily enabled them to dilute their anxiety over the big question of when, where, and if Peter's regiment was going to be posted abroad. Now that the Pacific theater had been opened in the war, Monica's greatest fear was that her Peter would be sent to Asia to fight "Japs," whom she conceived of as subhuman beasts equipped with state-of-the-art weaponry. Germans and Italians were at least recognizable as peoples; Japs were not. The unimaginable distance around the globe that separated England from Japan allowed mythmaking and atrocity stories to flourish on a scale that dwarfed the exaggerated tales of German horrors against Belgian children (they supposedly ate them) based on the real, and brutal, German occupation of Belgium in the Great War.

An intimation of Peter's imminent departure came in August, when he was inoculated against smallpox, and the jab caused severe inflammation of his arm and a fever of 102 degrees, so that he had to spend a precious weekend in bed at the mess in Raynham Hall, from where he wrote dispiritedly:

> This is the first Sunday I have spent in Mess since we were
> married, consequently I am thoroughly fed up and bored.
> However the Battery is in such a fit of depression at the
> moment that to be up and still stuck here would, I suppose,
> be worse.

The smallpox inoculation tantalized but gave no clue, except that the posting, when it came, would likely be somewhere outside Western Europe, which left most of the atlas in play for the rumormongers.

In September I was baptized at the Fakenham parish church, and laden with such a raft of given names (Jonathan Mark Hamilton Priaulx) that I've been trying to lose all but one of them ever since. They were particularly burdensome at my boarding school, where they were taken as evidence that I was trying to live far beyond my means. I think that my only godparent to show up was Uncle Peter, whose leaves from the Royal Navy seem to have been a good deal more generous than those of my father from the army. (But Uncle Peter ended up fighting Japanese kamikaze pilots from his aircraft carrier, so perhaps the scores were even.)

Given that, for soldiers, so much of the Second World War was passed in ignorance, monotony, and uneventfulness, occasionally punctuated by sudden bursts of violence, it's hardly surprising that the best-remembered English poems of the period are about the deeply ominous boredom of army life, like Alun Lewis's "All Day It Has Rained" and Henry Reed's "Naming of Parts":

> All day it has rained, and we on the edge of the moors
> Have sprawled in our bell-tents, moody and dull as boors,

and:

Today we have naming of parts. Yesterday,
We had daily cleaning. And tomorrow morning,
We shall have what to do after firing. But to-day,
Today we have naming of parts.

So it was for the Sixty-Seventh Field Regiment RA: an endless succession of exercises, schemes, and courses, until it seemed that the
army had run out of ideas on what you could do with an artillery regiment. In October, the men were ordered to become agricultural farm
laborers. The War Office was requisitioning a large chunk of southern
Norfolk (Breckland), near Thetford, to turn it into an artillery range
and "battle area," although the land was still under cultivation and
crops of carrots and sugar beets needed to be harvested. Who better to
do this than 140 overtrained, underworked gunners?

This brief taste of life on a farm seems to have planted the seed of
a persistent daydream of my father's about becoming a farmer himself
when the war was over. A few weeks after his beet-pulling exploits,
he would borrow a copy of Henry Williamson's *The Story of a Norfolk Farm* from Boots the Chemists' circulating library in Kilmarnock,
Scotland—a book that would haunt and sustain him for the duration.

The regiment's move to Scotland came on November 17, first for a
seven-day course on "bombardment" at Rothesay on the Isle of Bute,
then for a course that lasted several weeks on "combined operations,"
meaning amphibious warfare involving all three armed services—
army, navy, and air force—with the gunners clambering in and out of
landing (or "assault") craft, real and imaginary. The imaginary landing
craft were at landlocked Kilmarnock, the real ones at Inveraray on Loch
Fyne. All this Scottish training was in preparation for the regiment's
imminent departure for a secret destination overseas. Before that happened, everyone had to be granted a spell of "embarkation leave," and
the solemnity of saying goodbye to the British homeland was formally
underlined by an inspection of the troops by King George VI, now a
customary ritual for all departing army units.

My father came home between the end of the bombardment course
and the beginning of combined operations to pick up my mother and
me for a stay in Scotland. We went by train to Edinburgh, apparently,
where we lodged for a couple of days at the North British Hotel, and
there met up with some of Monica's cousins from the Shetland Islands.

Then we took another train to Kilmarnock, where we were to stay for nearly three weeks. Our quarters were a set of rooms in, as my father would describe it in his 1995 notes, "a rather weird and glum house" with an overtalkative landlady "who stuck dirty fingers or whatever into Jonathan's mouth." These rooms were shared with Hal Brading, a newlywed subaltern, and his wife, who "later turned out to be a bigamist—and may also have been a fille de ville." I very much hope that I spent my first Christmas in the company of a bigamous sex worker in that weird and glum household.

I was a Truby King baby, as more recent arrivals have been Spock babies. Sir Frederic Truby King (1858–1938), a grim-visaged New Zealander with a distinctly Hitlerian mustache, cast a baleful shadow on the early lives of many in my generation. His vastly influential book, *Feeding and Care of Baby,* first published in 1913, was a punitive gospel of discipline and strict by-the-clock convention, designed to produce warriors of high moral "character" and, for King was a keen eugenicist, improve the race. "OBEDIENCE in infancy is the foundation of all later powers of self-control." Do not cuddle your baby for more than ten minutes in a day. From the beginning set inflexible mealtimes four hours apart, and never feed the child at night. Ignore crying. Never allow access to a "dummy" or "comforter." Keep your infant out-of-doors in the fresh air as much as possible. Under the heading of "Masturbation," King warned that a baby's hand straying near its genitals, however innocently, could, if unchecked, lead to a lifetime of moral degeneracy.

My mother believed that King was the great authority on babies, and kept a copy of *Feeding and Care of Baby* close to hand, but mercifully was too soft-hearted and impulsive to be a slave of the book's multitude of strictures, and probably thought she was failing as a responsible parent whenever she broke with King, which was daily and often.

Kilmarnock's population was swollen by regiments of soldiers waiting to be shipped abroad (Combined Operations Headquarters, a War Office department, had a base in a village five miles from the town), and troops from all over Britain crammed the pubs, drowning their anxieties in beer and Scotch. For most of these visitors, the best-known fact about Kilmarnock will have been that it was the birthplace of Johnnie Walker whiskey, with its slogan "Born 1820—Still Going

Strong" alongside the sketch of a striding Regency buck in knee boots, tight white breeches, and a tail coat in hunting pink, who holds a monocle to his right eye. To balance this image of youthful high spirits gained by tippling, Kilmarnock's grandest Victorian public house was the alcohol-free Robertson's Temperance Hotel, later the Kilmarnock Arms.

With me in the pram, my mother wandered through the unfamiliar gray streets of the town in fogbound apprehension. This was not the last time we would see my father, for he was due a week's embarkation leave at Thorpland Cottage in January, before he sailed to wherever he was sailing to—a destination that was kept as tightly hidden from him as from my mother.

When my father eventually came home to the cottage, to plan for a future together was my parents' last best hope of salving the torment of indefinite separation. The White House, Hempton Green, was up for sale. Its owners, a bakery family named Feak, gave Peter and Monica the keys, and they spent a day looking over and memorizing the property, planting each room with dreams.

The White House was hardly ideal: its most modern features were its connection to the Fakenham mains water system, so water came out of the taps and didn't have to be fetched in a bucket from a well in the garden, and its wiring to the electricity grid. It had no telephone, though, and the lavatory in the bathroom was a primitive chemical toilet whose contents had to be emptied each week by somebody whom my mother called the "foo-foo man." In 1967, when I was a lecturer at the University of East Anglia in Norwich, I visited the White House for the first time since I was eight and was disappointed by how poky and ugly it was in its unimaginative squareness and absence of all decorative charm. It had evidently been put up by a jobbing builder sometime in the nineteenth century, and the best one could say of it was that it was a house, and was painted white, if only on its front wall, which looked stolidly out over the green. The paint effectively obliterated the contrast between chipped flint pebbles and local red brick, which had at one time been the house's chief distinction.

But in January 1943, with my father at the rented cottage on embarkation leave, the White House was a happy discovery that could be invested with hope for my parents' reunited future. The house was up for auction on February 16, when Peter would be back in Kilmarnock, leaving my mother to do the bidding. Granny, flush with money from the sale of the Gap, volunteered to buy the White House for all four of us—a proposal rejected by Peter with something close to horror. (To my mother he wrote that such an arrangement would only exacerbate Granny's "introspection" and discourage her from making new friends and a new life for herself as she ought to do.) He named £950 as the top price to which he was prepared to go—the sum dictated by his mother's legacy.

After an early lunch at the cottage on Sunday, February 7, Monica drove Peter and me to Fakenham Station. Everything was now up in the air: the purchase of the house, Peter's eventual foreign destination, and the overwhelming question of when and if husband and wife would ever meet again. Drooling in my carry-cot, I was already sublimely indifferent to the drama of my parents' leave-taking; much more important in my view was the huffing black beast of the locomotive belching pent-up steam and coal smoke from its twin funnels, and the uniformed men trying to contain it with waved flags and shouted warnings and announcements. At seven and a half months, I was already an old hand at trains, and railway stations for me were sites of pleasurable terror.

There must have been a last kiss through the lowered window of the otherwise unoccupied first-class compartment; then my father was gone, lost in the acidic-tasting fog of steam that enveloped the rapidly disappearing train. As it turned out, it would be one month short of three years before my parents set eyes on each other again.

His first stop was Norwich, just twenty-five miles down the line, where he would wait for several hours before catching another train to Ely, then one to Peterborough, then the overnight express from London to Edinburgh, which he'd leave at Newcastle-upon-Tyne and change for the slow, stopping, cross-country train that would take him back to Kilmarnock the next morning. In Norwich, he lingered in the tearoom of the Bell Hotel, on whose headed writing paper he penned a long love letter to Monica:

My own darling—thank you very, very much for a lovely leave: it couldn't have been better if you'd tried ever so hard—going to bed earlier couldn't have made it nicer! I shall always remember all of it—every moment of it.

We must only hope that there'll be more to come yet and a soon end to this war—then all our life will be one long leave and money or no money, we shall make the most of it, every moment of our life together.

On the auction front, Granny had dreamed up a smart ruse. At some prearranged point, Monica should drop out of the bidding with a posture and facial expression of acute disappointment, and leave the rest to Mr. Dewing, a locally well-known house agent who had recently valued the White House for my parents, and whose late entry into the bidding should scare off Monica's rivals.

The auction took place in a room at the Crown Hotel, Fakenham, shortly after Monica and Mr. Dewing planned their conspiracy in his office. Monica would go up to £750, then hand the bidding over to Dewing, who went on to win the house for her two bids later at £770.

As Peter wrote next day:

My Own Most Precious Darling,
    The King's visit is put quite in the shade!!! I have never heard of such clever chicanery in my life! I do congratulate you, Dearest, with all my heart.

Granny's trickery earned my parents some lasting ill feeling in Hempton Green, particularly from the Feaks, who had expected their house to reach £1,000 (too steep a price, according to Dewing's valuation), but, as my mother put it to Peter:

Apparently it's the done thing to be a dirty dog at Auctions, but everybody is very put out if you're the sort of dirty dog they don't expect you to be or if your dirty dogginess is not forestalled by worse on their part!

Although wartime was inflating the cost of housing in much of the countryside, Hempton Green was probably too far from any city except Norwich (never a prime target for the Luftwaffe) to benefit from this temporary boom.

Crowded troopships were meat and drink to the Luftwaffe and the German Navy, so elaborate plans for evasive action had to be made, beginning at Kilmarnock, where the Sixty-Seventh Regiment boarded a special train that took them to Liverpool via Glasgow, Edinburgh, and Newcastle-upon-Tyne, a route designed to mislead any watching fifth columnists. Under cover of darkness the train then turned southwest and snuck into Liverpool, pulling up beside the requisitioned troopship, the *Duchess of York,* formerly a Canadian passenger liner that would carry a few other regiments beside the Sixty-Seventh to Algiers in North Africa.

Here I should introduce Lance Bombardier Richard Whitfield, who would later publish his own memoir of life in the Sixty-Seventh, titled *The Eyes and Ears of the Regiment,* a valuable book, tartly observant, with a refreshing cynicism about the officer class. Before he enlisted in the regiment, after Dunkirk, he was a junior clerk in a Leeds accountancy office, and his account of the war, seen from the perspective of the other ranks, is a world away from my father's, though Whitfield was a member of a neighboring battery (446) to 265, and the two men probably knew each other by sight.

What Whitfield remembers of the *Duchess of York* is that everyone was seasick and the decks were slippery with other people's vomit. The ship was one of four Canadian duchesses, collectively known as the drunken duchesses because they rolled and rolled in almost any sea except a flat calm. When Whitfield's *Duchess* slipped her moorings in Liverpool, she steamed only as far as the mouth of the Mersey estuary, where she dropped anchor and commenced to roll and live up to her infamous reputation.

Other ranks occupied windowless quarters below the waterline, while officers traveled cabin class with their own private dining room. My father shared a spacious cabin with another captain in the regiment. In his first letter to Monica from the ship he extolled the quality of the cuisine on offer: "I have made a vow not to be sea sick, the food is far too good to miss any meals." Whitfield was unimpressed by the food available to ORs.

Next morning (March 1) the *Duchess* got properly underway, sailing northwest across the Irish Sea for Belfast, where she joined a convoy of eight merchantmen, shepherded by two destroyers and four corvettes and heading for either Canada or the United States. Another feint by the *Duchess.* She continued this western course with the convoy for three days, before abruptly turning southward and gaining two RAF flying boats as escorts. Whitfield again:

> Three or four days later we were joined by two Tribal class destroyers and in the evening a Catalina flew over signaling and dropping flares. The next day we were joined by a submarine and passed within six miles of Tangiers and then through the Straits of Gibraltar. The journey took us nine days in all and we were all pleased to see Algiers at 16.30 hrs.

The several regiments aboard the *Duchess of York* on March 10 had come to an already conquered territory: four months before, on November 7–9, 1942, the American-led Operation Torch had made simultaneous landings on the harbors and beaches of Morocco (including its Atlantic coast) and Algeria. The ambition and scale of the attacks were enabled by the fact that these coasts were defended by French colonial troops whose loyalty to Marshal Pétain's Vichy government in France was doubtful to say the least. Some towns and cities readily surrendered, while others fought tenaciously for a day or three before giving in to the force majeure of American manpower and matériel. The British tried to keep as low a profile as possible because, as President Roosevelt had pointed out, bitter Anglophobia had spread through France and its colonies as a result of wanton British bombings and shootings (as at Mers el-Kébir, Algeria, where 1,200 French sailors died in a five-minute burst of gunfire that scuttled a considerable part of the Vichy naval fleet in order to prevent it from falling into Nazi hands). In Operation Torch, many British soldiers came ashore wearing miniature Stars and Stripes on their sleeves to muddy their national identity.

Torch's object was to create a secure base from which to attack Tunisia, nearly four hundred miles east of Algiers and occupied by German and Italian troops. Tunisia was swelling fast with foreign soldiery— shiploads of Axis reinforcements from Tunis in the north; Rommel's Afrika Korps, closely pursued by General Bernard Montgomery's Eighth Army, from the Libyan desert in the south; and American, British, Polish, and Free French forces from the west. A *Chicago Tribune* reporter, quoted in Rick Atkinson's lucid and enthralling *Libera-*

tion Trilogy, said that the Tunisian conflict was "a bits and pieces war," while General Sir Harold Alexander, appointed to serve under General Eisenhower as commander in chief of the British contingent, wrote to Montgomery that he was "very shocked. There has been no policy and no plan. The battle area is all mixed up with British, French, and American units."

The fighting was all over the map: in fertile plains of wheat, date palms, and olive groves, on the southern desert, and in forbidding mountains of bare rock and shale with, here and there, a scrub pine clinging to what little dirt it could find to spread its roots. February had been a bad month for the Allies, who had been forced into retreat on several isolated fronts, each many miles from the others. March was better, and in April the war cohered into a broad push from south to north as the Allies began to drive the enemy into the Mediterranean Sea. By May, when Tunis at last fell to the Allies, the British Army alone counted more than seventy thousand dead, wounded, or missing.

The Sixty-Seventh Field Regiment made the long eastern trek from Algiers to Tunisia in convoy, towing their guns behind them on poor roads and in lousy weather. My father wrote my mother, saying that March in North Africa compared unfavorably with March in England, with its icy cold, heavy rain, high winds, and mud into which trucks sank to their axles. On top of the foul weather, the convoy was regularly harassed by German Stukas, flying low in tight formations, and the men grew into filthy, unrecognizable mud larks.

Of course my father wanted to shield my mother from the brutality and derangement of war—from the host of young men whose lives were exiting. From now on, my father's letters to my mother changed in character. Official censorship forbade him to reveal where he was and what precisely he was doing, but Peter took this injunction a great deal further than was necessary. Reading his letters in the twenty-first century, one might think that his wartime activities consisted primarily of shopping trips in search of dressmaking materials in unnamed African cities, along with the tiresome pen pushing required by the military bureaucracy—bumf, short for bum fodder, but always genteelly spelled by my father as "bumph," as if it derived from the Greek. Accounting for his spare time, he describes nature walks in the company of his friend Lieutenant Gerry Scrivener, and lists the birds and flowers they saw together. Of actual warfare he gives barely a hint, and when such hints do occur, their only purpose is to stress how extraordinarily safe life is in an artillery regiment compared to those unfortunates in tanks or, even worse, the poor bloody infantry.

My father needed to write his daily letters and aerograms as much for his own sake as for Monica's. He preferred to write them in his private trench, neatly dug for him by his batman Ransome, complete with a long shelf of compacted soil on which to keep his books and photographs along with every letter he'd had from Monica, carefully stacked and bound with rubber bands; and sometimes with a rock-built fireplace opposite his camp bed. Here, he could keep the reality of war at one remove and live instead within the alternative reality of his marriage; remembering lying with Monica, hidden in the long grass of the uncut hayfield beyond Thorpland Cottage; sharing with Monica her concerns for his mother-in-law's loneliness and depression; making sweet pillow talk.

Six feet below ground, working by the light of a storm lantern, the air of his snug burrow smelling of paraffin, freshly turned earth, and St. Bruno Flake pipe smoke, and with a bottle of NAAFI Scotch close to hand, Peter clearly took a writerly pleasure in inhabiting the world created by his own words—a world in which he could spend a blessed hour or two in exile from the war. His letters are long and commodious; ten or twenty pages, space enough to stretch, and settle down, and feel comfortably at home.

No one who has read my father's writing (especially his published writing—his monthly pastoral letters in three consecutive parish magazines, or his papers on privateering for *Transactions of La Société Guernesiaise* and the *Mariner's Mirror*) would accuse him of having an admirable prose style. His writing is so impregnably knotty, hedged and ditched with defensive qualifications, that it's a trial to read, particularly as he shows little sense of the natural rhythms of the language of ordinary speech, vesting his all in the Latin syntax that was drummed into his head in the 1930s.

Which is why I read his wartime letters with something close to astonishment, for they are lucid, simple, and have an emotional eloquence that I did not know he possessed. His guard is down, his tone intimate and trusting. So his private letters are a revelation. The few letters he wrote to me when I was away at boarding school were almost as chilly as his privateering statistics, but his letters to my mother radiate warmth, passion, and candor—except about the war he was fighting in, and for that I have to rely heavily on Lance Bombardier Whitfield of 446 Battery. Whitfield says that the Sixty-Seventh took up its first fighting position in Tunisia on the edge of the farming town of Goubellat, forty-six miles southwest of Tunis, which overlooked a broad plain of agricultural land surrounded by mountains. Each battery was assigned to provide covering fire for a different infantry regiment: 446 for the North Staffordshires, 265 for the Loyal North Lancashires, "the Loyals" for short. In *The Eyes and Ears of the Regiment,* Whitfield tells of an incident on March 31 that involved my father:

> Whilst we were at the Goubellat positions 265 battery sent an FOO[*] with a Loyals night patrol, when they were ambushed and lost eight men. It was something that had not been tried before and not to be repeated. The FOO party consisted of Capt. Raban, Bdr. Davis and L/Bdr. Chance. When they realised that the patrol was completely surrounded they lay down in the ditch in the dark to avoid the bullets which were flying around and discovered that some Germans were also lying in the same ditch. Fortunately the Germans did not recognise them as the enemy and they kept quiet until the Germans had escorted their prisoners away and they then came back independently without compasses or guide by the direction of the Pole Star.

Not a hint of this dangerous escapade appears in Peter's letters, which are full of rain and mud, and what he thought he was doing without a hand-bearing compass in the dark of the Tunisian night, at the end of its rainy season, beats me. That the sky on March 31 was clear enough for him to identify the polestar was a lucky accident. Rick Atkinson in the first volume of his Liberation Trilogy does mention that the American troops in Tunisia were short of compasses, and perhaps this shortage applied to the British too. Even so, I'd've thought it would not have been beyond the ingenuity of Peter, let alone that of his enterprising batman Ransome, to improvise a rough-and-ready magnetic compass for use on that patrol.

---

[*] Forward observation officer.

Three weeks later the gun batteries moved north to a place named or nicknamed Banana Ridge, a few miles closer to Tunis, where an intense and concentrated battle took place, beginning with a German assault on Allied artillery positions on the ridge. Of 265 Battery, Whitfield writes that "30 enemy were killed and a scout car and motorcycle captured." He also says: "The Battery lost three killed, thirteen wounded and six captured." Again, Peter keeps mum about this in his letters home.

The one engagement he describes to Monica is with a herd of cattle, mistaken by the infantry he is supporting (he calls them "the feet") for a large German patrol of "about 60 men and three light armored cars." Unable to see this target for himself, he takes instruction on its whereabouts from an infantry officer over the radio, and finds he is shelling cows grazing on the edge of Goubellat Plain (this is at lunchtime, in full daylight). The feet continue to insist that the cattle are German soldiers and that Peter's guns are taking a satisfyingly heavy toll.

> The official report was that a large daylight patrol was severely handled by British Artillery and forced to withdraw. Unfortunately I never could persuade the feet to send out a patrol of their own & collect the fresh killed meat! That is an example of the type of war we've been playing at.

Tunis fell to the Allies in one last frenetic battle on May 7. A week later, General Sir Harold Alexander (later to become Earl Alexander of Tunis) cabled Churchill to say that the entire North African coast was now in Allied hands. During that week, my father was sent to a military hospital in Tunis, suffering not from some honorable war wound but from impetigo, a skin infection more common in children than adults, which in his case had been brought on by sleeping in the same clothes for too many days and nights, not helped by the constant miasma of dust in which the race north to Tunis had been fought.

Circumstances had turned the hospital ("the food is excellent") into a curious institution, where German medics worked alongside their Allied colleagues ("to see the orderlies mixing in together you wouldn't know we were enemies. Of course that's just as it should be"), and several wards were full of German casualties ("the wounded Huns are rather different—as they seem to have a fixed idea that this is only a sideshow in any case & and the loss means nothing to them. They'll have to alter their views somewhat when the final figures are published!").

In fact, Tunis and its sister port Bizerte, forty miles northwest, were like a tables-turned version of Dunkirk three years earlier. Rick Atkinson says that the Allies had roughly 250,000 POWs on their hands, and that "an announcement from Berlin that remaining Axis troops 'will be withdrawn in small boats' brought derisive hoots from German and Allied camps alike." Instead of being rescued from their plight, as 338,000 British and French soldiers had been in 1940, the quarter million prisoners were shoveled into overcrowded trucks under armed guard, given meager rations, and taken to Algiers, from where they were shipped to POW camps in Britain, Canada, and the United States.

On May 29, now stationed thirty-seven miles southeast of Tunis on the Gulf of Hammamet, Peter was able to describe his peaceable, even sybaritic life of touring the countryside alone in his truck, swimming in the afternoons, and shopping for provisions.

> We all got so fed up with the lack of eggs and so forth that I've rather taken the job on myself. I was very lucky in my first effort as I managed to buy 250 eggs, but alas when I went out for more today there were none. However I persuaded the Arab to keep me 150 for tomorrow and 4000 for next Saturday!!!

His only complaint about these expeditions, half sightseeing and half marketing, was that lettuce seemed strangely hard to find. In the same letter, he owned up to misleading Monica about his soldierly activities:

> I still feel rather guilty about keeping you in the dark about our being in action, but there was so very little danger attached in the first five or six weeks that I considered it better so that you should have less to worry about. Precious, I won't do it again, honestly!

That promise was broken as soon as he next found himself in the combat zone, at Anzio, from January to May 1944, where he outdid himself in his artful evasion of what he was really up to in the war.

Only after the liberation of Rome, where Peter was able to slake his thirst for operagoing, which had begun in Leeds with his bus and motorbike trips to Harrogate in 1940, did he write to Monica, "As you probably guessed, we were in the Anzio show."

Love and my father. Peter was a good son of the rectory, obedient to the high church conventions of his father, and he had a natural bent for theology. The only club that I know he was a member of was the Seven Years Association, a group of young Anglo-Catholics, founded in 1933 with the object of revitalizing the Church of England by supporting missionary work in the British colonies, especially those in Africa. During the war, he sought out and made friends with a succession of Anglican army chaplains, with whom he liked to argufy (his word) and, with a chosen few, discuss his prospects of taking holy orders/becoming a priest. This was tricky ground because he lacked a university degree. On July 1, 1943, still camped on the shoreline of the Gulf of Hammamet and living a life of forced leisure, he wrote a letter to my mother that was really a sermon, addressed as much to himself as to Monica, on physical and spiritual love.

> My Darling, both of us have seen marriages partially or wholly failures and we can both find reasons for that—but . . . can we, or rather can I avoid the same pitfalls that so many others can't, or don't. So long as I have any self-respect left, I can, my Darling, because you, the most perfect wife in the world, have made my life, my aims and my desires. My whole being centres on you, to have your love and to cherish it—Love in the fullest sense—and, knowing that your love is mine completely and entirely, (a love perfect in every way, my own Darling,) I can only increase my love for you as I realise yours for me more and more fully. My Beloved, my love for you is infinite and you have given me yours so completely, so unselfishly, that, knowing it (your love) to be so full I cannot possibly ever disregard it in any degree at all.
>
> "Love" to so many people means something physical, or spiritual or of short endurance. To us it means everything worth living for—physical, spiritual, oneness in all our senses

and infinite, that will, surely, last beyond Death. Our spiritual love—the joy of being with you, of understanding and appreciating your likes and tastes—the perfectness and calm that I experience only when I'm with you—the knowledge that we don't need "language" to convey our thoughts to one another—the complete "oneness" that binds us, not only when we are together, but also when we are apart—this spiritual love must be more than a gift that will die with our bodies: the materialist would deny this, but what is there material, earthy, of a temporary nature about this gift—born into material bodies, this, (the essence of our souls,) once created can never wilt or die with our bodies because it is a creation in itself of the soul, it is an "advancement" (awful word!) and since it is the creation of something outside the earthy world, it cannot die with this world.

And so on, for nine pages. This letter of Peter's may or may not count as a classified heresy, but it's certainly a long way away from the usual Christian definition of carnal and spiritual love, eros and agape, in which agape represents the selfless, purely altruistic love (as in Love thy neighbor—or thy enemy—as thyself). The almighty hypothesis on which Peter hangs his argument is that our temporal world, in which everything must die, is contained in a space that is beyond time, where neither moth nor rust doth corrupt, and from where a compassionate God can gift a human couple with incorruptible love that will last forever even as their mortal erotic passion eventually dies. This love seems to be exclusive to the couple in question and arbitrarily denied to, say, Granny and her colonel or Peter's father and his mother.

Yet Peter's readiness to view his own existence sub specie aeternitatis, rather as I imagine the suicide bomber does, was an advantage to him as a soldier. When members of his battery began to trickle home in the autumn and winter of 1945, those with Norfolk connections often showed up at the White House at teatime, as I well remember, and remember, too, their reverence for my father's coolness under fire; when enemy shells and bombs came shrieking overhead, no other officer, they said, showed such equanimity in situations of extreme peril. To have a blessed eternity almost within touching distance must have made it a good deal less difficult to be brave.

Chapter 18

THE CHARGE NURSE was in my room, along with an underling she had brought with her, who was on the periphery of my vision from the wheelchair, straightening my bed. I had never seen the charge nurse before, but her palpable air of command signaled her expectations of deference from patients like me. After she had introduced herself ("Good morning. I am the charge nurse here"), she went straight to the point—which was Paul's cardboard hamper of comestibles lying open on the floor. She crouched in front of it and pulled on a pair of disposable latex gloves, making herself look like a TV detective on the hunt for evidence at a crime scene.

"At this time of year we have to be on the lookout for flies," she said, fingering every fruit in turn, feeling it between forefinger and thumb for soft spots of incipient decay. Suspect items were carefully transferred into a yawning plastic bag.

I remembered how Simon, electro-stim Simon, had told me that I was "obsessed" with my own privacy, and thought if that were true I should now be in a state of outrage at the charge nurse's invasion. But I wasn't; I was just lost in wonder at the cool professionalism of her operation as she demonstrated to me that this room, which I had thought was "mine," was not mine at all but the hospital's, and therefore her personal domain.

Finished with the hamper, she moved on to the closet where I'd hung my civilian clothes and hidden Paul's half crate of six bottles of red. "Do you know what he's got in here?" she asked her attendant nurse as she pulled a bottle by the neck out of the box and held it aloft. "Wine!"

I thought I knew where she was going next, to tell me to ask Julia to remove the wine from my room and take it home with her. In which case, I'd reply that Julia was a minor, and that if I did the charge nurse's bidding, I would be inciting my daughter to commit a criminal act.

But the charge nurse took the wind out of my sails by returning the bottle to the box in the closet. When I checked forty-eight hours later, the wine was still in its ineffectual hiding place, and remained there until I left the rehab ward a few weeks afterward. In this little pantomime about institutional power, the charge nurse showed admirable restraint and economy in her methods.

I should, as I remembered later, have paid more attention to the way she entered the room. Most of the nursing staff on their first visit made a show of interest in Julia's big photographic prints that were thumbtacked to the walls, and one had (correctly) identified the image of the McCullough Memorial Bridge over the Coos River and the entrance to Coos Bay Harbor on the Oregon coast. That bridge was one of many that had connected up Oregon's otherwise isolated harbors and fishing villages during the New Deal, under the Works Progress Administration, and the series of bridges along Route 101 was a collective memorial to the achieved ambitions of Roosevelt's cabinet of wise men (and one woman, Frances Perkins) in the 1930s. When the charge nurse walked into my/her room, it was as if the walls were blank, the prints perfectly invisible. No mention of thumbtacks, though I feared they might be a target, despite Julia thoughtfully having secured permission from the nurses' station. Someone must have tipped her off about the offensive hamper and the wine in the closet, and it was clever of her to limit herself to those two well-planned objectives in her raid.

Chapter 19

———————

MY MOTHER AND I moved into the White House in April 1943, where the absence of a telephone underlined just how far she had become disconnected from Peter, whose letters from abroad often arrived in clusters, succeeded by many days of obtrusive silence that could turn on an instant into terrifying intimations that he was dead. Monica kept her ear cocked, with a mixture of hope and dread in equal parts, for the soft slather of falling letters as they came each morning and afternoon, pushed by the postman through the flap on the front door. The same hope and dread accompanied her reading of the daily paper and her waiting on the time pips for the BBC Home Service news. "Trying not to worry," honored in the breach if not in the observance, became Monica's full-time occupation for more than the next three years.

On April 1, 1943, she wrote:

My very own & dearest Beloved,
    The news is still very good & I try so hard not to worry
& to trust instead—I don't expect you hear the news? So you
can't reckon up how much, through guessing at your probable
whereabouts, I can follow your movements.
    Sometimes the wireless & the paper give bare facts but more
often they go into detail about actions on the different fronts
that are too vivid in the pictures they give—yet I'd rather
know & understand how much you are going through & what

conditions you have to put up with, however bad it makes
me feel & sometimes I see or hear bits of news that make my
heart feel like lead for the rest of the day, but always I have that
feeling that you will be alright which is more cheering than
anything else could be—and helps me along.

The wan ending of that paragraph betrays Monica's true state of
mind. She was always a chronic worrier, and her attempt to finish the
sentence on an upbeat note rings patently false. The Royal Mail's failure to deliver letters on time between Britain and the various foreign
fronts was a major cause of low morale at home, where, as people well
knew, war news was an inscrutable mixture of ascertainable facts and
sometimes ludicrously optimistic propaganda. Peter's tale of how he'd
spent one early afternoon shelling a herd of cows peacefully grazing on
the rim of the Goubellat Plain, only to find it reported as an attack on
a large enemy patrol, sent packing by the Royal Artillery, was evidence
enough of the corruptibility of print and broadcast news. As for Peter's
letters, Monica was up against his own rigorous self-censorship as well
as the official censors. At the White House the fog of war was pea soup
thick and baffling.

One day, not long after my father was shipped to North Africa, Sam,
the bellicose Staffordshire bull terrier, feeling short of company, made
an impressive leap over the fence around my playpen, and joined me
on my blanket, where my mother found us snuggling up to each other
a little while later. This was, I'm sad to say, curtains for Sam as the dog
of the house. With humans he was by all accounts unconditionally
affectionate; it was only with other dogs that he became a menace,
and he evidently recognized me as a human, if a small and insufficient
member of my species, or he would've had me for his breakfast. My
mother had doted on him and he was a lovable companion for her,
so his departure from the house must have added to her loneliness in
Peter's absence. Years after he left she would speak of Sam with tender
regret. Granny, who thought him a terror, and called him "that dog,"
was delighted to see the back of him.

In her daily letters to Peter, Monica recorded the position of every
piece of furniture in the White House so that he could make a complete imaginative reconstruction of their new living quarters, from
their Indian rugs to the dominant blue of Granny's room between

the "nursery" and the big marital bedroom. The White House looked out over Hempton Green, an unusually broad reach of common land, on which grazing, or "turbary," rights came with the house. Toward the northeast end of the green, about a hundred yards from our house, stood a Victorian building of flint and stone, more chapel than church, with a tall witch's hat belfry just large enough to hold a single bell, together with a parsonage, to which my mother paid a visit to ask about finding domestic help in the village. The door was answered by a woman whom my mother called "The Vicaress," and described as "a dear" but "rather dirty"—hardly surprising since the vicarage had neither running water nor electricity.

Nurse Moore who had delivered me at Thorpland Cottage was staying at the White House to help us all move in, and was the first to try out an 8:00 a.m. Holy Communion service. Monica to Peter: "Nurse went to Church last Sunday and came back saying 'Smell me!' She said our little church in the Rectory garden was fairly drenched with insense [sic]. The padre there rings bells like HP does. Like the shrine at Walsingham, it's full of pictures." High-church Anglo-Catholicism, with its bells and smells, evidently reigned in Hempton Green, and it slightly surprises me that when my father came back from the war he didn't latch on to Holy Trinity Church at Hempton as a spiritual home away from home, but drove us every Sunday through a small labyrinth of overhung lanes to the Church of St. Mary the Virgin in Colkirk, where the building was large, ancient, beautiful, crowded with antique brasses and memorials, and whose churchmanship was middle-of-the-road Anglican. I see now that St. Mary's, along with the village of Colkirk, was exactly the kind of church and parish of which he would have loved to become the rector himself had the opportunity ever arisen in the course of his clerical career, which it didn't.

My own earliest, most persistent memory of Hempton, dating from about the time I graduated from a pram to a pushchair, is of the village idiot—a boy in his early teens, tethered by a longish rope to a creosoted wooden stake with a swivel on its top. His stake was rooted on the green midway between the church and the row of tiny, terraced farm laborers' cottages that bounded the green's northeastern end, one of which must have been the idiot's home. On any fine day when the temperature allowed, you'd see the idiot capering, gibbering, at the end of his tether, and we'd have to pass close by him on the mile-long

footpath to Fakenham, which, past the idiot, took us along the southern bank of the River Wensum.

The idiot (I knew no other name for him) had worn his own path,
a perfect circle, into the mixture of grass, gorse, and bracken that surfaced the green. With his stream of noises, some angry, others apparently friendly, he seemed to me half beast, half human, like a Roman
satyr. He inspired in me first fear, later fascination, and later still, when
I was six or seven, a feeling of kinship, though I'm not sure if I identified myself more with the boy or with his tethered state—life at the
end of a rope. Round and round he went, and, inspecting his old terrain on Google Earth from four-thousand-plus miles away, I think I
can still see the remains of his circular path just north of the church
on Hempton Green.

Chapter 20

AROUND MIDNIGHT. THE usual nocturnal noises of the unsleeping hospital: an occasional rattle of gurneys in the corridor beyond my curtained picture window; alerts and summonses broadcast from the nurses' station and its scattered network of loudspeakers; faint snatches of conversation and laughter. I was trying and failing to fall asleep.

Under the duvet cover I felt my right hand slowly clenching and unclenching, fingers and thumb moving as they used to do. A miracle of resurrection! With my left hand I clicked on the light and pushed the duvet away to expose what my other hand was doing. Nothing at all was the depressing answer. The hand was flaccidly inert, and, as what my eyes could see battled with what my nerve endings could feel, the sensation of movement began to die in my head. I was not entirely disappointed, for surely my conviction that I was making and unmaking a fist so long as the hand was out of sight intimated a return to normal life in the not-so-distant future? I badly wanted to talk about this with both Kelli and Simon in the hope that they'd recognize it as a known symptom of the brain reconnecting itself to the stricken limb.

I picked up the Kindle from the bed table and went into *Postwar*. I used to deride electronic books as an inferior and debased technology compared with their print versions, but the stroke had made me change my tune. In print and paper, Judt's book was just short of a thousand pages—not quite a Gibbonian *Decline and Fall* length, but getting on that way. Hard to read in bed with two hands, let alone one. The near weightlessness of Kindle books endeared them to me now

as it had never done before, and *Postwar* in electronic form happened
to lay out its paragraphs as if they were independent building blocks,
with full double spacing at their tops and bottoms, which drew my
attention to how self-contained each stage of Tony Judt's argument
was designed to be. Every paragraph was a miniature argument in its
own right, achieving a crisp point at the culmination of three, sometimes four sentences, before the reader moved on to the next broad
step.

Reading Judt was exhilarating because he could see the wood and
the trees in one and the same moment. The wood in this case is the
landmass of Europe and its offshore islands; the trees are the individual nations and their politicians and peoples, closely observed over
a period of sixty years (1945–2005). No country is robbed of its par-
ticularity, its thisness, but Judt is always aware of the place it occupies
in the emerging pattern of his narrative, which is as complex as Henry
James's "figure in the carpet"—a pattern whose vital key is withheld
until the final paragraph of the epilogue. Titled "From the House of
the Dead: An Essay on Modern European Memory," it is about how
firsthand experience of the Holocaust shaped the continent's future
and why "it seemed so important to build a certain sort of Europe out
of the crematoria of Auschwitz."

Considered simply as a self-imposed course on intellectual rehabilitation (a subject not on the curriculum of the neurological rehab
ward, sadly), *Postwar* was ideal reading. It was a history of my (and
my father's) lifetime on my own home subcontinent that forced me to
confront my inbred insularity and ignorance of my European neighbors (a condition that afflicts all too many modern Europeans, as the
book shows). So many strange names to pick up and integrate into this
elaborate and many-faceted story! So many crossings and recrossings
of national borders! Such a multitude of minor themes slowly swelling
into major ones! To follow Judt as closely as his book deserved, one
was required to be sufficiently fit mentally to sign up for this intellectual marathon. I was unfit, but found *Postwar* very hard to put aside.

That night, Dr. Clawson's message on my door saved me from
unwanted demands for my vitals and other intrusions. I went on reading myself to sleep, and woke to find the light still on, my gift shop
spectacles still attached to my ears, and the Kindle fallen to the floor.

Chapter 21

THE BRITISH FIRST Infantry Division included nine regiments from the Royal Artillery, one of which was the Sixty-Seventh Field. The First Division was held back in North Africa while most of the rest of the Allied troops went on to invade Sicily in July and mainland Italy in September 1943.

Postwar, the Italian campaign has been criticized as the most irrelevant and most incompetently wasteful of human lives in the Second World War. Winston Churchill was its prime cheerleader, and both FDR and General Eisenhower were deeply skeptical of its value or utility, suspecting that Churchill was more interested in maintaining the British Empire and its routes of access through the Mediterranean than he was in defeating Hitler's domination of mainland Europe. The reasons given for invading Italy were: it would give access to airfields progressively nearer to Germany; it would give the Allies effective naval control of the Mediterranean Sea; it would divert a very considerable number of German troops from the eastern front, where they were facing Stalin's advancing Red Army; and mounting a mass shipment of Allied troops from North Africa back to England would be close to a logistical impossibility and would seriously impede the plans now underway to invade Normandy in the spring of 1944. When Churchill said "Rome is the bull's-eye," he was obviously mistaken. Berlin was the only real bull's-eye, while Rome was of precious little strategic importance in modern times. Churchill, one imagines, may still have been in—somewhat rusty—thrall to the Latin teachers from his school days at Harrow.

When the option to invade Italy was reluctantly conceded by the politicians, to assuage what seems to have been a Churchillian whim, many of the generals, both American and British, who were charged with carrying it out, saw the Italian campaign as likely doomed from the start. General George C. Marshall, Roosevelt's chief of staff of the US Army, later to become secretary of state under President Truman and the author and chief executor of the Marshall Plan, said that "invading Italy . . . 'would establish a vacuum in the Mediterranean' that would suck troops and matériel away from a cross-Channel attack,"* and General Bernard Montgomery protested that the plan for invading Sicily would turn out to be "a first-class military disaster."

Despite the multitude of cock-ups made by the Allies as they landed on the beaches of Sicily (including the disastrous Operation Ladbroke, a pet scheme of Montgomery's that involved 144 troop-carrying gliders, in which everything went wrong, causing a third of all Eighth Army casualties during the landings), the expulsion of the Germans from the island was accomplished in six weeks. During that time, Mussolini was overthrown by his own Fascist Party, and, broadly speaking, Italians thereafter saw the Allies more as liberators than enemies, and the Italian military surrendered.

War news in the summer of 1943, as it reached both Fakenham and Tunisia, was upbeat, and my parents—even the habitually cautious Peter—spoke in their letters of being reunited in a few months. When the Red Army decisively won the Battle of Kursk in July, forcing the Germans into a "fighting retreat" on their eastern front, it seemed that the Nazis should be on the brink of imminent defeat. On October 1, writing from an olive grove near Tunis where 265 Battery was camped in a state of suspended animation, Peter was making holiday plans, apparently for 1944. In these letters I make a predictable appearance as the apple of my mother's eye, and in my father's, equally predictably, as the cuckoo in the love nest, who will be parked on his granny (when she finds her own house to live in) as frequently as possible.

Their correspondence had become their marriage: it was where they

---

* The quotation is from Rick Atkinson, *The Day of Battle: The War in Sicily and Italy, 1943–1944* (New York: Holt, 2007), 13.

made love; discussed income tax; painted, wallpapered, furnished, and planted their new home; chatted about everything from politics to changing nappies; it was where they lived in and for each other, a perfect marriage in which their occasional and slight disagreements were lovingly made up on the same day, in the next letter. Their first four years of married life, so dominated by physical separation and the intolerable anxiety of war, set an Olympian standard for the "honourable estate" of "holy Matrimony," as the Book of Common Prayer describes it. Reading these letters, I tremble for the flesh-and-blood couple who will have to live up to the ideal they are setting for themselves in their writing when they eventually meet again in person. Letters, however intimate or conversational, are formal, considered verbal artifacts, and my parents' letters are like arias in a libretto—moving when performed onstage with an orchestra, but touched with the absurd when acted off it.

In Tunisia, the regiment was killing time as best it could. Richard Whitfield reports that in June the regiment handed over all its "first-class vehicles" (including his Bren carrier) to the Fifty-First Highland Division, which was bound for Italy; dogsbody jobs, like spells of a few days guarding (mostly Italian) prisoners of war, were found for a few unlucky subalterns and many other ranks. Whitfield, an accountant's clerk in peacetime, is fond of figures and percentages: "Our time was spent roughly 25% bathing, 25% exercises, 25% firing and 25% Tunis." As in Lincolnshire, my father was called on to attend a string of dull courses, whose main highlight was the commute through the desert— solo drives on which he could place himself elsewhere, mostly in the White House, Hempton Green, overlooking his and Monica's cows, goats, and chickens as they exercised their turbary rights.

It was at this period that I began to consistently lose weight, growing a few ounces lighter every week. The first doctor that Monica consulted made a tentative diagnosis of tuberculosis. The second said rickets and prescribed cod liver oil and as much sunshine as possible ("Rickets!" Monica exclaimed to Peter in a letter, not because the disease was incurable, but because in her mind it was exclusively associated with children from city slums, the lowest of the low). The third, a pediatrician in Norwich, came up with celiac, of which I had some at least of the known symptoms. In 1943 the causes of celiac had not yet been discovered and the diet of bananas, first trumpeted by the American pediatrician Dr. Haas in 1924, was still very much in vogue. In 1944, yet another, more observant pediatrician, the Dutch Dr. Dicke, noticed that in the famine of that year when bread became almost unobtainable in the Netherlands, the death rate of children diagnosed with celiac dropped from 35 percent to zero, and deduced from this remarkable statistic that the disease must be a response to glutens, especially those in wheat, barley, and rye. Dicke's deduction still holds today. Just as I was a benighted Truby King baby, so I became a benighted Sidney V. Haas banana-eating celiac case. Though I didn't have celiac, as both modern doctors to whom I've mentioned the diagnosis have told me ("Once a celiac, always a celiac"). No wonder I spent my early childhood vomiting into the Elsan chemical toilet: it was, I bet, those squishy black bananas.

On his visits to Tunis, my father shopped for "undies" to send to my mother, and on at least one occasion consulted an Englishwoman ("old . . . at least 44") who was perusing the same counter, on which nearly all the underwear displayed was black. Given my father's chronic shyness, and his distaste for shopping for anything except secondhand books, I find this scene almost impossible to imagine. He must've been desperate. But the woman was friendly; she guided him to matching bras and panties in inoffensive white. Peter's courage in the shop must have equaled anything required of him in battle, to which he'd be returning all too soon.

The war resumed in earnest for the British First Division on November 26, 1943, when all units assembled at a transit camp at Bizerte. Two days later, the Sixty-Seventh Regiment embarked on HMS *Cuba,* a Cunard liner requisitioned as a troop carrier. Richard Whitfield writes that

> conditions on the ship were appalling, being far too overcrowded, an army of cockroaches that invaded everything, shocking food and the ship's blankets were lousy. We discovered that the ship was sent out from England equipped for three weeks and had been on duty for seven months without refitment of any type. Breakfast consisted of bully beef in rice pudding. French bread was available if you bribed the cook.

The *Cuba*'s destination was Taranto, on the eastern instep of Italy, and it was a feint designed to fool German intelligence. Taranto was where the British First Airborne Division had landed (not by parachute but from ships of the Royal Navy) in early September. By December, much of southern Italy was now occupied by the Allies, and the First Infantry Division traveled by train (in cattle trucks, says Whitfield, but that may have been true only for other ranks, I suspect) to Bari and Barletta, heading north along the Adriatic coast as if to reinforce Montgomery's Eighth Army. At Barletta the division abandoned that pretense, piled into vehicles, and abruptly drove west up the valley of the River Ofanto and into the southern Apennines.

Whitfield again:

> The inhabitants of Spinazzola [the mountain village where the regiment camped] seemed hostile and sinister. All the men wore black capes and black hats and huddled about in groups on the street corners exactly like wicked uncles or Bolshevik spies. The dirty whitewashed house walls displayed many black crudely painted "Viva Duce"s and the only social life was created by an empty shop filled with crude notices in English by the Communist Party. The town was filthy. Each house had a pig tethered up outside its door, and consequently the streets flowed in sweetly-distilled manure. The children were barefoot, hungry and in rags. There was a great demonstration on the first night of the Regiment's arrival when the town's principal whore was forcibly removed for safety reasons.

My father's take on his first days in Italy is more genteel and less sharp-eyed than Whitfield's. For security reasons he is not permitted to say "Italy," though he manages to drop obvious hints about the radical change of landscape and style of life. On December 8 he writes:

> I can reassure you that though I'm fairly fully occupied, it's in more comfortable surroundings than I've had for some time— good food, really decently served, and a real bed to sleep in! (Mattress & so forth, though the blankets & sheet are mine, which takes away a little of the thrill! Ransome does very well in his laundering but it will be nice to see really white sheets & blankets & a proper pillowcase!) And, in between times, the company is good too—not to mention the fact that I can

now enjoy a real wash in a real basin with piping hot water—
I almost feel civilised!

Continuing the same letter four days later, he has obviously arrived in Spinazzola: "Amongst other things that have prevented me [from writing], is the rain, with an incredible amount of mud that has put a very new complexion on life!—especially as I asked for 'undies', Darling, but when I saw the stock they showed me I had to very hastily turn away & say 'No thank you!'—they weren't exactly indecent, but either they were left-overs from Queen Victoria's day or else the Young Idea—anyhow they wouldn't have suited you at all, Darling, being a sort of pantaloon!" He mentions that "at a later date" he will tell her something "rather amusing" about this shopping expedition, "but it isn't a thing that bears repeating at the moment!"

On December 15, with the battery moved to a more comfortable campsite on flat, dense turf at Minervino Murge, eleven miles north of Spinazzola, Peter complains of the continued rain and cold but boasts of how, as mess secretary, he has organized the batmen into a crew of builders who have installed a handsome stone open-hearth fireplace and chimney set into the wall of the mess tent. My father's brick-and-canvas private quarters abutted the back of the fire and caught its heat. Two of the batmen were bricklayers in civilian life, and made a fine job of substituting mud for cement to glue the sandstone blocks together. When the fireplace was finished it was large enough for all ten to sit comfortably around the centerpiece of blazing logs, and in the next ten days, the men's messes—sergeants' and other ranks'—would be similarly equipped, much to Peter's satisfaction.

Finally, on December 18 the order came down from divisional HQ that the word "Italy" was now permitted and that troops could change their return addresses from "BNAF" (British North Africa Force) to "CMF" (Central Mediterranean Force), which let my father come more or less clean in his letters:

You can guess what a joy it is to be in a civilised country again,
tho' that doesn't mean cleanness in the towns as you know!
But to see farms & hedges, woods, stone walls and real towns
and villages, each with its church overtowering the lot—white
people, women who don't scuttle into the shadows on your

approach (I'm no "chaser," Darling, nor yet do I find any interest in appraising the features of those who pass by, but I do hate the blatant insinuation that to look on a white man is akin to walking through dung!) In all my dealings so far, I must say I've found the Wops pleasant & their children are just as bad as the Arabs in their insistent demand for biscuits or cigarettes, but they are human & do speak a language that could, no doubt, be understandable when mastered. I had thought Italian was going to be easy, with my smattering & mixture of Latin & French, but it's not so. I can go into a shop & ask for stockings & so forth but have little hope of understanding any reply that goes further than Yes or No! It ends up in a stalemate usually, tho' I'm slowly improving. The story I have to tell you that had to wait until this time was of my visit to buy you face powder & so forth—the girl behind the counter was professing to speak English, which I admit she succeeded in doing better than any retaliation I could make in her own language, but on being shown some powder that seemed rather expensive I remembered the correct phrase to indicate something about being "piuttosto caro" (rather dear) but wishing to be more emphatic I decided that I wanted to say "far too dear" & concocted "piuttosto carissima"! It was only after I left the shop that I realised why this caused her to blush! (It's all right, Beloved, my honour is unblemished!)

My father's vocabulary was liberally sprinkled with words that have since become taboo: "wops," "wogs," "Ities," "frogs," etc. He was a child of his time and place: the early 1940s, the army officers' mess, and the white-supremacist British Empire to which he belonged. The disparaging names for these supposedly inferior races were on the one hand facetious and jokey; on the other they represent the way in which war coarsens the language with brutal oversimplifications.

My father was surprising himself in his first-sight love for Italy, seeing in it a kind of Platonic ideal of how the countryside should be: a small-scale agrarian society, presided over by its conspicuous Christian churches—each preaching a theology very close to his own. As an

Anglo-Catholic, he found it natural to genuflect toward the altar when he crossed the aisle of a church, and there was a familiar homeliness in the smell of burning incense. His father, H. P., was an Anglican who in his churchmanship was as close to being Roman Catholic—including saying the core of the mass in Latin—as it was possible to be without taking the vow of celibacy and acknowledging the pope as God's emissary on earth.

Peter took walks around Minervino Murge in a landscape to which even *The Countryman* (a magazine that he had recently added to the stock of old *Lilliput*s and dog-eared picture papers in the officers' mess) would have awarded its seal of approval.

To Monica he wrote:

> I had hoped I'd never see any olive trees again when I left
> Africa, but they're not at all unpleasant here, being much more
> organised & well laid out, in orchards, walled in, & the soil
> decently ploughed around—there's none of the haphazard
> farming that was such an eyesore before.

Such orderliness was close to godliness in Peter's mind, and the "overtowering" churches dominated both the land and its strict, economic style of cultivation, its farming implicitly rooted in its theology.

Christmas was coming, and the regiment seems to have given itself over to preparations for the holiday. By tradition, Christmas dinner was supplied and served by the officers to the men, though there's no mention of who got to do the washing-up afterward. Peter writes of spending whole days shopping for ingredients, drinks, and more underwear and a nightie for Monica in Minervino. Whitfield reports that a "large stone barn" was requisitioned as a dining hall and hung with decorations:

> Christmas Day was a roaring success. There were streamers and
> sugared almonds from Barletta. Yew branches from Castel del
> Monte, 2 quarts of NAAFI beer per man, 200 litres of delicious
> local wine, pork and turkey and Xmas pudding from the NAAFI,
> 11 local turkeys, homemade stuffing and figgy pudding. The cel-
> ebrations lasted for a further three days.

My father offers up his own schedule of festivities for Boxing Day: drinking parties that, like Northwest Indian potlatches and other gift-giving ceremonies, entailed the gracious donors taking not-so-covert revenge on the recipients.

> This morning we had the sergeants in to a drink before lunch, & this is, I'm afraid, where I may get unstuck—the "cocktail" I mixed was potent, consisting of 2 parts Brandy (wood alcohol I should think), 2 of Whisky, 2 of Vermouth, 1 of Gin for so long as it lasted, 2 of lemon! It worked with extraordinary rapidity, and now, this evening, we've got to go to their mess and be their guests. I shall be very, very careful of what I drink, and shall probably go up with a couple of bottles of beer for myself! I warned them all this morning that I'd been to far too many parties in Sgts. Messes & have a fairly comprehensive knowledge of their mixtures!

No wonder the war seemed far away, though the month was earning the title "Bloody December" as the Allies sought to penetrate the Winter Line of German defenses 140 miles to the northwest, and the Adriatic port of Ortona, which marked the east end of the line, was being named "the Italian Stalingrad" for its house-to-house and street-to-street fighting and the shocking number of both German and Allied casualties there during the Christmas "holidays."

On January 3, 1944, the Sixty-Seventh Field Regiment crossed the Apennines and set up a new camp outside the ruined town of Battipaglia, which had been pulverized by USAAF bombing in September, when Lieutenant General Mark Clark's Fifth Army landed on the beaches of Salerno, eleven miles to the northwest. Nearly five months later, a fleet of DUKWs (amphibious trucks) and other shallow-draft landing craft was being assembled at Salerno, and similar flotillas were marshaling at Naples and two other ports. It was obvious to the troops that yet another amphibious assault was planned for them in the very near future, though no one yet knew where. Richard Whitfield says that he and his mates believed that they were heading for the Yugoslavian coast, where they would reinforce Marshal Tito's Partisans.

After the landing ships were sorted out, too little rehearsal time was left for exercises. Whitfield says that only a couple took place, on consecutive days, January 18 and 19, the first American, the second British. The American one was "a complete fiasco" that involved the sinking of twenty overloaded DUKWs (a likely underestimate; Martin Blumenson, an official historian for the US Army, says that forty DUKWs went to the bottom) and the loss of "two battalions' worth of guns and signal equipment," while "few troops landed in their correct places, all were late and some never [landed] at all." The British exercise didn't go much better: "The infantry were landed by the Navy on the completely wrong beach. There was a demand for further training and exercise but there was no time to do that." The Sixty-Seventh Field went aboard LST (Landing Ship, Tank) 301 that same afternoon. LST 301, an ungainly but efficient sea monster, built in the United States and on loan to Britain under the terms of the Lend-Lease Act, was crammed with four hundred troops, along with the regiment's trucks and guns, when it put to sea at one minute after midnight on January 21. Once safely offshore, the men were told that they were bound for Anzio ("the birthplace of both Nero and Caligula," writes Whitfield).

Anzio is about 120 nautical miles from Salerno, and the huge convoy of 374 ships took twenty-five hours to get there, which gives them an average speed of barely five knots. They crawled toward their destination, trying to make as little giveaway white water wake as possible, and allowing for the blunt, roll-on, roll-off bows of so many of their number. They were lucky with the weather. The voyage was made in a light fog—just enough to make them difficult to spot from the air.

This slow progress allowed my father to spend the whole of January 21 writing a very carefully phrased letter to my mother, which reads as if he put it through multiple drafts to get it right. Recent amphibious landings, on the southeast coast of Sicily and then again at Salerno, had gone so badly, causing many hundreds more fatalities than had been expected, that it was only prudent of my father to anticipate his own death at Anzio. What he now needed to do was write something that would serve as a last (though theologically optimistic) letter if he was killed the next day, but wouldn't unduly upset Monica with intimations of his likely death if he happened to survive the landings.

The letter begins with his usual salutation, "My very Own Most Beloved Darling," and thanks her for her recent batch of "five most perfectly lovely airletters," which promise the arrival of both a home-made cake and a home-knit sweater. He goes on to warn her of his latest consignment of underwear: "Oh! Darling, I'm afraid you will be horribly disappointed in the undies when they arrive, as they're neither very smart nor of good material—but I will get you some that are better just as soon as possible, perhaps without at the same time lining an Italian's pocket with paper lire!" He advises Monica about their joint income tax return, which will fall due in April ("Poor Darling, You do have a time trying, very ably, to cope, with these abstruse business matters"), and instructs her to write to Mr. Porter, the manager of their local branch of Lloyds Bank, who should have all the documents she'll need. He tries to alert her to the burgeoning egotism of their nineteen-month-old son: "I suppose nothing will shame him at all & that he will always regard the world & its other occupants as simply a provision for his own support & enjoyment!" The facetious exclamation point doesn't even begin to disguise his real anxiety about what was going on back home in his presently fatherless family. He commiserates with Monica on her having to find yet another adoptive home for Sam, the Staffordshire bull terrier; he and the wing commander had fallen out, but Monica thought she'd found an army major who was keen to take the dog on.

Only after all these issues have been addressed in detail does Peter get around to what is chiefly on his mind. Enlarging on a simile of Monica's in which she likened their situation to a couple taking a walk "around the block," momentarily losing sight of each other in the crowd and then immediately regaining it, but always with the assurance that they were both circling the same block at the same time, Peter writes:

Our love is there always joining us—making us a unity in its strength and intensity. If, for a time, we stand still or get jostled back, we can both find deep consolation in knowing that, at last, we shall be united again, forever and for all eternity, in the love that God has given us to cherish and to increase so that we know, even now, that it is the greatest and most precious of all things in life and afterwards. If it's a long time before we meet again, we both shall find patience and comfort in that—you with J to comfort you, to ease the burden of the present, and I in the knowledge that no matter how bleak the moment may be, how futile or helpless it may seem, nothing can prevent our love, nothing can ever come between us. And both of us put our faith and hope in the belief that God is with us, caring for us, and that He will answer our prayers. No other man on this earth can have had such love as you have given me, Dear Heart, nor found, with you to help and comfort me, to console and encourage me, that life is not a day to day business at all but a prelude to paradise, where love overrules all else. The unity and perfection of our love will outlive us, Beloved, and will find its complete consummation only when we are together for all eternity: though now, we believe our love to be complete, it will never be complete, Darling, in the full sense, as we shall always find deeper and greater means of unifying our Heart, Soul and Body even more closely in this life and afterwards. There can never be any limits to our love or to its increase, Dearest—it is infinite, and nothing can ever alter it or Us. I love and adore and worship you above all the world—every part of you, the love of your Heart, so deep and pure and strong, and all of your Soul and Body—all an expression of the whole that makes you so very much more than the most perfect wife that any man could ever have or pray for or create in his imagination. If it weren't so, J would not be what he is, an image of yourself in his every expression, in his perfection. And, if he has a little devil inside him on occasions, it can only be his heritage from me, Darling—a devil that you've purged me of, & are doing so for him too! This does not mean that you have made me perfect too, Beloved, but that you have given me a capacity for loving, for seeing life in a truer and finer perspective, for realisation of what love means, that I would never have had without you. You mean all the world and more than that to me, Dear Heart, you are my life and I must be away from you, cheering me, encouraging me; and in your arms, or in my happiness; and your love is my one comfort, the only comfort I need when the sweet and perfect memories I have of you, I forget all else but the eternity and strength of the unity that God alone is able to give us. May He answer our prayers and bring us together again soon, and in the meantime, give us the courage of our beliefs.

God bless you and keep you and Jonathan always, my Beloved Darling. I love you, my own, with all the strength I have, every atom of my love, of my Heart, Soul and Body is yours forever. I love and adore and worship you above life itself, my own Sweetheart. Forever your very own Peter.

Where another writer might have chosen a more explicitly religious word, like the "hereafter" or the "afterlife," my father twice settles for the common or garden "afterwards," as if personal resurrection followed death as naturally as drinks follow seeing a movie. To a non-believer like me there's something preposterous in his view of life and death, but I can't help but admire the unquestioning sturdiness of his faith—a faith of which I have no doubt at all.

In his grim, funny, unforgettable poem "Aubade," Philip Larkin describes religion as "That vast moth-eaten musical brocade / Created to pretend we never die." My father chose never to notice a single moth hole in the brocade, until he was deep in his forties and the moths began to attack, first in timid ones and twos, and then in swarms. His air of absolute certitude used to madden me when I was in my adolescence and he was smugly trotting out old favorites from his stock of godly quotations like "Theology is the queen of the sciences, old boy, queen of the sciences." How he had managed to fight in a brutal world war, killing people on a daily basis with his field glasses and slide rule, yet was seemingly immune to the doubt that haunted so many of his generation, I couldn't fathom. It took the arrival of the moths for me to appreciate the sheer strength of the fortifications of faith he'd built around himself, just as they started to crumble.

Chapter 22

THE REHAB WARD psychologist was in my room. The last time I'd encountered her was a couple of days after our initial interview, when she'd ducked her head around my door to ask me to tell her how her lame story about the forgetful woman in the supermarket had ended. I told her. Obviously she had a box to check on her official patient form that was labeled "Short-Term Memory." "Thank you," she said, "that's all I need to know. Bye!" and withdrew her head from the door. This time around she had fully entered the room and perched on the edge of the bed, as if positioning herself for a confidential heart-to-heart.

"We've just had our weekly Monday meeting, and we talked a lot about you! We think you are very depressed."

I was astonished. For the last ten days or so I had been fielding phone calls from old friends like Paul Theroux, Bob Silvers of *The New York Review of Books,* and Gary Fisketjon of Knopf, all of whom had remarked on their surprise at my good humor about my current circumstances, and they were right; I was surprising myself with my elation at having come out of the stroke alive and with, apparently, a still-functioning brain and memory. I was all too intimate with the black dog of depression and the paralysis of mind that it inflicts. In the rehab ward, I often felt frustrated and sometimes became angry at being treated by strangers as if I were an unruly child again, but—at least when my door was shut against unwanted intrusions—I was not depressed.

I said, "And Dr. Clawson was at your meeting?"

"Yes."

"And he thinks I'm depressed?"

"Yes."

"So tell me, what symptoms am I showing of this so-called depression?"

She enumerated them. Item: I never showed up in the communal area by the nurses' station to eat my meals. Item: I kept the long curtain pulled between me and the corridor outside my room. Item: I didn't interact socially with the other patients on the ward. Ergo: I was clinically depressed.

I quailed before the sheer bulk of the explaining that I'd have to do to get myself off this particular hook. Clearly the psychologist didn't have the faintest inkling of the daily pattern of a writer's life. Most important of all, she didn't recognize that both reading and writing are intrinsically sociable activities even though both take place in private solitude. Neither reader nor writer stops being a functioning member of society just because each is sitting alone in a room, where both find themselves called on to make moral and social choices that are more subtle and consequential than nearly all of those they habitually encounter in everyday life.

But trying to interest the psychologist in this argument was like trying to force a filet steak, singed blue to rare, down the throat of a vegan. She wasn't having any of it. Putting on a show of patient placation, as if soothing a toddler, she asked: "So what book are you reading now, then?"

"Among others, mostly about strokes, I'm reading *Postwar* by Tony Judt."

I would have given a great deal to see the faintest glimmer of recognition in her eyes: the book had been widely and admiringly reviewed, had appeared on several national best-seller lists, and its author, a magnet for controversy, had been a "public intellectual," often seen and heard on television and radio. But to the psychologist he was apparently an obscure nobody.

I tried to extol *Postwar*'s ambitious geographical and political range across Europe, east and west, its satisfying intricacy, and its always-acute moral consciousness, but my voice came back to me as a string of feeble bleats, vain as those of a lost sheep.

As for my nonappearance at mealtimes in the communal area,

God knows but I'd tried that too. Every conversation that I overheard was about symptoms and the regime of prescription drugs that each patient was taking. Because I was in a hospital, did that mean that I had to participate in hospital small talk when I could be reading Judt, or, at breakfast, skimming the news from the online *New York Times* and indulging myself in the Obituaries page of *The Guardian*? I'd been addicted to obituaries for more than forty years, reading them for English lives satisfactorily completed and boiled down to a few hundred words, like model ships in bottles, or lives rudely interrupted in mid-career by an accident, a crime, a suicide, a cancer. The best, funniest, most resourceful obituaries had been in the *Telegraph,* but they were now hidden behind a paywall, and though I missed their ironic humor I wasn't quite prepared to subscribe to the paper's reactionary politics. The *Telegraph,* unsurprisingly, had always been Granny's daily paper.

I told the psychologist that, accustomed to solitude in my working life, I found the company I kept in the hospital almost too much of a good thing. Four forty-five-minute sessions with different therapists each day provided me with more conversation than I was used to, and that was only the beginning. Richard, the wine-bibbing nurse and University of Michigan English graduate, had taken to dropping in on my room during lulls on his schedule. Or the cleaners, mostly Somali and Ethiopian women who showed up in the afternoons with their mops and pails and with whom I talked about their children and the slippery ladder of college entrance, a topic that seemed to engross them all. I listed names as evidence of my gregarious hospital life: Richard . . . Pat from Maine . . . Kelli . . . Kathy (she and her husband owned a boat, a pocket-size motor cruiser that they kept on moorings somewhere along the Snoqualmie River and in which they'd made small but intricate voyages to the American San Juans and Canadian Gulf Islands) . . . Trish . . . Shannon . . . Robert . . . Simon . . .

Simon. It must have been Simon who had brought the psychologist to my room. But that was entirely my own stupid fault for alluding, however distantly and hypothetically, to the Washington State Death with Dignity Act. "I don't mind you talking to me like that," Simon had said, but I couldn't, not really. Just by uttering the phrase "Death with Dignity," I had placed the weight of the multimillion (multibillion?) dollar Swedish medical empire on Simon's back, and had I been standing in his shoes, I too would have done as he did and tipped off Dr. Clawson, just on the off-chance that one fine day I might be found hanged in the en suite bathroom. I knew that he knew I knew, and he knew that I knew he knew, and so our regular electro-stim sessions became noticeably more constrained and formal. Golden rule: never mention suicide in a hospital, especially not in a Catholic hospital, or any hospital where God and medicine work cheek by jowl.

Chapter 23

JUST AFTER MIDNIGHT, Saturday, January 22, 1944, between two and three miles offshore from the low and marshy coastal plain where Anzio and its twin town of Nettuno, three miles to the east, meet the Tyrrhenian Sea. The sea is calm, visibility good, and the light onshore breeze is barely sufficient to carry the faint sounds of anchor chains rumbling from their lockers, shouted commands, and the low throbbing of marine diesel engines, to the sleeping or deserted seaside towns. Five miles to the northwest of Anzio, a beach code-named Peter is slated to be the landing ground for the British First Division, now incorporated as part of the American VI Corps. The beach, fringed with maritime pines, will give access to the Padiglione Woods, where tightly clustered cork oaks grow among the scrub pines and where, in this considerable stretch of evergreenery, many artillery batteries might be persuaded to disappear from enemy sight. LST 301 is in the process of anchoring on the ten-fathom line offshore, with the Sixty-Seventh Field Artillery Regiment aboard, as fast-moving patrol boats chivvy the arriving ships into position.

Seven miles down the coast another, larger fleet is assembling in the darkness: American troops, who outnumber the British by three to one, are readying themselves to land inside the Anzio harbor and on the beaches east of Nettuno, code-named X-Ray. The soldiers aboard the ships, living now on the toxic cocktail of fear and adrenaline, exchange terse, profanity-laced jokes to keep their spirits up. Everyone is counting down the minutes to go before a replay of the Salerno landings—the blaze of artillery and machine-gun fire, the casualties to be measured in the several thousands, the gut-wrenching deaths and injuries of best friends.

The landings are set to begin at 0200. At 0153, two Royal Navy vessels open the proceedings with a continuous barrage of five-inch rocket shells, 1,500 of them in five minutes, six per second. As they explode, the shells are sufficiently earthshaking to detonate many of the land mines that the Germans have left buried on the beaches, and the air is filled with the sound of breaking windows falling from their frames into the streets. But their primary effect is visual: for five minutes Anzio and Nettuno stand violently illuminated, as if by some giant, rapidly pulsating strobe. Eerie white light bounces off the white stucco buildings of the twin towns, converting them from three to two dimensions; a single black page ornamented with blindingly white rectangles.

An intelligence officer reported that this weird *son et lumière* entertainment "made a tremendous noise, achieved no good results, and was prejudicial to surprise," according to Rick Atkinson. (At the same moment, ships from the US and Royal Navies mounted barrages at Civitavecchia, forty miles up the coast from Anzio, and Terracina, down to the southeast, just to confuse the Germans. Dummy landings were also staged off the coasts of Corsica and Sardinia.)

After the show was over, the entire American fleet waited with bated breath, but nothing happened, except for a single, hesitant stutter of machine-gun fire from the southeastern end of the X-Ray zone. A gun crew aboard one of the destroyers accurately pinpointed where the muzzle flashes were coming from and shelled the position. Obedient to the moment, a few figures stepped out from the scrub at the far edge of the beach, their hands held above their heads in surrender. Trying to shield themselves from the unforthcoming fire by putting the bulk of the ship between themselves and the shore, infantrymen clambered down the nets suspended from the ship's seaward beam and took their places in the open landing craft.

Atkinson catches a GI saying, "It ain't right, all right. But I like it." The landings had started.

To the north, LST 301 was among the first vessels to go ashore, its massive steel doors wide open and its landing ramp fully extended beyond the bow. Major Bill Kerr, 265 Battery's commander, a regular member of the bridge four, and my father's friend, stood on the lip of the ramp, ready to step onto the beach as early as possible. When he felt the ship's stern shudder as it scraped the bottom, he confidently stepped forward into what he thought would be ankle-deep water but turned out to come up to his chin, with the edge of the ramp pressing hard against his neck. Even if the ship was traveling at one knot or less (as it almost certainly was), it cannot have been fun to experience the brunt of the 328-foot, 1,625-ton ship pushing him forward in the ice-cold January sea. Apparently Bill Kerr, closely followed by the rest of 265 Battery, was the first member of the British division to set foot on Peter Beach.

The cause of this unexpectedly high water was an uncharted sand-bar, not the gently shelving beach, which still lay a hundred yards or more ahead. Somehow Kerr managed to find handholds on the ramp and cling on, dog-paddling with his feet, to allow the ship to carry him to the shore, where he was able to come out upright, shivering and sopping wet, and make a preliminary recce of the terrain, searching for positions for gun pits and forward observation posts. He was a lucky man, and fate didn't punish him on this occasion by exploding a mine beneath his feet. When he and my father were bridge partners, they almost invariably won; when he and my father were on opposing sides, my father's diary entries were apt to read, "Lost ⅔d" or "Lost 5/—."

The division of British and American troops meant that each faced a different landscape to hold and defend, and in this the British got much the better bargain, for they landed on the edge of the Padi-glione Woods, which, though described in the US official history of the Anzio campaign as a mixture of "bog" and "scrub," actually have distinct hills according to the contour lines on maps of the area, where high ground was at a premium for military purposes. The American force looked out over the Pontine Marshes, once an infamous malarial swamp before Mussolini reclaimed it as rich agricultural land with a collection of sturdy farmhouses, villages, and a model Fascist market town, Aprilia (which Allied soldiers immediately renamed the Factory for its industrial appearance). But after the fall of Mussolini in September 1943, the Germans did their best to revert the land to a watery, mosquito-ridden, malarial bog. The grandiose, forty-foot-deep Mussolini Canal remained, along with an intricate labyrinth of drainage and irrigation ditches—ready-made trenches for German and

Allied troops to crawl around in a ferocious war of attrition, World War I–style.

The present invaders were now just thirty-four miles from Rome and well behind the enemy's front line at Cassino, eighty-five miles east-southeast of Rome. In the near distance, about fifteen miles away but looking much closer as the crisp, sunlit January morning broke, the British and American troops could see the Alban Hills (a.k.a. the Colli Laziali) rising to three thousand feet above the coastal plain. Whoever commanded those hills would control the road to Rome that skirted them on their western side, and on this day they appeared free for the taking, with no sign of a German military presence. Major General Ronald Penney, the commander of the British First Division, pointed at them with his cane and said that it looked as if he could take them with a walking stick.

But Penney was answerable to the American in charge of the Anzio operation, Major General John Lucas, who answered to the American lieutenant general Mark Clark, who in turn answered to the British general Sir Harold Alexander, who answered to Winston Churchill. Poor Lucas confided to his diary: "I can win if I am let alone but I don't know whether I can stand the strain of having so many people looking over my shoulder."

Lucas at fifty-four was older by six years than his immediate superior, Clark, but he both looked and felt much older than his actual age (and he would die in 1949, aged fifty-nine). His temperament was cautious, meticulous, and admirably reluctant to risk the lives of young men in the pursuit of his own glory. Every description of him notes his small gray mustache and the corncob pipe from which he was inseparable. He had the soft voice of a kindly grandfather.

His mission at Anzio was, as he understood it, to establish a firm beachhead in the face of fierce German opposition. When he met virtually no opposition at all, he concentrated on building the perfect beachhead, with excellent lines of supply and a fully functional harbor, whose would-be destructor, a German mining engineer wearing the uniform of a *Leutnant,* had only just arrived in Anzio with the mission of sabotaging it within the next fortnight. Lucas's orders beyond the bridgehead phase were vague and ambiguous: to advance either "to" or "toward" the Alban Hills. He chose "toward," and took his time.

Not so the German commander of the Italian theater, General Kesselring, who first got news of the Anzio landings at his headquarters just outside Rome at 3:00 a.m. on the twenty-second, and between 5:00 and 8:30 a.m. had summoned troops from southern France, Germany, the Balkans, northern Italy, and the Cassino front to head for the Alban Hills immediately. Kesselring's chief of staff would later write in his memoirs that "the enemy remained astonishingly passive."

Late in the winter night of that first day of the landings, the headlights of trucks moving in convoy were spotted by the Allies as German troops began to converge on the hills in what Kesselring would call "a higgledy-piggledy jumble." The window of opportunity opened by the complete surprise of the amphibious assault was already starting to close, but the Anglo-American force still had a fair chance to seize the hills tomorrow, Sunday the twenty-third, or even Monday. After that the Germans would be in full possession of the high ground ahead, with all the military advantage that would give.

But Lucas would not be rushed. He knew his own tiredness and constitutional frailty; and by the end of the long, long Saturday, between midnight and midnight the next day, he knew that he'd achieved a triumph of complex military logistics, a history-book example of a successful amphibious invasion. During the afternoon both Lieutenant General Clark and General Alexander had swept into Anzio from Naples in a fast patrol boat to review the troops and offer Lucas their warm congratulations. But the best testimonial to Lucas's skill came, improbably, from the captured mining engineer, a Leutnant Seiler, who had watched the landings almost from the moment they began. In the words of Blumenson, the former US Army official historian with Lucas's VI Corps:

> Seiler watched the landing operation. The smoothness of the work amazed him. He heard no words of command, yet everything went beautifully—"like clockwork," he said.
>
> The beach was congested with matériel, and troops were moving around smartly, unloading, adjusting, correcting—"like a big market," Seiler said, "like a big business without confusion, disorder, or muddle."

After the two catastrophic rehearsals for Anzio earlier in the week, the real thing turned out to be a general's dream. Blumenson sums up Lucas's achievements:

> By midnight of January 22, the VI Corps had about 36,000 men, 3,200 vehicles, and large quantities of supplies ashore—about 90 per cent of the equipment and personnel of the assault convoy.
>
> Casualties were extremely light: 13 killed, 97 wounded, and 44 missing. The VI Corps had taken 227 prisoners.

Remembering Bill Kerr's near brush with death as he clung to the lip of LST 301's exit ramp, it seems fair to say that relatively few of the listed dead, wounded, and missing men met their fates as a direct result of enemy action, though in the afternoon six Luftwaffe fighter-bombers managed to penetrate the air cordon laid on by the USAAF and the RAF and sank a landing ship, then strafed the streets with machine-gun fire. The casualty tolls in the rehearsals (most of them caused by the capsizing DUKWs) were roughly as heavy as those incurred at Anzio itself.

Wynford Vaughan-Thomas, the BBC war correspondent "embedded," as we'd say now, with the British First Division, described walking through the town that first afternoon of the landings in his 1961 book *Anzio:*

> DUKWs were already chugging in from the big Liberty ships lying out to sea, and long lines of tramping men were marching through the empty streets. Notices were sprouting in profusion on every telegraph pole as the army lost no time in imposing its own geography on the newly occupied country. Bull-dozers flung aside the rubble near the quays and engineers festooned every wall with endless rows of signal wire.
>
> But just off the main highways the town was deserted, looted and abandoned. The Germans had cleared out the inhabitants and left nothing but haphazard wreckage in the houses they had once occupied.
>
> As I wandered through the side-streets I felt that not even Pompeii seemed as deserted as newly captured Anzio, away from

the dust and engine noise around the harbour. I had a sensation of almost indecent eavesdropping into the pathetic secrets
of ordinary family life.

I picked my way over the rubble into what had been a small
private school. The schoolbooks had been tumbled into the dust
and the carefully filled report forms flung into untidy heaps which
would have vexed the heart of the headmistress. But would anyone
now care if T. Ghilberti had won Honours in Ancient History?

It should be explained, perhaps, that after the fall of Mussolini, the
Germans had declared much of the Italian coastline, including Anzio
and Nettuno, to be an exclusion zone, promising dire penalties for
anyone found there unless they could produce official papers that registered them as belonging to certain reserved occupations, like farming
and bread making. Everyone who entered Anzio in the small hours
of January 22 was met with the alluring smell of freshly baked bread.
So the bakers, at least, must have been happy with this unexpected
invasion.

Waking on Sunday morning, most of the senior officers cast pos-
sessive eyes on the town of Albano and the easily defensible hills sur-
rounding it, eager to put the beachhead behind them, but Lucas saw
only the need to strengthen and fortify the position he'd created yesterday. Already the beachhead stretched along the coastline for about
sixteen miles, from the west bank of the Mussolini Canal in the southeast to the south bank of the Moletta River in the northwest, with
Anzio-Nettuno at the center.

Lucas set up his first headquarters in Nettuno, on an upper floor
of No. 16, Piazza del Mercato, from which he was quickly evicted by
an unexploded bomb that lodged itself in his ceiling, forcing him to
move to the wine cellar of a nearby osteria, twenty feet below ground,
clammy, and lit by bare low-wattage bulbs. From this dark hidey-hole
he rarely surfaced to visit his troops, and perhaps the gloom of his
surroundings helped to fuel the pessimism with which he viewed his
mission.

He had an academic turn of mind, having spent the 1920s as an
instructor in military science for the University of Michigan ROTC,
followed by another instructorship at the Field Artillery School, Fort
Sill, Oklahoma, before becoming the professor of military science and

tactics at the Colorado Agricultural College's ROTC program. He now set out to create a textbook example of an amphibious landing translated into an ideal defensible space: a semicircle like a math-class protractor, with its base superimposed on the harbor and shoreline and a radius of roughly eight miles in every direction. Into this he slotted a multitude of details like improvised roads, corduroyed with wire netting, that could be used by any vehicle from a jeep to a tank; dumps for everything from ammunition to grocery supplies; sites for field hospitals, troops in reserve, troops temporarily withdrawn from the line in need of rest and recuperation, and the ubiquitous smoke pots that were manned by Indian soldiers. Blumenson writes:

> During the day the smoke-generators produced a light haze, at night a dense low hanging cloud.
> Though the liberal use of smoke made German artillery fire inaccurate and unobserved and forced German pilots to drop their bombs haphazardly, the protective smoke was disagreeable, terribly smelly and black and greasy, coating clothing, skin, and nostrils with a thin mask of carbonized oil that stifled breathing and made everybody feel dirty.

As Robert Graves, Siegfried Sassoon, and other memoirists of World War I made clear, there was always a radical division between "the line" and "behind the line." The line meant mud, blood, rats, inedible rations, and the continuous, unbearable noise of war, while behind the line meant an incongruously peaceful world where nightingales sang and everyone wore pajamas to bed—which might well be in a fully functioning French hotel. Behind the line was where the generals, staff officers, and members of the military bureaucracy lived, sheltered from the German artillery by an intervening range of hills that abated the very sound of war to a harmless rumble. What made Anzio—and similar amphibious operations, like the disastrous Allied landing and long, losing battle at Gallipoli in 1915—so different was that there was nothing behind the line except the sea. Everyone, from the private in his trench to the general in his underground bunker and the wounded on their gurneys, was on the line here, though it's true that the two most senior officers involved with the beachhead, Generals Alexander and Clark, maintained their sleeping quarters, messing arrangements, and offices in their own version of behind the line: the vast eighteenth-century palace at Caserta, twenty miles north of Naples and a considerable journey, by road then sea, to Anzio. Clark kept two fast PT boats (max speed forty knots) on hand to make the trip, which, under ideal conditions, with a merely rippled sea feeling as hard as reinforced concrete beneath one's spine as the souped-up torpedo boats planed across the water, would still take the best part of two hours, and that's not counting the tricky thirty-mile trip by jeep from Caserta to the mouth of the Volturno River or the time spent in the motor launch to the PT boat. This little odyssey turned Alexander and Clark into battlefield tourists. On their intermittent visits they usually arrived early in the afternoon and left a couple of hours later, in time for dinner at the Caserta palace.

"They came, they saw, they concurred" was the beachhead phrase for what Alexander and Clark achieved on these outings, which invariably led General Lucas to confide his deepening depression to his diary. "I have done what I was ordered to, desperate though it was." "The situation changed so rapidly from offensive to defensive that I can't get my feet under me." "Apparently some of the higher levels think I have not advanced at maximum speed. I think more has been accomplished than anyone had a right to expect. This venture was always a desperate one and I could never see much chance for it to succeed, if success means driving the Germans north of Rome." "My head will probably fall in the basket, but I have done my best."

No sooner had Lucas achieved one of the most successful landings in the history of warfare than he was being blamed by his superiors for failing to get a move on into the Alban Hills—an advance he thought of as potentially suicidal for his entire corps. Relations between the British and American partners in the alliance rapidly turned sour and peevish, a condition not helped by Lucas's personal Anglophobia, or by the nickname bestowed on him by the British troops, Corncob Charlie. (A "Charlie," or "proper Charlie," in Brit vernacular is a born fool.) Clark disparaged Penney as "a good telephone operator" (He'd previously served as Alexander's chief of signals). Penney reported to his diary after a meeting with Lucas, "Complete gaff, no decision." And so on.

Underlying this international split was the justifiable argument that the whole Italian campaign, and Anzio in particular, was an unfortunate sop to Churchill's romantic, schoolboyish taste for brave but improvident adventures (like Gallipoli, which he had authored and championed twenty-nine years before as Britain's first sea lord)—an argument endorsed by a number of Englishmen as well, including General Sir Charles Richardson, the deputy chief of staff to General Clark, who briskly dismissed Anzio as "a complete nonsense from its inception."

Further down the chain of command, Americans and Brits mingled a lot more amicably. Given the relative absence of cover elsewhere in the area, the Padiglione Woods became a favored place to park artillery units of both nations. As my father wrote on February 2:

> Occasionally we get American rations which are always very exciting, being done up in cardboard cartons (it's a treasure dip, really, seeing what's coming out next!) & they go in for fancy stuff like boiled sweets, pressed fruit bars, sweet biscuits & so forth, & usually a small tin of meat, (NOT Spam!) is included. It makes a great change from stew, bully and biscuits!
>
> But I must say, Darling, I _am_ looking forward to the arrival of your cake—it should be here in about 3 weeks time with any luck!

Peter also took to going off to hobnob with his American opposite numbers, taking with him a couple of bottles of Scotch to make himself welcome and to trade for American military luxuries like cans of camouflage paint for his guns. As part of his campaign to persuade Monica that life in a war theater was as boringly uneventful as life during peacetime, Peter wrote to her on January 24, promising to get his hair cut that afternoon. "It's pretty terrible at present & is beginning to turn up at the ends!" In the event, the haircut had to wait until the morning of January 26, when he wrote:

> I haven't heard the BBC news recently to know just what you're hearing, but it can be nothing but good! Last night I had my full quota of sleep—ten hours! and this in my camp bed and in pyjamas; I was so warm that it wasn't till I got out that I discovered the ground was white with hailstones, but they're all gone now & the sun's shining once more. If it wasn't for a

strongish wind, it would be perfect now, & it isn't nearly as cold as it has been in other places. I feel almost civilised again now, as I had my haircut at last this morning—long, long overdue!

This haircut helps to date Peter's only appearance in the international news media, in a story titled "Vignettes from the Italian Front," written by John Lardner, one of Ring Lardner's several sons who followed their father into the writing trade, and published in the February 14 issue of *Newsweek*. The story, short as it is, goes as follows:

> The British were drawing a bead with 25-pounder guns on the Germans across a stream called Fosso della Molotta [*sic*] when we arrived at one coastal farm hamlet.
>
> They had an observation post upstairs in a bake house. A battalion commander was staring out a window at the Germans in a farm building 2,000 meters northward. Genially he needled his observer, a young captain called Peter who needed a haircut and smoked a pipe, as he studied the Germans through field glasses and called signals.
>
> "Drop three-oh minutes and add one hundred," said Peter without taking his pipe from his mouth.
>
> "Drop three-oh minutes and add one hundred," said a sergeant through the telephone.
>
> A gun spoke behind us and a few instants later we saw black puffs near the objective.
>
> "You're slicing your drive, Peter," said the colonel. "A bottle of beer you don't hit that house where the Jerrys are having lunch."
>
> Peter chewed his pipe and said: "More one-oh minutes repeat."
>
> The gun talked again. Looking along the level brown and green sea marshes, we saw one shell drop against the right wall of the house and another nestle against the left wall. The house shimmered queerly and changed shape.
>
> "You won't need your putter," the colonel said.

In the second week of April, Arthur Rose, a lieutenant in A Troop and a solicitor in peacetime, spotted a torn and ragged copy of the magazine lying with the dust and cigarette ends on the top floor of the San Lorenzo tower, which had been used as an observation post by both the British and the American artillery. Lardner's portrait of my father caused a good deal of amiable ribbing in the mess. Peter was obviously bucked by his mention in the press; he showed the piece to Bill Kerr (the major who prematurely jumped from the lip of the LST in the darkness of early morning), and "it tickled him not a little!" as my father reported to Monica. But Peter's nature as a stickler for details and judicious qualifications led him to add six numbered footnotes to his transcription of Lardner's story:

i/.   On Jan 25 we had no beer in the bridgehead!
ii/. There never was a bet!
iii/. I never hit the building properly whilst the reporters were there—they walked away—bored!
iv/. It was 9:30 AM and the Huns don't lunch at that time!
v/.   My first correction is a fiction—for "Drop" read "More"—technical point!
vi/. The haircut and pipe are true facts! It makes a "nice" story!

Facetious, yes, in this instance (cue the multiple exclamation points), but the notes capture the zest for qualification and correction that was part of my father's nature. He couldn't resist the impulse to put Lardner right, but with its talking gun and the colonel's running golf metaphor this really is a nice story, redolent of its period and of leisurely English sangfroid as seen by an American sportswriter (Lardner's profession in peacetime). But as a report on the Anzio situation, it was seriously outdated long before it was published in *Newsweek,* let alone by the time it was discovered in April in the San Lorenzo tower. It is true to that brief, early moment of triumph at the successful landing before the Germans reestablished their positions in the Alban Hills and made hell for the Allied troops on the beachhead, whom they were determined to drive back into the sea.

As the Wehrmacht made counterattack after counterattack, helped in the air by the dwindling remains of Göring's Luftwaffe, my father's attitude to journalism and journalists hardened from amusement to contempt. When my mother wrote to say that the papers were comparing Anzio with Verdun, the longest, bloodiest, most fatality-ridden battle of World War I, my father advised her to cancel her subscription to the *News Chronicle*. On February 16 he wrote:

> And now Darling, for the news that you have been waiting for & may have guessed at already, but which I'm now allowed to tell you that I'm in the Anzio area:—I'm so afraid, from the harum-scarum newspaper reports that you will have an entirely wrong picture, Dearest, & think of nothing but air raids and fierce fighting. I've referred to "war correspondents" before, but when I had some in my OP three or four days after it had begun, & was able to show them a real live German (a long way away) they reacted like children as if they'd never seen one before—it was an eye-opener to us all, and I know how because of that, one of the reasons for hair-raising reports, My Precious—no one but an unimaginative idiot could ever discuss war as anything but unpleasant, but, at the same time, the things you read in the newspapers are the rarity & <u>not</u> everyday facts. War is noise—a lot of noise, but, thank God, I have so far been spared from being personally involved in that part of it which makes headlines—& believe me Dearest they are the exception. I'm writing this by my "dugout"—six feet deep, dug into the side of a hill, &, but for the odd plane droning in the skies could almost believe myself in England on a Sunday afternoon.

His opinion of the press matched that of General Alexander, the commander in chief of the Italian campaign, who had visited the beachhead on a cold, wet February 14, then called in the war correspondents to give them a severe dressing down. He held his press conference in General Lucas's gloomy underground headquarters beneath the osteria in Nettuno, that grim catacomb whose only comfort was the bouquet of wines maturing in their big oak casks. Wynford Vaughan-Thomas, the BBC man, was one of the correspondents in attendance, and he described Alexander's manner as that of a "headmaster disappointed at some misdemeanour in the Upper School."

He admitted that the Beachhead landing hadn't gone as he had hoped: "We wanted a breakthrough and a complete answer inside a week. But once you are stopped it becomes a question of build-ing up and slogging." He insisted that it was the people with guts and determination who were going to win when it came to a slogging match. The correspondents listened politely—generals are bound to sound more optimistic than the man in the fox-hole—but when General Alexander went on to say that the reports sent from the Beachhead were causing alarm, there were emphatic protests. General Alexander looked sternly at the protesters. "Were any of you at Dunkirk?" he asked. "I was and I know that there is never likely to be a Dunkirk here."

Alexander actually went a good deal further than that, at least in Rick Atkinson's book, which has him saying that the correspondents' reports were filled with "pessimistic rubbish," and that he was "very disappointed that you should put out such rot." He threatened strict censorship, apparently unaware that reports from Anzio were being censored in both Naples and Algiers; then, after he left the beachhead, he had second thoughts and made no further mention of censorship.

When not standing in an elevated observation post, calling shots down to guns hidden in the woodlands at his back, my father was immersing himself in a genre of literature spawned by the war: books about England, profusely illustrated with woodcuts. Monica, no doubt with me in tow, haunted Priest's bookshop in Fakenham, scouring the shelves for additions to Peter's already quite extensive collection. Anything with "English" in its title was a likely candidate—English Villages, English Canals, English Churches, English Windmills, En-glish Farmhouses. The intent of each book was to remind servicemen overseas of the land they were fighting for, always conjured in sweetly nostalgic prose.

On February 21, my father, anticipating his and Monica's third wed-ding anniversary, which would fall on March 13, wrote:

Thank you, <u>very, very</u> much, Dearest, for the lovely wedding anniversary present you've got for me, I am looking forward to it especially as I really do enjoy all Robert Gibbings' work, his wood-cuts particularly. No! Darling, I shall never tire of books about the country and the land—every single one you've sent me is a treasured companion, & the arrival, the other day, of the "Countryman" is still giving me hours of pleasure, as they all do.

It interests me that Peter singles out Robert Gibbings as a favorite author/artist. In Britain at least one tends to think of "war writing" in terms of Cyril Connolly's magazine, *Horizon,* or John Lehmann's *Penguin New Writing,* where the war was addressed directly as personal experience. But for someone in a trench at Anzio, as for people crowding down escalators of stations on the London Underground after the air raid sirens had gone off in the middle of the night, there was another kind of war literature, of which Gibbings's *Sweet Thames Run Softly* was among the first and best when it was published in 1940.

The book was presented as a modest and leisurely downstream drift in a homemade flat-bottomed punt named *Willow,* equipped with rowlocks and a pair of oars ("for I was brought up by the sea and have an instinctive scorn of 'prodding the mud'"). Four wooden hoops ran from stem to stern, over which a big tarpaulin could be spread to provide Gibbings with his nightly living quarters. Along with the usual supplies he packed a microscope and a wooden glass-bottomed box through which he could survey the underwater life of the river. His Huckleberry Finn–ish aim was to go with the flow, letting the current of the Thames (by then greatly reduced in speed by forty-five locks and weirs that turned the river into a succession of slow-moving pools) carry him wherever it chose. Every so often he'd extend an oar to avoid an obstacle or a collision with the bank (to borrow Lord Salisbury's metaphor for the ideal conduct of foreign policy, but Gibbings meant it literally).

In the summer of 1939, when Britain was in a frenzy of war preparations and Austria and Czechoslovakia had already been invaded by the Nazis, Gibbings was embarking on the most unhurried and peaceful voyage imaginable. He briskly excused himself from the coming war, saying, "I was over age. Besides, I had met a bullet in the last war." Not that he meant to laze; he was just liberating his time to devote himself to sketching and note-taking along the way.

The result was an exercise in free association, digression piled upon digression, in which the private life of the caddis fly or the routes taken by migrant birds (both described with the precision of a professional naturalist) suddenly yield to a conversation with a yokel met on the riverbank (a blizzard of apostrophes on the page marking every dropped *h*), or a memory of Tahiti, or Ireland, or a long-ago feast with fine wines ("Lafite 1924, Haut-Brion 1924, Margaux 1920; imperials, magnums, jeroboams of them"). The wood engravings, of which there are too many to count (at least by me), come as necessary reminders of the book's essential theme: land- and waterscapes of the Thames Valley, including studies of its birds, its aquatic vegetation, its bridges and thatched cottages, and some of its human residents. In this last category, there's a curious full-page illustration in which a large swan dominates the foreground while three nude young women disport themselves in and on the edge of the water in the middle distance. One is equipped with swan's wings and either has just landed or is about to take off, the second is running away from the viewer, cradling a baby, and the third is swimming on her back with her head and shoulders raised sufficiently clear of the water to fully expose her breasts (it looks like an impossible way to do the backstroke). This engraving is justi-fied by a cursory account of Vedic swan-maidens. "How I do seem to wander from the Thames," says Gibbings in mock surprise at the way his mind takes him.

Gibbings was rather lamely orthodox in his pursuit of the sexu-ally exotic, voyaging to the South Seas, to Tonga and Tahiti ("Where the Gauguin maids / In the banyan shades / Wear palmleaf drapery / Under the bam / Under the boo / Under the bamboo tree," as T. S. Eliot put it, making Tahiti sound already old hat and ripe for music hall parody in 1927). At fifty, Gibbings was a bit too old to be chasing naked naiads, but he claims to have induced one to climb aboard his boat, which she does only after sending him on a fruitless errand from which he returns to find her modestly clothed in a rug he has converted into a poncho. They have a cup of tea together; then, after distracting him with another ruse, she returns to the water and addresses him by his full name. "'Good-bye, Robert Gibbings,' she called. 'You see, I know who you are.'" So this little episode turns out to be a sly attempt to advertise his own celebrity, which he does several times in the book, as when walking in Oxford he's approached by an older man and his son.

"Excuse me," said the elder, "didn't we see you on the television a little while ago?"

"That's quite possible," I replied. "I've done several perfor-
mances."

"Under the sea, making drawings on celluloid?"

"Xylonite," I corrected.

"May I shake your hand?"

"You may, indeed," I said, giving it to him.

"May my son shake your hand?"

"He's welcome," I said.

Sometimes Gibbings's style shows signs of having been consciously
"antiqued," as when he uses the phrase "I would fain"—a verb for
which the *Oxford English Dictionary* is hard-pressed to cite any usages
later than the sixteenth century. But he had a foot in so many camps
that it's hard to pin him down to any time, taste, or space: he was
at the tail end of the Arts and Crafts movement (and never more so
than when he owned the Golden Cockerel Press from 1924 until 1933,
publishing lavish, leather-bound, limited editions, some printed on
vellum, of books like *The Four Gospels* and *The Canterbury Tales*); he
stood on the raffish fringe of G. K. Chesterton and Hilaire Belloc's
Catholic back-to-the-land movement, the Distributist League, and
very probably knew both Chesterton and Belloc; he kept a foot in
London's metropolitan bohemia, another in a succession of country
cottages sprinkled across the landscapes of England and Wales (his final
berth a cottage on the Thames in Berkshire, shared with his divorced
second wife's sister, Patience Empson, who went on to guard his legacy
after his death in 1958), and yet another in the islands of the South
Pacific, which he visited for long stays of up to a year at a time. Plus,
he was the BBC's nature expert on radio and television, the forerun-
ner of David Attenborough, as Attenborough himself acknowledged.
Online, there's a Pathé News clip of him clowning for the camera in
1945: a big, jolly, loose-limbed, uninhibited man with an untidy shock
of hair, who, as he plumps himself down on the riverbank, allows his
feet to spring aloft as soon as his ass hits the ground—he looks like
Humpty-Dumpty.

Sweet Thames Run Softly was published in time for Christmas 1940,
the darkest period of the war, when Britain was clinging to its independence by its eyelids. It became an instant and surprise best seller
for its publisher, J. M. Dent, precisely, I think, because it conjured so

many liberties now lost: the freedom to loaf and wander at will; the freedom to enjoy now-banished luxuries, like the French wines itemized by Gibbings; the freedom to travel abroad, as in his memories of Tahiti; the freedom to indulge in the author's very sociable form of solitude in nature. Reading the book, one could vicariously share the experience of one of the world's notable free spirits, and rejoice in the peace that he found there, naiads and all.

Reprinting followed reprinting. Alongside the Dent edition with its gilt-on-green cloth binding was a much cheaper two-and-sixpenny hardback version, issued in 1941 by the Readers Union book club, which brought *Sweet Thames* to a new and more impoverished class of reader. Even after the war it went on selling steadily through the age-of-austerity 1940s. Gibbings would write and illustrate more river books, including ones set on the Wye in Wales and England, the Lee in Ireland, and the Seine in France, but none of them came close to achieving the enormous success of his book on the Thames.

Chapter 24

BY SPRING 1944, peace was being anticipated before the end of the year. Even cautious Peter wrote of being home by Christmas, and *Sweet Thames* only intensified the appeal of this prospect, as it spelled out what peace could mean for a rurally nostalgic world.

At war-weary Anzio, Wynford Vaughan-Thomas laid out the German plans for the beachhead with clarity and admirable economy:

> The great battle down the Anzio-Albano road, the centre of the Beachhead drama, resolves itself into three acts. First, a prelimi-nary attempt by the Germans to cut off the 3rd Brigade of the British 1st Division. Then, with stronger forces available, the Germans press on to seize the Factory area and Campoleone. From this start-line they finally drive forward with every ounce of power they can muster in a stupendous all-out effort to smash through to the sea. Each act of the drama has its own crisis, sur-prises, unexpected failures and equally unexpected successes.

The first of Vaughan-Thomas's "acts" was attempted on the night of February 3–4, the second on February 7–9, and the third began just before dawn on February 16. That February brought more rain and cold to western Italy than usual, sometimes frosting over the surface of the water in the "wadis," a term the British imported from their experience of the dry watercourses of North Africa (Americans were inclined to call them "draws," but "wadi" quickly became the generally accepted word for them).

Looking at the battlefield from the coast, one saw only an unbroken, level agricultural plain that stretched to the foot of the low mountains to the north. But seen up close, the plain became a labyrinth of ditches, some very deep and few marked on the available maps. The wadis could trap tanks and turn soldiers into amphibians—salamanders, slithering along the bottoms of the ditches on their stomachs, clothed in soft mud and becoming unrecognizable as human beings. More than anything, the wadis gave Anzio its reputation as a terrifying place to fight, because they enabled the enemy to crawl through the sparsely defended Allied front at night, then open fire with machine guns from positions behind the line.

Peter must have done his fair share of wadi-crawling to get to his observation posts, but he neglects to mention this aspect of his soldiering in letters to Monica, where he insists, rather too emphatically, that he is as safe as houses, despite everything awful that she may have read in the newspapers. "My job is to see without being seen," he writes, adding that whenever he looks at the enemy, it is through a periscope that he carries with him everywhere. "I am neither an infantryman nor yet in the Tanks." He doesn't seem to realize that he has given himself away by sending her the *Newsweek* clip by John Lardner, which makes clear that the artillery observer is positioned far ahead of the guns whose shots he calls. In one letter he writes that he is feeling "human again" after his "weekly wash." If that's true, he must have stunk like a skunk and been caked from head to foot in dried mud before the wash took place.

Monica must have found it hard to reconcile Peter's relentlessly cheerful letters with Wynford Vaughan-Thomas's sober communiqués from Anzio on the BBC News. On February 28, Peter wrote, "And now, to show you just what a fool of a husband you've got, I will tell you the only disturbing news you might hear from Dorcas [the wife of a senior officer in the regiment who also lived in or near Fakenham] or other sources. I must tell you in any case, to ease my conscience." But he was not about to confess to her the many acts of self-censorship in his previous letters; this was to say that he had declined the offer of a promotion to major.

Three days ago I was asked "There's a vacancy in another
Regt. You may not get it, but, if it was offered, would you take
it?" . . . I suddenly had to think seriously what it would be
like to be whisked off & be landed in a unit in which I've no
interest or friends at all. Thinking about it since then, I realise
more and more fully that my sole interest in this Army—the
only thing that keeps me going, is the fact that after five years in
the Regt, I am established—& it has taken me most of this time
to get where I am. I would find it an impossible task to take
over a battery of 200 men & 9 other officers, none of whom
I know, & settle down as I have here—it would be hell, & all
my thoughts & feelings would still be here. So, this morning, I
have recanted my first decision, & said definitely that I am not
prepared to leave the Regt & so far as I'm concerned promotion
is "off"—privately I reckon I can possibly outlast the "power
that is" in hope that his successor does not adopt the same line.
He is of course a regular and cannot be expected to understand
that a civilian turned soldier has more interests than putting up
a crown.[*]

He says that he feels "very guilty about all this," and knows that "if
I were doing my duty, I should not hesitate to accept." "I know too
that the extra income should influence me—in my selfishness I console myself that it would only be a difference of £60 with Income Tax
deducted." He then likens himself to "the oldest member of the club
[who has got his] special chair by the fire and intend[s] to stay there."
There's a good deal of smoke-screening in this but what it really boils
down to is "all my thoughts & feelings would still be here."

His battery had become a substitute family for my father; at last he'd
found a place where he really fitted in. At twenty-five, he was unusually young to be offered this promotion, and the contrast between
the life of an inept primary school teacher at Cradley Heath, which
he had been miserably enduring just five years before, and the success he was enjoying in the army now, must have been balm for his
soul. And, as it turned out, he did outlast the "power that is": almost

* That is, on his epaulets. In the British Army an embroidered crown denotes the rank
of major.

exactly a year later, in February 1945, Peter reported to headquarters in Cairo to find that he had been promoted in his absence, on the voyage from Italy to Egypt, and had become the commanding officer of 265 Battery.

Several days after the Anzio landings, the British First Division tried to open an important salient.* A patrol of Grenadier Guardsmen marched and drove their Bren gun carriers north, up the road to the Factory and Campoleone, a small town about eight miles ahead of the present front line, that they expected to capture without difficulty. No one anticipated that the Germans would have yet been able to muster enough men to mount more than a skeletal defense of the two towns, so it came as a very unwelcome surprise that the Factory was fully occupied by Germans with tanks. The patrol, now under heavy gunfire, retreated behind the embanked "Flyover," a disused railway line that bridged the Anzio-Campoleone road, from where they'd come. The British had discovered how unnervingly close the Germans already were, and in what alarming numbers.

Over to the west, across the Pontine Marshes, the Americans were finding out the same thing. General Lucas ordered a two-pronged breakout from the beachhead: Americans were to take the town of Cisterna to the northeast, and the British objective was to overrun Aprilia and occupy Campoleone. Because these two attacks had to take place simultaneously, the operation was postponed for twenty-four hours when a jeep carrying three company commanders from the Grenadier Guards, along with the secret battle plans they were to share with their opposite numbers in the Scots Guards, took a wrong turn and landed up in enemy territory. All the company commanders were killed, and the secrets-no-longer fluttered in the wind. General Penney made the decision to hand over the attack on Campoleone to the Irish Guards, who managed, at great cost of life on both sides, to drive the German occupiers out of the Factory but were pinned down a mile short of Campoleone.

---

* A salient, a word beloved by military historians, begins as a bulge in the front line and can then swell into a peninsula. The narrower the salient, the more vulnerable it is to attacks on its flanks, which can transform it into an island surrounded on all sides by enemy troops. This particular salient was named "the thumb" or "the pencil," and, as Carlo D'Este genteelly notes in his *Fatal Decision: Anzio and the Battle for Rome,* "some gave it a very rude nickname indeed."

In the American sector, a stealth attack on Cisterna was to be made by two battalions of a unit called Darby's Rangers, after their colonel, William O. Darby. Handpicked for their toughness and readiness to take risks, these officers and men had been trained as commandos in Northern Ireland in 1942 and had since won battle honors in North Africa, Sicily, and Salerno. Their mission this time was to creep up a long, deep wadi in darkness and surprise the Germans in Cisterna before dawn. That didn't happen. The Germans took advantage of the twenty-four-hour delay to entrench themselves more closely, and in even greater numbers, around the beachhead. Vaughan-Thomas wrote: "Out of 767 men in the Rangers' attack only six returned. The rest were killed or captured by the Germans."

By late February Winston Churchill was lamenting: "We hoped to land a wildcat that would tear out the bowels of the Boche. Instead we have stranded a vast whale with its tail flopping about in the water." In allowing Lucas just two divisions to take Anzio, the American and British generals who doubted the maneuver ensured its difficulty. So long as the Germans had the freedom of the Alban Hills, and suf-ficient supplies of both men and war matériel, the beachhead would remain just that, sprouting salients one day, then shrinking the next, but never more than a perilous toehold. It was a First World War battle being fought a quarter century too late. Lucas predicted that his two divisions—more than seventy thousand men—would end up being pushed back into the sea. He turned out to be wrong, but only nar-rowly so.

On February 16 before first light, the Germans launched a tremen-dous artillery barrage from the Alban Hills. This was the prelude to the third act of Vaughan-Thomas's Anzio drama, the "stupendous all-out effort to smash through to the sea." But my father was otherwise engaged, for February 16 was one of the rare days when he found time to write two letters to Monica. His usual work schedule, or so he claimed, was forty-eight hours on duty at his observation post, taking short naps whenever the opportunity arose, followed by three days off, and the great German onslaught happened to coincide with one of his off-days.

While the Germans opened a major salient in Allied lines just a mile or so away, my father was preoccupied by thoughts of Fakenham and, in particular, by a visit to the White House paid by the fiancée of his older brother, Nick. Her name was Mary, but my parents called her The Disaster, not least because she was separated from her husband and seeking a divorce; she also had a young son—not Nick's—in tow. Her latest offense had been to make a proprietorial tour of the White House, earmarking all the best pieces of furniture that their mother had left to the two brothers, so that they could be shipped to her new home.

> I'm terribly sorry that I ever urged you to have her over & I hope she will never set foot in the house again but I'm afraid that is probably not to be the case. I'm afraid I cannot & will not express overmuch sympathy with Nick tho' I'm prepared to do whatever can be done to help him—to call him a fool is possibly not quite fair, because I tend to think that circumstances have always been rather against him—hence his slightly quizzical temperament & lack of balance in his general attitude to worldly matters: I am terribly sorry for him (which sounds odd after my previous remarks!) & am selfish enough to thank God that he is overseas now: like you, I tend very much to the thought that he's too proud to ask for legal or family help & so would rather marry her & hope that, honour being satisfied, that will be the end of the matter. At the same time, I'm prepared to have news from him that he is really in love with her—God forbid!

And so on, and on, in the neat, fluent, closely spaced penmanship whose only defect is to darken and pale at irregular intervals—a problem with the pen, not the writer. The writing never betrays, by the merest tremor or hesitation, the deafening turmoil of shelling and being shelled that was going on just outside his trench and causing trickling cascades of earth to fall inside it.

This shivering trench, just 168 cubic feet in volume, was Peter's shrine to Monica. Her letters, some loose, others in rubber-banded stacks, were all around him, lightly scented with her lipstick. Framed photos of her were arranged on the earthen shelf beside his camp bed, along with the books about England she had sent from Priest's.

He used the sweater she'd knitted for him as his pillow and swore he could find her presence in it. At ten o'clock each night that he was not on duty, they kept their regular "tryst," an hour-long exercise in marital telepathy, which, as they assured each other, perhaps rather too emphatically, really worked.

But, as he wrote to her, opining, argufying, grumbling, so confident in his declarations of love fully requited, he could keep her there with him in the trench, foggy with pipe smoke and the burnt wood smell of spent Swan Vestas. Each "Darling," "Dearest," and "Sweetheart"— those banal endearments—was a magical invocation for him, bringing the Italian dugout closer to the White House (*his* house!). As the noises of war boomed around him, with waves following waves of German infantry in field-gray uniforms, yelling their World War I cries of "Sieg heil!" and "Gott mit Uns!" and breaking through the Allied lines in the tangle of barbed wire and decomposing bodies that lay between the Factory and the Flyover, Peter calmly finished his first letter of the day to Monica—a mixed bag of love, income tax returns, power of attorney, and outrage at the assault on the White House by his brother's fiancée.

> And now, Dear Heart, I will write that quick line to HP & then settle down to write you a <u>proper</u> airletter, all about yourself & not of such vile matters as this is so full of! Thank you again, my Own, for all your lovely letters, for the love you put into them and for the nearness of You and your dear self—all that I prize and cherish and worship above all the world, that they bring to me. God Bless you, Beloved, & keep you & J safe always. Don't worry! I love you, my Darling, above all the world and with all the strength of my Heart, Soul & Body & I live only for the days of unutterable happiness that lie ahead of us when you are with me to share our Unity in its fullness again. Your very own most adoring Peter.
>
> xxxxxxxxxxxxx

He then wrote to his father in Hadzor, and by some miracle of the usually benighted postal service got a reply just six days later. H. P. dismissed Nick and Mary's engagement as an "infatuation" and indulged in a quite funny if mildly unchristian quip: "He says she is divorcing the husband for cruelty, but if he was cruel to her I think he deserves the VC."*

When he finished writing to his father, Peter reached for a fresh air letter and resumed work on his epistle to Monica. As he'd promised, this letter was more about her than him, and I appear in it in my increasingly usual role as the gooseberry in the garden, a conspicuous impediment to my parents' lovemaking.

> Yes, Darling, I will always try to be with you at six o'clock at J's bathtime—but I certainly won't do a "Good dog, lie down!" stunt & retire to the basket chair with a hurt expression or the remark "Mummy doesn't want me, Jonathan." You will find me harder to dispose of than that, Precious, & J will be old enough by then to know when he's playing gooseberry & will tactfully retire to the bathroom whilst we try and make up for lost time, holding close to each other & forgetting everything but the present, the expression of our love flowing through our lips and our eyes and the pressure of our hands. And when J comes back he too will find his part in our love—the love that can only be found in a family that knows happiness as no other family ever can.

It's a measure of my father's innocence of child psychology that he could conceive, even facetiously, that a boy aged three would be capable of mounting a "tactful retirement" from the scene rather than a total meltdown. He was, after all, the youngest son of his father's second marriage, and the war had deprived him of any experience of my own transitions from babyhood to toddlerdom to walking, talking, thinking childhood. The circumstances were against us (as Peter remarked of Nick), and I would give him no quarter when he eventually showed up in my life. He and I would be strangers to each other until late in my adolescence and his late forties, when, with my financial independence taken care of, thanks to a generous local-government student grant, we fell into a sort of reserved mutual regard, especially when we found we had certain books in common.

Peter had just reached the top of the third page ("poor Darling!")

* The Victoria Cross, awarded for acts of valor.

when the war intervened and he had to break off. He continued the
letter on February 19—the beginning of the end of the all-out German
assault on the beachhead—and apologized for the interruption. By
the afternoon of February 16, 1944, the first day of the enemy's attack,
my father might have been spotted wriggling on his stomach up some
muddy wadi or another, en route to his observation post, periscope
ready to hand.

Chapter 25

RICHARD HAD PREPARED me for my next encounter. Dr. Clawson was off this weekend and a locum was substituting for him—a doctor approaching the end of his professional life, whom the nurses had to shepherd through his appointments. I'm not being coy when I say I can't remember his name, but he was the only member of the Swedish medical staff to send me a bill for his services after I left the rehabilitation ward, and it's his bill I recall, which I paid with the greatest ill humor, and the near certainty of his double-dipping. I had been summoned to his office for no good reason so far as I could tell, and sat in my allotted chair facing him across the desk. A nurse was in attendance, providing the guy with notes on patients and the occasional whispered prompt. Many decades of hospital doctoring had equipped him with the false condescending smile that went with the job.

"Ah yes, um . . . Jonathan," he said. "You're the one who used to be a writer."

The smile was now a mixture of condescension and self-congratulation. "Used to be" went off in my head with the force of a grenade. I tried to respond to the remark as if it were a joke. "I very much hope that I'm still a writer." I looked him between the eyes and said, "I very much hope that I'll write about this—about *you*—when I get out of the rehab ward. You'll make what they call 'good copy,' you know?"

He was not a fool. Looking discomfited, he said that he was looking forward so much to his own impending retirement that he was liable to attribute his own feelings about ending his working life to other people, and apologized to me for any offense he might have caused. Tempting as it was to say that I was evidently more content in my vocation than he was in his own, I suppressed the impulse to say it out loud and mumbled some kind of acceptance of his apology.

If there was any further conversation between us about my medical condition, I have no memory of it because the "used to be" has rankled so deeply in my mind in the years since that interview. Sheila Hale's *The Man Who Lost His Language* helped me to put the locum's remark in context, for he belonged to a generation of physicians who believed that stroke victims were destined for the scrap heap. "You don't want to spend the rest of your life tied to an infarct," said the odious Dr. X. "Put him in a home."

Dr. Clawson's locum was from the same mold. In his day, research on strokes was the most unsexy specialism of the medical profession—by definition, a stroke was incurable. With hearts, there was the exciting possibility of transplantation or the intricate and prestigious business of open-heart surgery; with cancer, the wide-open field of treatment with new drugs, chemotherapy, and, again, surgery. But strokes were irreparable and there was nothing that the surgeon's scalpel could do for them—until the new doctrine of the "plasticity" of the brain and its capacity to improvise its own reconstruction. By the end of the twentieth century and the beginning of the twenty-first, the stroke was becoming an almost fashionable area of inquiry and not a career dead end.

So I was lucky. Electro-stim Simon with his armory of gadgets and his inexhaustible enthusiasm for books of popular neuroscience was a child of his time, someone who could see in every stroke an opportunity for experiment and hope. And the locum was a child of his time too. As am I.

Meanwhile, in the rehab ward, Richard was my temporary best friend. It was he who bought me my prescription red wine in boxes and he who took to dropping in to my room for conversation and complaints about other members of the hospital staff, usually with disposable cups of coffee for us both.

"You're looking browned off right now . . ."

"Oh, you know how it is . . ." And he went on to describe an encounter with an officious nurse who had just upbraided him for not wearing his ID card.

Richard put me in mind of Holgrave in Hawthorne's *The House of the Seven Gables,* a character who, by the age of twenty-two, had begun and ended a peculiarly American set of unrelated careers, having already been

first, a country-schoolmaster; next, a salesman in a country-store; and, either at the same time or afterwards, the political-editor of a country-newspaper. He had subsequently travelled New England and the middle states as a pedler, in the employment of a Connecticut manufactory of Cologne water and other essences. In an episodical way, he had studied and practised dentistry, and with very flattering success, especially in many of the factory-towns along our inland-streams. As a supernumerary official, of some kind or other, aboard a packet-ship, he had visited Europe, and found means, before his return, to see Italy, and part of France and Germany. At a later period, he had spent some months in a community of Fourierists. Still more recently, he had been a public lecturer on Mesmerism . . .

Holgrave's "present phase" is being a "Daguerreotypist," an occupation that Hawthorne fancies will last no longer than his previous jobs, though the novelist stresses that "amid all these personal vicissitudes, he had never lost his identity."

Richard had wandered through rather fewer walks of life than Holgrave, but the connections between them were equally hard to figure. He had studied English at the University of Michigan, where he had also got himself entangled in Scientology. This disappointed me as a former faculty member of two university English departments: surely a competent critical reader of the language should not have been taken in by L. Ron Hubbard's pulp science-fiction writings, where Scientology began. Richard claimed to have been kidnapped from Ann Arbor by a couple of Scientologists in a van who spirited him away to their Florida headquarters for punishment (his offense to the Church of Scientology was not satisfactorily explained). In the torrid heat of a Clearwater, Florida, summer, Richard had been sentenced to clean a filthy shipping container with a toothbrush and other similar impositions. He then worked for a restaurant-supply business in Paris, France.

"Paris!" I said.

"Well, it was on the outskirts of Paris . . ."

I caught a look in his eyes which might have signaled: Uh-oh, this guy's a European who may know France better than he should.

He was a freelance agency nurse, paid by the hour with no benefits, and therefore earned considerably more per week than his in-house colleagues. Bored with the tedium of general nursing in the neurological rehabilitation unit, Richard was talking of his next move, to become an anesthetist, for which he'd have to do at least two years of advanced training to become a certified registered nurse anesthetist or CRNA. In 2019, 10 percent of CRNAs reported making more than $200,000 a year—a fat salary for an English major and way above the ceiling for nurses in general.

Richard was clever, moody, quick to pick up allusions, and addicted to living high on the hog. An oenophile, he was also a connoisseur of automobiles. In my third week on the ward, another nurse told me that Richard wouldn't be coming in to work that day because his car had been totaled in an accident, though Richard himself had not been hurt. Next day he appeared, looking a little paler than usual, and told me that he'd been T-boned by a woman driver coming without looking from a side street. He seemed pretty sanguine about this and was just waiting for the woman's insurance company to name the size of his settlement. As soon as he got his hands on the check, he bought himself a brand-new Audi. I had expected him to buy some run-of-the-mill Ford or Toyota, and found it hard to see a nurse, even an agency nurse, in the luxury car market.

I tried and failed to imagine Richard's life outside the hospital. Where other nurses talked of "we," indicating an invisible partner in their lives and thus leaving an opening into which I could stick my nose, Richard spoke only in the first-person singular. I had no secure opinion as to whether he was gay or straight; I assumed he was childless, but that too may possibly have been a misapprehension. I warmed to his air of self-containment, and sympathized with his frequent expressions of discontent with the institution's elaborate bureaucracy.

Despite his onetime enslavement to the Scientologists, he seemed an enviably free spirit.

Early in our relationship he told me that he'd ordered a book of mine from Amazon, but never mentioned it again, so I presumed he either hated it or didn't read it; I would have liked to know which one, but free spirits must, I suppose, be free not to tell.

Chapter 26

On January 27, 1944, five days after the landings at Anzio, General Alexander wondered aloud to General Clark whether General Lucas was the right man to command the beachhead, or whether they needed more of "a thruster, like George Patton." On February 17, Clark issued an order, moving Major General Lucian Truscott from his command of the Third Division to second-in-command, under Lucas, of VI Corps.

Lucas wasn't deceived. Even as his painstakingly constructed beachhead was proving its strength against German penetration, the British were plotting to deprive him of his command of the operation. He correctly intuited that Truscott would very soon supplant him, and that Churchill, Alexander, Penney, and other senior British officers had conspired to engineer his removal. Five days later, on February 22, Clark—with considerable reluctance—relieved Lucas of his command and installed Truscott in his place. That evening, Lucas wrote in his diary: "And I thought I was winning something of a victory." It was a deeply hurtful end for Corncob Charlie.

Wynford Vaughan-Thomas quotes his own diary on Truscott's first press conference:

> We've got a new head at Anzio, tough, Barrymore-profiled General Truscott, husky-voiced and with slightly greying hair. But he looks—as we hope every general should look—like a two-fisted fighter and not like a tired businessman. He was honest, outspo-

ken and completely realist. "No," he said, "I don't reckon that everything is for the best, we're going to have a tough time here for months to come. But, gentlemen, we're going to hold this Beachhead come what may." And he stuck out his jaw in a way that convinced you that any German attack would bounce off it.

One of Truscott's first actions was to move his HQ from Lucas's dank wine cellar in Nettuno to the ground floor of another building from where he could see the battlefield and the troops could see him. Unlike Lucas, he made regular and frequent visits to the beachhead's front line, and, though he was afflicted with a serious throat ailment that he self-medicated with cigarettes (up to eighty a day) and silver nitrate, he seems to have improved everyone's morale, even if he did little or nothing to change the character of the battle.

Stalin said that machines win wars. By mid-1944 the Allies were vastly outperforming the Axis powers in producing planes, tanks, ships, trucks, guns, and ammunition. My father told Monica that for every German shell that fell inside Allied lines in Italy, twenty were fired by the artillery batteries on his own side. Vaughan-Thomas put the ratio at one to ten, but the point is essentially the same. In the Alban Hills, ammunition was at least as strictly rationed as, say, jam in England.

When darkness fell in Anzio each evening, the Allies put on a dazzling fireworks display to taunt the Germans, as tracer rounds lit the sky in a silver blaze; an insolent show of conspicuous consumption that the Germans could not possibly respond to in kind. So, too, with aircraft. Vaughan-Thomas reports that when the weather cleared on March 2, Allied bombers were at last able to show themselves.

Two hundred and forty-one Liberators, 100 Fortresses, 113 Lightnings and 63 Thunderbolts swarmed into the skies. Cisterna, Velletri, Carroceto—there was hardly a moment when the earth around these places was not shaking with the demoralizing thud of exploding bombs. The Allies unloaded an even greater weight of high explosives than on 17 February, during the crisis of the Beachhead.

Those of us who watched the attacks, lying behind the broken farmhouses of Isola Bella, were ourselves continually shaken and deafened by the unbroken drumroll of the heavy explosions. Overhead the sky was filled with the glitter of the winter sun. The great flight of aircraft looked strangely beautiful, remote, and efficient as they came up from the south in an endless stream, jettisoned their load of death with a clinical detachment and swung back for more. For hour after hour the procession continued in the clear sky.

The Allies had very nearly depthless resources, especially in the manufacturing cities of the United States, beyond the bombing range of their enemies. In 1944, the city where I'm writing this, Seattle, was enjoying an enormous boom as workers poured in from the south and the east to take up jobs in the elaborately camouflaged hangars of the Boeing Company at the city's southern end, birthplace of all the B-series war planes, like the B-17 Flying Fortress. Seattle then had much the same blackout regulations as London and Berlin, but no bombs ever fell here.*

This manufacturing supremacy effectively meant that all the Allies needed to do now was wait until German and Japanese supplies of men and matériel eventually reached vanishing point, so Anzio turned into a grim, slow battle of attrition that wasted men's lives by turning them into mere collateral damage in the war of the machines. Salients opened and shrank, usually with huge losses of life, but the military situation remained a humiliating stalemate for both sides.

My father admitted as much in a letter to my mother dated Wednesday, April 26, 1944:

My Very Own Most Beloved Darling,
    At the moment I'm suffering from an attack of complete ennui, when life seems so empty that I don't know where to

---

* A Seattle native and friend, a lawyer named Henry Aronson, who's half a dozen years older than I am, remembers the city in wartime: "Blimps dangling chains designed to entrap low-flying aircraft, the night sky streaked with crisscrossed beams of light from searchlights manned by troops—one such anti-aircraft battery was located on a vacant lot about a block from my grandparents' home near Twenty-Ninth and Spruce—I delighted in hanging around with the soldiers, who seemed equally delighted by a neighborhood kid in shorts. Also blackouts (with neighborhood wardens), and car headlight covers with slits that emitted a small amount of light. Another memory, 'victory gardens,' those little patches we all had to increase domestic food supply—I grew killer carrots and radishes." The parallels with European cities are unmistakable.

turn next to find something to distract me—I seem to be
completely empty: do you feel like this sometimes too, Darling?
It's a horrid feeling and as a result I've wasted two hours this
afternoon doing nothing, feeling that if I did start my letter
to You I should find nothing to write about! Which is of
course quite wrong once I really settle down to it & snap out
of this mood. And now, to interrupt me, the mail has just this
moment been brought to me to ease my "emptiness." Darling,
3 lovely Airletters from you waiting to be read and a packet of
newspapers! . . .

I'm now writing this outside my dugout tho' it's not quite
as warm as it has been lately with a little breeze. The valley
is looking much nicer now than it did a few days ago, all the
trees and bushes are showing green fringes, and the ground
is carpeted with patches of yellows, blues and whites of wild
flowers: I picked one of a small bunch of orchids not 50 yards
away from here last night, which I'll be sending on to you when
it's properly pressed—in a few minutes, before the setting sun
drives me inside again, I'm going to inspect a clump of what I
believe to be daffodils at this distance—just budding—if they
are, I'm afraid I shall pick them & construct a vase from an
old shell case to adorn one of my shelves, as otherwise, they
will very shortly be the victims of our "malaria drive" which
includes clearing all the banks of the streams of "undergrowth"
to stop the larvae having a chance of breeding: although it isn't
necessary yet, I've already got my net waiting for when the
season really begins.

The word "ennui" makes its first appearance in his letters here, and
it's a reluctant admission. The stale impasse of the military situation
at Anzio seems to have worked its way inside my father's head, despite
all his efforts to brighten the tone of the letter with nature notes on
the glories of the Italian spring. Two days later, still in the same foul
mood, he refers to himself as "sitting around like Mr. Micawber" (one
of literature's great comic manic-depressives), waiting for something to
turn up, and confessing that his continuing ennui is making the end of
the war impossible to imagine.
Sandwiched between these two air letters was another, dated

April 27 and written on proper writing paper that was destined to go by sea and arrive several days later than its companions, with whom it shares its general tone ("the days drag on somehow"). It's worth mentioning because it does shed light on my father's preeminent wartime friendship and his later career in the Church of England. The friend was Gerry Scrivener, whom Peter first met in Worcester in 1939 when they were both freshly commissioned in the Territorials. The son of a prosperous Staffordshire farming family, Scrivener was more worldly, funnier, and more skeptical (especially of army bullshit) than my conformist father, and his tastes ranged from orchids to fast cars. In the spring of 1944, Scrivener had just been promoted from lieutenant to captain (very belatedly, Peter thought). Just recently, his sister had been killed in England, and he was in sorrowful bereavement.

In the letter, Peter describes their successful orchid hunt that morning, and how Scrivener identified the "daffodils" that Peter had spotted from a distance as flag irises. He mentions how he and Scrivener used to drop in, most evenings, to each other's trenches and tipple Scotch together, and I can guess how his friend in mourning must have found solace in my father's company: Peter was always good at lending a sympathetic ear to other people's misfortunes, though that was not a talent he invariably practiced when it came to his own sons.

On the twenty-seventh, the regimental padre had stopped at Peter's dugout for a "chat." The flag irises were now installed in "a cartridge case cut down to the suitable dimensions of a vase & they look rather nice & have a very faint scent that is slowly filling the dugout, & with photographs of you nestling under them the effect is very pleasant: I shall get some more tomorrow & and another 'vase' so that I can have them both ends of the dugout—there won't be much room for myself!" In this floral marital bower, the padre arranged himself as best he could and soon came around to his point. He "wanted to know if I'd ever thought of going into the church."

It was a by-no-means new question. Peter's letters are full of army padres on recruitment drives, showing up in his tent or trench on the pretext of passing the time of day, only to offer him a job that was not actually theirs to give. His father was an Anglican clergyman, as had been his grandfather and many of his ancestors. So far, so good. But he was lacking in one thing usually considered as a sine qua non for the profession, a university degree, and preferably one from Oxford, Cambridge, or Durham, the oldest institutions in the country where theology had always been close to the heart of a classical education. Peter's dirty little secret was that he'd only been to a teacher-training college. So these visiting padres reopened the wound of which he was most ashamed, his educational mediocrity.

He disposed of this particular padre by taking "him along to see Gerry's orchids, as he's a great wild flower expert, so that I had to stay & chat for a bit & now here I am again, able at last to settle down to write this."

I met Gerry Scrivener once. Sometime in the early autumn of 1945, a very few months before my father returned from Palestine, he visited us in the White House, dressed (to my disappointment) in civilian clothes, with a cravat at his neck. My mother had prepared me to address him as "Uncle Gerry," as if he were part of the family. On arrival, he kissed Monica on the cheek with, I thought, perfect aplomb and propriety—although neither word was yet in my limited vocabulary.

His car, parked outside our front door, smelled expensive when you stepped inside it, a masculine scent of leather, cologne, machine oil, and tobacco. Its engine hummed smoothly and didn't growl like AUP 595. In my memory it's a big green convertible with the canvas hood closed (another disappointment), which may or may not be true. Uncle Gerry, who said he was "famished," drove us to the Crown Hotel in Fakenham—a Jacobean coaching inn—for lunch. He'd spent all morning driving up from Evesham, a journey of more than 160 miles, mostly then on country lanes, with farmers' tractors and slow-moving convoys of army trucks as unyielding obstacles.

The lunch went well, its grand ritualist surroundings keeping me on my best behavior while my mother and newly adopted uncle talked of Peter and Palestine, topics of equal remoteness to me. I wanted the elderly waiters to take my uncle for my father because he was showing to me a paternal sweetness and solicitude. Then the pudding course arrived. It was rhubarb tart, and one tablespoonful of the fibrous strings of rhubarb triggered the vomit button in my tummy that sent an overflowing fountain of sick into my mouth—an emergency that my mother was long used to dealing with. She rushed me from the table to the ladies' lavatory while I tried and failed to stop flecks of vomit from leaking between my lips onto the hotel carpet.

With my mother's hand cupping my forehead (our usual posture for these events), I stared at the cobwebby craquelure on the stained porcelain bowl, and at the brand name of the toilet, SIMPLICITAS, a word that was anything but simple to me, over which I'd puzzle long after we left the ladies', and threw up my hotel lunch, my elevenses, and my breakfast in a series of uncontrollable retches.

Reentering the dining room, face washed, mouth rinsed, I saw that Uncle Gerry was looking at me with new respect, as if I might at any time repeat my performance over his neatly pressed gray flannel trousers. He was smoking a postprandial cigarette.

That Scrivener had returned to civilian life while my father still languished in Palestine was probably due to their respective ranks as captain and major (to which Peter had been promoted in early 1945). Captains were two a penny while majors commanded a far larger body of men (in the Royal Artillery a whole battery, not a troop) and were therefore more valuable for keeping a steadily disintegrating regiment in order.

On the too-short car ride home, I caught Uncle Gerry's anxious eye on me in his rearview mirror; no doubt he had his immaculate leather back seats in mind.

But there's a problem here. Gerry Scrivener's name was frequently on my mother's lips at the end of the war when my memory begins, but after my father returned, his name appeared less frequently until it disappeared completely. I think they remained friends of the sort who exchange annual Christmas cards but little more.

Given the military emphasis on comradeship—as the American Veterans of Foreign Wars and the American and Royal British Legions neighborhood posts attest—one might think that sharing experiences of combat together would make for lifetime friendships, but this was clearly not the case for Peter and Gerry, for whom six years of war was their university (another place and age where people tend to make friends for life). I wonder if for both of them, they simply had too much in common—Dunkirk, Tunisia, Anzio, and Palestine, all associated with deep anguish of one sort or another. It is the artilleryman's lot not to know who or what or how many, if any, people he has killed, and so go through life with a perpetually uneasy conscience. It's worth saying that Richard Whitfield (the lance bombardier) dedicated his 1995 war memoir to "all the members of the 67th Field Regiment RA with whom I shared a comradeship, and still do, rarely found in civilian life." It may well be that those whose job it was to obey orders and not to give them find life afterward easier to bear—though that hardly accounts for the braying braggadocio of generals like Bernard Montgomery, who never tired of reliving his famous victories on television in the 1950s, armed with a swagger stick, which he rapped peremptorily on his wall maps of his greatest battles.

Chapter 27

A SUNNY MORNING on Hempton Green. I was in my pushchair. My mother and I were on our way to Fakenham when I caught sight of David in the middle distance. David, though we'd never been introduced, was my beau ideal, largely because of his hugely covetable hat—a khaki felt fedora, creased and dimpled in all the right places, with a narrow leather hatband and (this made it perfection itself) a chin strap. His bold red neckerchief was held in place by a leather woggle, like a small napkin ring, through which the neatly rolled loose ends had been fed. Both sleeves of his military-style jacket were decorated with embroidered proficiency badges for tying knots, first aid, woodcraft, swimming, making a fire with two sticks, and heaven knows what else. He walked with an ashplant staff as tall as he was, and wore short khaki trousers to match his hat. He can't have been much older than twenty because the skin on his cheeks and chin looked so soft and unblemished that it must rarely or never have seen a razor. This man-boy failed to entrance my mother half as much as he entranced me.

"He's the scoutmaster," she said, rather curtly, as I thought, then muttered more to herself than to me, "He's a conchie. Either that or his mother pulled some strings to keep him out of the war."

"What's a conchie?" I asked.

"I expect it was his mother. When a husband dies, his wife becomes a widow, and widows can get very lonely with only themselves in the house. So they didn't send David away to the war like they did your daddy."

David's exoticism and glorious attire eclipsed everything else on Hempton Green that day. I had no desire to join the knot of village children clustered around a bicycle, and I wasn't going to be scared by the idiot on his tether. But I very, very much wanted to be a Boy Scout.

My mother told me that I would have to become a "cub" first, and she didn't think that I would be allowed to join the cubs until I was a big boy of six or seven. I asked her if cubs wore the same hat as David did, and was told, to my great disappointment, that she thought not, that she believed they wore berets. I had no time for berets, I wanted only a real Boy Scout hat, and made a private resolution to search for one in the shop windows of Fakenham.

And she had never told me what a conchie was.

Chapter 28

———

THE FIRST THING you discover when you are abruptly transformed into a hemiplegic is the terrible, unwieldy weight of your own body. From infancy to senility, I had always been a featherweight for my height (six feet), and when I arrived at the rehab ward I clocked in at about 125 pounds. I was also a lifelong weed—throwing a ball "like a girl," as my schoolmates said with contempt—and, though I spent quite a lot of my adult life either pulling up sails and tensioning their sheets with the help of a winch, or trying to cast artificial flies accurately to trout, I never developed any real strength in my arms. It was a shock to find that having a paralyzed half body made the simple task of lifting my new lopsided self out of the chair into a feat comparable to lifting a Volkswagen Beetle with one hand. God knows how difficult that must be for the averagely overweight person.

Leaning as far forward as you can in your wheelchair, you have to push down as hard as you can with your good arm on the chair's armrest and coordinate that movement with an upward thrust from your good leg until you can stand upright. Luckily, this gets easier with every inch of elevation gained. Then, balancing for a moment on one leg, you must transfer your handhold to somewhere close to your destination (bed, toilet seat, conventional chair, whatever),* swivel your

———

* I've had handrails installed in various tricky places around the house—the stairs, bathrooms, and exterior steps—and thank the gods of the auto industry for providing overhead straps to hang on to when getting into the passenger seat of all the cars I've met so far.

torso sideways, and gently lower yourself into place. My two advantages in this maneuver are my weight and my keen sense of balance, gained no doubt from all those pitching, yawing, rolling boats in my past.

Meanwhile, Kelli was teaching me to walk again, in the long corridor that led from the gym back to the rehab ward. The unbroken line of windows on the north side yielded a view of the tallest building west of the Mississippi, now dwarfed by the post-1960s skyscrapers beyond, like a metaphor for aging: the older you grow, the more you shrink. The southern side of the corridor was equipped with a long handrail, to which I was hanging on for dear life, my right foot resting on a small wooden trolley with brakes that kept Kelli occupied as she crouched beside my feet.

What she required of me was this sequence: transfer my weight onto my paralyzed right leg, whose foot was on the securely braked trolley, then take a step with my good left leg and restore my weight to that before she eased off the brake and I could drag my right leg forward, bringing the trolley with me underfoot. Repeat, ad nauseam, until exhaustion and pain in my left calf became unbearable. I was so frightened of falling that I had the shakes, and each hesitant, foot-dragging step felt like the overture to a sudden collapse onto the floor.

From the rehab ward direction came a woman I had grown to recognize being pushed in her wheelchair by a therapist. As we passed, the woman said, "Standing upright now—that's good to see!" In my funk I tried to produce a grin, and probably succeeded only in making a contorted eye-popping grimace.

The woman, whose name I never knew, reminded me tantalizingly of an old friend, Caroline Blackwood. Caroline had died in a New York hotel room in 1996, aged sixty-four, of lung cancer brought on by a defiant lifelong addiction to cigarettes. Like Caroline, the woman in rehab was skeletally thin, and looked as if she'd been through the wars. Her face had the same huge searching eyes, prominent cheekbones, and overinsistent survivor's smile. I wanted to know her, but felt deterred from saying so by my instinctive antipathy to her husband, who regularly showed up at the hospital, looking always as if he had important business elsewhere, and spent more time in the hallways holding a smartphone to his ear and talking in conspicuous sotto voce than he ever spent with his wife.

The husband, who looked to be in his late forties, had the air of not so much visiting as maintaining routine surveillance over her. A bad man to tangle with, I thought. But she and I continued to make friendly acknowledgments of each other when we passed, and when our gym appointments coincided I felt a distinct lifting of my spirits.

"You want to rest for a while?" Kelli said.

"Yes, please, a good long while."

She had left my wheelchair parked by the wall a few steps behind us. So we sat and stood side by side looking out over Seattle, while Kelli, full of plans for her upcoming trip around the Caribbean, told me that she was flying to Miami tomorrow and staying there overnight before embarking on her cruise ship in Fort Lauderdale the next day, and yes, she was going to read the David Foster Wallace essay on the plane.

"I'm going to miss you while you're gone."

"Don't worry, you'll be in good hands."

But *whose?*

I got an answer to that question the following afternoon. By 2:00 p.m. I'd finished lunch, a sort of open salad sandwich with too much romaine lettuce, and I needed to pee. Going to the bathroom was still a humiliation for me since I had to call for help and be transferred from the wheelchair to the lavatory by a nurse or nurse's assistant—a man by preference but sometimes, of necessity, a woman. I telephoned the nurses' station and was told that someone would be with me very shortly.

At 2:20 no one had shown up, so I phoned again and got the same reply. Ten minutes later, and still no helper, I began to get rattled because at 3:00 I had an appointment with a physical therapist I hadn't met yet. So I decided to go it alone, not altogether without qualms. Wheeling myself into the bathroom, I succeeded in pulling first my elasticized tracksuit bottoms, then my underpants, from beneath my buttocks, and then made a competent job of transferring myself to the toilet seat. But getting back into the chair was not so easy, as, placing my left hand on its seat and levering my body round so that I faced the shower at the far end of the room, I miscalculated the distance and sank almost to the floor, just catching myself, mid-fall, with my good hand.

Now, bare-assed, and in no position either to hoist myself back into the wheelchair or to reach the big red emergency button by the side of the toilet, I had to holler for assistance. No one came to my rescue, though I could hear footsteps in the corridor. I upped the volume of my cries for help until at last a woman opened the bathroom door and began to upbraid me in no uncertain terms for getting myself into this shaming pickle. "Are you allowed to make bathroom transfers on your own? You're not supposed . . ."

With a show of effort that I thought excessive to the task at hand (I was not so heavy as all that), she restored me to the chair and asked me, in a voice of reproof, if I had (a) wiped myself and (b) pulled the plug.

"Yes of course," I said testily, as my dislike for this offensive Good Samaritan mounted.

I got the wheelchair turned around and headed for the doorway, passing the small corner handbasin that lacked a towel.

"Now wash your hands!"

"I am just about to."

The much larger and better equipped basin was situated beyond the bathroom door, in the bedroom. As commanded, I washed my left hand there, then transferred myself onto the bed, where I lay flat, arched my bum into the air, and wriggled my way back into respectability, every movement coldly observed by my tormentor.

"Right, now we can go to the gym."

Until that moment it hadn't crossed my mind that this woman might be my new physical therapist and Kelli's temporary replacement. I'd thought her to be a stray member of the hospital staff who had just been passing by.

"No," I said. "Not after this calamitous introduction. I can't take therapy with you. I'm sorry, but I just can't. You'll just have to put it down to my embarrassment."

She didn't say a word, but left the room, closing the door behind her with a louder-than-necessary *ker-thunk*. As soon as she'd gone, her words kept on replaying inside my head, with "Now wash your hands!" as their dominant motif. For the third time that afternoon I called the nurses' station and asked for the name and phone number of the therapists' supervisor. "You want Michael Pirkle, the therapy manager," said the voice on the other end.

Mr. Pirkle answered on the first ring and said he'd be happy to visit me in my room sometime in the next half hour. He arrived promptly, sprucely dressed in a suit and tie, and had a cautiously diplomatic manner that I attributed to his probably having come to his position via a business administration degree rather than from a background in any sort of therapy. He sat across from me in the ratty armchair by the window, silhouetted by sunlight, as I told him the story of my encounter with Kelli's substitute.

But I lost faith in my story even as I told it, so loudly did it ring in my ears as a banal case of making a mountain out of a molehill. When I got to "Now wash your hands," I heard my own voice making an infantile complaint to the therapy manager whose time I was wasting.

My trouble was that I no longer knew my own mind, and couldn't hold a thought in my head for more than a few minutes before it was flatly contradicted by its opposite. My capacity for rational judgment seemed to have capsized on me, just as my tear ducts had gotten out of my control. I could—at a stretch—justify a welling of tears over Julia, on the cusp between leaving school and starting out on her freshman year of college in California, but there was no justification at all for the copious shedding of sentimental tears over reruns of imported British crime and comedy dramas on PBS that I happened to run into on the wall-mounted TV in my room. When you find your eyes misting over at the sight of Judi Dench in some long-outdated episode of *As Time Goes By*, it may be time to call for professional help, but I doubted that the rehab ward psychologist would be up to the job.

I had no way of telling if the stroke was the cause of my brain turning into mush, or if the stroke was merely coincidental and the real cause was my reintroduction to life in a prison substitute, for the first time since I was unwillingly sent off to boarding school at the age of eleven. Certainly my symptoms now closely resembled those I experienced then, a kind of mental unraveling and an achingly deep self-mistrust.

When Mr. Pirkle got up to go, I again apologized for troubling him.

"No worries," he said. "It's what we're here for."

Shortly after he'd gone, Richard looked in, and I told him about my encounter with the therapist, this time recasting the story as farce, with me in the role of booby and the therapist as termagant.

"I'd say she was just frightened," Richard said.

Of course she was, and why couldn't I have seen that at the time?

Chapter 29

FIRSTHAND ACCOUNTS OF Anzio, like those by Blumenson and Vaughan-Thomas, make much of the putrefying smell of death that hung over the battlefield and mixed with the oily odor of the smoke machines. Both the Germans and the Allies did what they could to retrieve and bury their dead, but the closeness of the two front lines and the exposed position of the narrow no-man's-land that separated them meant that many cadavers were too risky to salvage. So they hung spread-eagled in the ubiquitous coils of barbed wire, first bloating into wrinkle-free obesity, then spilling their innards and shrinking around their skeletons as blowfly maggots and internally generated bacteria went to work. Some remained ghoulishly lifelike, sitting with their backs propped against a rock or tree, still cradling their rifles and Bren guns, from which they were inseparable in rigor mortis. As winter gave way to a warm Italian spring, the stench from the blackening bodies intensified, and they turned into convenient landmarks for those directing artillery or sniper fire—and, as generally happens with landmarks, their new function soon outweighed their capacity to inspire shock or nausea.

Peter, of course, never mentioned the corpses or their stink in his letters to Monica, but he did welcome his temporary escape from the battlefield when he was granted a four-day spell of leave at a hotel halfway up the vertical cliff above the fishing and resort town of Amalfi. On April 4, he wrote:

Before I answer them [three newly arrived letters from Monica]
I must tell you my own news which is that I'm going on "leave"
tomorrow! My Precious, I have no right to push this news in
at the beginning except if we were going to share our leave
together when I should be more than excited! But somehow
it seems to occupy my mind far more than it should—I think
it's the prospect of a change, of being able to "getaway" for a
little & walk about, eat, sleep and laze without keeping alert
all or most of the time, & to break the routine of what is at
the moment a very dull existence (better that than many other
possibilities though!) As to the "leave" itself, I get four days at
the Rest Camp, so, including travelling, I shall really be away
for the best part of seven days—it isn't a "camp," really, but I
believe a rather pleasant hotel on a <u>very</u> pleasant part of the
coast, well within range of Naples, Pompeii and Capri to be
seen, I hope, with very little effort.

His only anxiety was that, because his leave straddled Easter weekend, all the shops selling women's underwear might be closed. In his
next letter, two days later, he reported his safe arrival ("a very surprisingly comfortable hotel in perfectly glorious surroundings") and how
he met on the boat from Anzio the two other officers ("very pleasant") with whom he was sharing a room. The LST apparently docked
at Salerno, where Peter took his new friends to the officers' club for
drinks and later commandeered a truck (probably a Bren carrier)
for his own use from 265 Battery's "rear party," who were stationed
nearby.

Mostly he drove alone, dogged by the melancholy awareness that
Monica wasn't here to share his leave.

If I try to think of you being here with me, then my present
loneliness is only the greater. So you have a husband torn
between what is a very nice place and life, that he wants to
enjoy but just can't, and his longing for you.

On Good Friday he took his truck to Naples and checked into
the "nondescript" officers' hotel because he hoped to spend Saturday

morning shopping for presents for Monica. He ditched his plan to
find an opera house to visit that evening, and instead lingered in the
hotel lounge, drinking kümmel and listening to the house orchestra.

> There's one thing that prevents me from getting any full
> enjoyment out of this place, that dissociates all connection
> between your being here and that is the overwhelming presence
> of khaki uniforms: whenever I start to think of what we'd do
> if we were here together, and dream of all the possibilities,
> somebody close at hand, with an unrefined accent of some
> thickness and little intellect, or with an all-pervading ability
> to talk of no matters other than the Army, brings me back to
> ground level with a bump that shakes all my visions into a
> hopeless blur.

His shopping trip was disappointing: he bought some stockings
("not silk"), a pair of dubious female pajamas, and a length of white
material that he suggested might be sewn into a "blouse or something." Returning to Amalfi after lunch, he stopped for an hour to visit
Pompeii and Vesuvius, which, less than three weeks before, between
March 17 and 23, had had a major eruption (the last on record as of
this writing) that destroyed three villages and much of a fourth, as well
as eighty or so USAAF B-25 bombers that were parked on the tarmac
at Pompeii Airfield.

As a result of this very recent disaster, Pompeii's famous ruins were
coated with a thick layer of volcanic dust and ash that Peter said he
had to "paddle through." The ancient city's inhabitants, caught in a
fast-moving (two hundred mile-per-hour) pyroclastic current of rocks
and gas that boiled their brains inside their skulls but left their clothing more or less intact, were eerily preserved as plaster of paris effigies in every imaginable contortion of sudden death. (The effigies had
been created over a period of nearly three hundred years by archaeolo-
gists who injected liquid plaster into the cavities left by the decom-
posed flesh and clothes in the hardened and compacted ash, though
the skulls and skeletons of the victims remained inside their plaster
likenesses.)

Peter was taciturn about his brief trip to Pompeii. Aside from saying that he spent only an hour sightseeing there, and that debris spewed from Vesuvius made driving on the coast road tricky, he made no mention of his reactions to the ruins themselves. I don't know if he got as far as the Garden of the Fugitives, where thirteen men, women, and young children are caught in the instant of their deaths, or whether he made the connection between the miraculously preserved dead of Pompeii and the unburied dead at Anzio. In any case, even if he did, he wouldn't have told Monica about it. In my father's reported war virtually nobody died, ever.

The next day, Easter Sunday, he planned to go to an improvised Anglican church with a roving priest in charge, for the early Communion, then spend the rest of the day sailing, but the hotel receptionist gave him his wake-up call an hour late, he had to attend the ten thirty Eucharist, and his sailing jaunt went by the board. Going to church turned out to be the highlight of his leave: "an extraordinarily nice service (with vestments and ritual after the fashion of your little church—excepting incense) in an extremely nicely decorated 'church'—which is a largish room converted in very good taste with altar hangings—so very nice that I took some snaps of it after the service, to the padre's great pleasure, as he'd wanted to get some photos taken."

On Monday afternoon, he caught his ship back to Anzio and his hole in the ground, to which Gunner Ransome had made many small improvements while my father was away in Amalfi, trimming back the roots that protruded through the walls, extending the earth shelves for books and pictures and lining them with paper, and reconfiguring the drainage beneath the wooden pallet floor. "I do wish you could see my dugout now, Darling—it really does look quite homely." With nothing much to do he lay in his camp bed till nine, then took a leisurely breakfast of bacon and eggs, telling Monica that it might be weeks until he was called back into action.

The attrition continued, with fewer and fewer shells being lobbed from the hills into the Allied lines, fewer German planes overhead, and a growing conviction among the Allies that the Germans could soon be forced to retreat. By mid-April, skylarks had arrived, and their continual breathless trilling could be heard high above the killing fields beyond the Flyover, shortly followed by the song of nightingales along the banks of the Moletta River and in the Padiglione Woods. On April 12, my father wrote: "There are quite a lot of wildflowers coming up here now—some very pretty ones which Gerry tells me all their names, but I never can remember them!"

At last, on May 23, the Allies broke free of the Anzio beachhead, first slowly and with difficulty, gaining five hundred yards on day one, then rapidly quickening their pace in a two-pronged attack agreed on by Generals Alexander and Truscott. The American Fifth Army would drive north-northeast through the gap between the Alban Hills and the Lepini Mountains to the heavily bombed town of Valmontone. So the German retreat would be blocked when they tried to flee along Route 6 to Rome, following their defeat by the Allies at Cassino and the Liri Valley. Alexander's plan was to annihilate the German divisions as a fighting force, and if the Fifth Army could hold Valmontone, it should be able to do just that. Meanwhile the British were to stage a diversionary attack, aimed at the western flank of the Alban Hills, to confuse the Germans over which way the Allies were trying to go to Rome.

But neither Truscott nor Alexander, the supreme commander of Allied forces in Italy, had taken into account the preening vanity of Mark Clark (nicknamed behind his back Marcus Aurelius Clarkus), whose personal destiny, as he saw it, was to become the sole conqueror of Rome, a city that he, like Churchill, viewed as a very great historic prize. In his memoirs, *Calculated Risk,* Clark recalled being "shocked" that Alexander had made his decision to cut off Route 6

without reference to me. I should point out at this time that the Fifth Army had had an extremely difficult time throughout the winter campaign and that we were now trying to make up for our earlier slow progress. We had massed all of our strength to take Rome. We were keyed up, and in the heat of battle there were almost certain to be clashes of personalities and ideas over this all-out drive. We not only wanted the honor of capturing Rome, but we felt we more than deserved it; that it would to a certain extent make up for the buffeting and the frustration we had undergone in keeping up the winter pressure against the Germans. . . . Not only did we intend to become the first army in fifteen centuries to seize Rome from the south, but we intended to see that the people back home knew that it was the Fifth Army that did the job and knew the price that had been paid for it.

There speaks the emperor, a man who never quite grasped the fact that the Roman Empire fell from its pinnacle in the world the better part of a couple of millennia ago.

On May 26, just as Truscott was anticipating a famous victory of his own—sending the Fifth Army, in all its considerable strength, through the gap between the hills, capturing Valmontone from the Hermann Göring Division. This would block the whole valley with sufficient troops to destroy the fleeing German army. But he was interrupted by the arrival of a staff officer, General Don Brann, bearing a disquieting new order from Clark. The job of cutting off Route 6 was to be left to a single infantry division together with the First Special Service Force, while the main body of the Fifth Army was to strike out to the northwest, skirting the west flank of the Alban Hills to take the shortest route to Rome. Truscott was incredulous. The new order effectively meant that the German army, now fleeing from Cassino, would not be pulverized and scattered at Valmontone, which had been the chief point of the Anzio landings in the first place. But it also meant that Clark would be remembered as the conqueror of Rome.

Truscott tried to raise Clark on the phone, but Clark had made himself unreachable. He also let a whole day pass before communicating his new plan to Alexander, his senior officer. Alexander, famous for his irreproachable, aristocratic good manners, appeared to take this breach in the chain of command in his stride, presumably to avoid an upset in Anglo-American relations.

On May 24, the second day of the breakout from the beachhead, Peter wrote Monica a letter of barely suppressed euphoria—not an emotion he usually went in for. Knowing that she would have heard the news of the breakout on the BBC, he tried to soothe her fears:

> I know you will have been worrying a lot, Beloved, imagining
> that I'm in the heart of a battle—I wish I could reassure you
> that I wasn't, but that would be a breach of security; it is very
> quiet where I am, & that's about all that I can say. I was on
> duty yesterday, & it was like any other day for me—so you've
> no need to worry, Precious! As usual I've spent today resting
> & having a good wash to get rid of the dirt—twice today as I
> unwisely joined in in a little cricket practice on the dirt track
> that runs by our position, & by the time we'd finished I was

just as dirty as when I came back last night—but, nevertheless, it was very pleasant pottering about, losing the ball at frequent intervals in the bushes and briars that abound here. Even more than usual, we wait for more & more news of how things are going, & when it comes, everyone pores over the maps & hazards a guess on further developments. But so much is based on unconfirmed reports that we never quite know . . . ! Can you realise how we feel, Darling—after these interminable months of waiting—doing nothing except wait, to know that things are moving, & though our particular part may be very small, to feel that we are helping in some way, & that "the bridgehead" at any rate, is on the move again without quietly waiting to be caught up with. It does give us a purpose, and consequently dispels the awful boredom of inactivity that was getting everyone down to some extent. And too, there's the promise of bigger things yet to come now—the Second Front [i.e., the Normandy landings], perhaps, and the goal of Rome ahead. It does give meaning in life, & too the hope of getting the war over all the sooner, taking an active part in it again—however little it may be!

By May 30, Peter was with the battery as it slowly fought its way along the road to Rome. According to a letter he wrote that day, he was *hors de combat,* sent to his camp bed inside a truck by order of the regimental medical officer: not as a victim of German gunfire but because the itching rash on his upper right arm, which had plagued him during the North African summer the previous year, had recurred. The MO prescribed a course of ten sulfanilamide pills a day, and bed rest, to clear the thing up. But the cure was worse than the disease. Sulfanilamide, an early antibiotic, had a grim list of side effects, though Wikipedia says, "Powdered sulfanilamide was used by the Allies in World War II to reduce infection rates and contributed to a dramatic reduction in mortality rates compared to previous wars."

The letter—for which Peter apologized two days later because it was written "under the influence"—had two anniversaries to celebrate: the first was his rescue from Dunkirk, which fell on June 1; the second was my birth on June 14, or rather my mother's devastating labor pains as she fought to produce me during my father's absence at Glenridding on "that damnable gas course." "My own Beloved—YOU ARE WONDERFUL!"

> And give Jonathan an especial birthday kiss from Dada (of course you will!!!) Tell him too that if the guns weren't making such a beastly noise at the moment making progress towards Rome possible, we hope, I might be a little more coherent!

That "progress towards Rome" was frustratingly slow for the British First Division, as Major D.J.F. Grant, a staff officer at the Royal Artillery headquarters on the beachhead, explained in his fluent twenty-one-page pamphlet titled *The First Divisional Artillery at Anzio,* which is dated October 1944 but wasn't published until late in 1945, after a string of skirmishes with the censors.

> To leave the beach head area where we had so long been penned in and harassed by shelling was a strange and exhilarating experience, and we could now all see the evidence of the destructive power of our artillery. The whole landscape was pitted with shell marks, ammunition blown up, dug outs fallen in. Not a tree bore any foliage, not a house was left standing. Roads and tracks were almost impassable for shell holes. Dead men and horses lay unburied where they had fallen. Compared with conditions within the beach head which we had thought pretty bad, this was complete desolation. The German dug outs and tunnels, some incredibly deep, were now occupied by our battery command posts and were all found in a disgustingly filthy condition.

Grant courteously acknowledges that at Anzio the Brits played second fiddle to the American-led advance. Clark, incapable of modesty, seized the entire campaign for himself and the Fifth Army, telling Alexander, or so he boasted, that he'd open fire on the Eighth Army, now commanded by Oliver Leese, if the British dared to challenge his claim to be the lone conqueror of the Eternal City. Questioned later, Alexander said that this outrageous threat had never been uttered in his presence, which suggests that Clark, or Clarkus, was indeed the very type of *miles gloriosus,* the braggart soldier of Roman comedies.
Meanwhile my father in his sickbed inside the truck, too close for

comfort to the incessant thunder of the guns in his battery, had other thoughts on his mind. During the four-month standoff at Anzio, the Sixty-Seventh Field Regiment had undergone a number of changes. Bill Kerr had been promoted to second-in-command of the regiment, though he kept his rank of major and still showed up for dinner and cards on bridge nights at the 265 Battery officers' mess. Major Derek Whitehouse briefly occupied the post of battery commander, but was soon succeeded by Major R. Gunn, whom my father called in his letters "the new major," first described as "a very nice man and a keen bridge player." On his second appearance, in a letter on May 22, the new major is held up as a military paragon:

> The Major knows his own mind & does all the suggesting
> himself, without asking what other people suggest! It's really
> rather refreshing—particularly as the Battery has lived &
> thought & acted on a personal basis for four years now,
> a condition that meant that everybody thought solely of
> themselves, their own troop, & hang the rest—the results of
> which are beginning to tell in a bad way. And too, of course,
> the Major is a gentleman!

That last sentence clinches the argument. For my father, few words in the language carried the resonant weight of "gentleman," and its meaning was strictly and precisely defined. Nobody could turn himself at will into a gentleman, any more than he could turn himself into a duke or an earl. Heredity was essential, though how many generations were required to make a gentleman was deliberately vague. Occupation was important: landowners, whether they farmed on their own behalf or lived on the rents paid to them by their tenant farmers, could qualify for the title; so could officers in the armed services, and members of the "learned professions," meaning theology, medicine, and the law. All gentlemen had gone to public schools and some would have graduated from one of the ancient universities, or, if farming was their profession, they might have attended the Royal Agricultural College in Cirencester, a town that my father insisted on pronouncing as Sister, with a slight stammer over the second *s*. Driving through Cirencester one summer afternoon en route for a cowpat-spattered field in Cornwall, where we'd pitch our army surplus tents for a fortnight, he pointed out the college as the alma mater of the "gentleman farmer."

For my father lived in an England of his own construction, where the Industrial Revolution had not yet taken place. His definition of a "city" was a town that had grown around a pre-Reformation cathedral as its center. No cathedral, no city—which excluded such places as Manchester, Birmingham, Leeds, and Sheffield but included, for instance, Ely in Cambridgeshire and Wells in Somerset. (Old parish churches that had been rechristened "cathedrals" in the nineteenth and twentieth centuries were regarded as parvenus by my father and therefore didn't count.)

Appropriately enough for someone whose immediate family had spent so much time in India, working first for the East India Company beginning in the mid-eighteenth century, then for the British Raj after the company was nationalized in 1858, Peter instinctively saw the English class system as a hierarchy of hereditary castes rather than classes. When Monica wrote to him saying that she was thinking of offering the spare bedroom in the White House to a bombed-out mother and child from London, he replied with a dire warning tinged with panic:

My Darling, just as you're unsympathetic as I am about any Italian or other family when husband & wife are still together, I'm a little inhumane about refugees from London. Unless you've already committed yourself to actually taking someone in, I think you want to be very careful & not have just anybody. I shall probably surprise you with what I'm going to say, but you will find it very much easier to take than get rid of a Cockney or any other working class wife, particularly if they're bombed out. I'm afraid my eyes are possibly too-wide open on this because living for practically five years with the men has taught me this. In action, or doing a job of work, they're grand, but, out of action (I mean out of working hours, or meeting them as men, seeing their constant unthinking grumblings & complete selfishness & incapability to do anything for themselves) they are quite a different proposition. I'm an awful snob, & possibly a little disillusioned & consequently cynical, but—be careful, Beloved, & don't let your humanity override "commonsense." I have every sympathy for people who have to suffer, but at the same time, I should be furious if, after doing all & more than is expected from you, you get no gratitude, & no help from the "refugee"—especially as there've been enough evacuation schemes already & such people really have little excuse for being where they are.

One reason offered for the Labour Party's landslide victory over the Conservatives in the general election held in July 1945 (when Churchill was still prime minister and Britain still at war with Japan) is that members of the British officer class only really met and mingled as close colleagues with working-class people in the Second World War, when the scales fell from their eyes and they came to comprehend the gross social and economic inequalities of the prewar world. I don't know how true or not this appealing idea is or was, but certainly my father would not have agreed with any part of it. In an earlier letter he had written of a subaltern who was trying to make friends with the noncommissioned men in his troop. "It's either his way or mine, and I shall have to give him a talking-to," my father wrote. He revered the rigid class division that the British Army enforced among its personnel, the strict prohibition of "fraternization" between officer and man. Only on rare holidays like Christmas was the rule relaxed, and even then it extended downward no further than the sergeants' mess.

Chapter 30

———————————

IT WAS EVENING in my room and I was suffering from a mild bout of cabin fever. On other evenings, Julia and I had had dinner in the ground-floor café attached to the hospital kitchens, where the food was the same as what came up to the seventh floor, but at least was a bit warmer. It was where the Swedish staff ate, some of them with their families, and the Naugahyde-upholstered benches in its booths reminded me, not unpleasantly, of our favored Mexican joint for weekend lunches on Fifteenth Avenue NW. Taking my Kindle with me (I was rereading Trollope's *The Way We Live Now*), I headed for the elevator, only to be stopped at the nurses' station counter.

"Where are you going?"

I told the nurse on duty that I was just going down to the café.

"Is your daughter down there?"

No, I said, finding the question both odd and somewhat presumptuous.

"Is she planning to meet you there?"

No, again. What was this obsessive curiosity about Julia?

"It says in your notes that you must be accompanied by your daughter—I can read it to you."

I asked if Dr. Clawson was still around. He wasn't.

"But he made that note—look, it's in his handwriting."

She was as they say only doing her job, and I knew that any further argument from me would lead us nowhere. But I chafed irritably at the fact that rehab could advertise itself as the "halfway house" between the hospital and home, yet the slightest show of independence led to one's immediate arrest, as was happening now. That Julia was now reckoned to be my guardian—the grown-up in the room—stung me keenly as an insult to my pride and reemergent self-sufficiency. I felt the scene at the nurses' station had come straight out of Ken Kesey's *One Flew Over the Cuckoo's Nest,* a ritual comic humiliation.

The next morning Dr. Clawson visited me after my solitary breakfast, and I asked him to release me from his constraints on my movements within the hospital, which he did with good grace, saying, "I'll do it right now before I forget."

The rehab ward was a statistical anomaly. Across the United States in 2012 the average hospital stay was four and a half days at a cost of $10,400 per stay, according to the Agency for Healthcare Research and Quality. But for inpatients in rehab wards, their stays were more likely to be measured in weeks, not days, though the institution of the hospital was geared to a much faster turnover of patients between admission and discharge. I was trying to figure out what effect, if any, this anomalous factor might have on the social relations between patients, nurses, and other permanent members of the hospital staff. In my own case, I realized that the friendliness I enjoyed with, say, Clawson, Richard, Kelli, Robert, Kathy, and Simon had been established in every instance by the briefest possible signals exchanged on our first meeting—a tone of voice, a casual remark, physical appearance, clothing, eyes that registered interest, a lopsided smile—and the same applied to those to whom I had taken an instant dislike . . . the resident psychologist, the charge nurse, the heavyset male nurse's assistant on my first waking morning on the ward and who'd plagued my life since.

The nursing staff who regularly migrated from ward to ward, and became habituated to dealing with four-and-a-half-day stayers, had, I thought, the best excuse for regarding patients as an undifferentiated class, childlike dependents with their aggravating demands, and individuated more by their symptoms than their personal characters. For the rehab therapists it was a different story: working one-on-one with a patient for forty-five or ninety minutes a day in the gym, each party was bound to form a relationship with the other for better or worse. As one did repetitive exercises with an arm or a leg, small talk became a necessary currency, and however slight might be one's physical improvement day by day, both therapist and patient could take justifiable pride in it, as they could share their disappointment in defeat. Kelli and I fell into a style of gentle banter that seemed, at least to me, to sustain us both, and when I eventually left the rehab ward, it was Kelli's cheering company that I would miss most.

And in the rehab ward, thanks to the patient tutelage of Kelli and her colleagues, I was making definite progress. At long last (about fourteen days after my admission) I was free of the humiliating necessity to phone for a nurse's assistant to help me from the wheelchair to the toilet seat in the bathroom, the word "Transfers" having been ticked on the whiteboard opposite my bed. My earlier bathroom fall, from which I had been rescued by the deeply unsympathetic therapist whom I never saw again, had counted against me and added to the days in which I wasn't permitted to make the "transfer" on my own.

My new freedom of the bathroom felt like an enormous step forward. No longer did I have to suffer the indignity of being helped by female nurses who, I always imagined, were suppressing their disgust at this horrid task; my own self-disgust rising in me during every second of the transfer. The least embarrassing person who regularly answered my call for assistance was Robert, whose unassuming good humor and friendliness made it possible for us to chat convivially while the deed was being done, which relegated the transfer from the first order of business to a contingent incidental.

Up till now, my "restroom" time had been strictly limited by the audible pacing of my helper in the bedroom outside, impatiently waiting for me to finish. At last, I could retire there, as I used to do at home, catching up on my reading with my new backlit Kindle. In Judt's *Postwar,* the Berlin Wall had just been torn down and President Mitterrand and Mrs. Thatcher were forming an alliance to, in Thatcher's phrase, "check the German juggernaut." There can be few better illustrations of the mind-body disjuncture than reading an elegantly patterned history of one's own time in the world while taking a leisurely shit.

Chapter 31

———————

ROME FELL TO the Allies on Monday, June 5, 1944. Hitler, whose adolescent dream had been to become an artist or, failing that, at least an architect, shared with Churchill an almost superstitious reverence for the Eternal City, and although other cities across Europe, from Dresden to Warsaw, Stalingrad to Coventry, were smashed to bits in the war without any regard for their people or their historical importance, Rome would be spared. On June 3 a message from the German high command in Berlin announced: "Führer decision. There must not be a battle of Rome." So Rome became an "open city," meaning that its defenders would peacefully move out when its attackers moved in. There was still gunfire, mostly from snipers, in the city and its suburbs, but neither the Allies nor the Germans mounted bombing raids, and all the ancient bridges over the Tiber were left intact.

At 1:30 a.m. on June 5, both Old Glory and the Union Jack were hoisted in Piazza Venezia to fly side by side, and later in the morning General Clark declared that this was "a great day for the Fifth Army," neglecting to mention the British Eighth Army or anyone else, so determined was he to claim the fall of Rome for himself. Rick Atkinson reports that "Churchill cast a blind eye on fraternal frictions, notwithstanding reports that some British officers were turned away from Rome at gunpoint."

But Clark's self-promoting triumph lasted for only a few hours. On June 6 at 6:00 a.m., German radio came through from Berlin with news of the Normandy landings. According to Atkinson, Clark said:

"How do you like that? They didn't even let us have the newspaper headlines for the fall of Rome for one day." In fact, Clark was lucky to get any headlines at all, for the Normandy landings had been postponed at the very last moment for twenty-four hours because of a once-in-a-lifetime June windstorm that was shredding the English Channel on the fifth (and was still making serious trouble on the sixth, though Operation Overlord went ahead that day).

Atkinson again:

At the Albergo Città, a BBC correspondent burst into the Allied press headquarters. "Boys, we're on the back page now," he said. "They've landed in Normandy." Eric Sevareid later recalled that "every typewriter stopped. We looked at one another."

Atkinson goes on to quote Sevareid, a news reporter for CBS, at greater length:

Most of us sat back, pulled out cigarettes and dropped our half-written stories about Rome on the floor. We had in a trice become performers without an audience . . . a troupe of actors who, at the climax of their play, realize that the spectators have all fled out the door.

Apart from that "Boys" from the BBC man, which makes him sound more American than British, this abrupt deflation of the fall of Rome in the media seems spot-on. The enormous loss of life and even bigger numbers of disabling head wounds and amputations required to capture the city became as nothing overnight. From June 6, 1944, till the end of the war, the entire Italian campaign faded into a minor sideshow as far as the media were concerned. So much for Clark's bloodthirsty eagerness to beat Oliver Leese to Churchill's bull's-eye.

On June 6, my father wrote jubilantly to my mother, with every sentence terminating in an exclamation point:

Well, Precious, here I am! And what a lot has happened since I last wrote!

It wasn't until late this morning that I heard the second front had begun, &, as I'd been expecting it to happen the previous night to coincide with the fall of Rome, I'd given last night as the last chance of it coming off at all! That good news added to our own has given life quite a different appearance! Especially as I'm now able to wear a soft hat all day without any thought of the tin one that's been such a headache for so long!

That afternoon he had made a short shopping trip into the city, finding Rome "practically untouched . . . what little real damage there is has been done by our bombers, I think." The RAF and USAAF had targeted Rome's rail marshaling yards, hoping to cut off the enemy's supply lines, but, as was usual in World War II, many bombs had missed their objectives by a mile and more, and the trains still ran, if not quite (as in the Mussolini proverb) on time. Peter's gift shopping: for Monica, two rolls of artificial silk, one "plain pink" and the other "flowered white"; for me, a "wooden elephant on wheels which, when pushed along nods its head and flaps its ears!" I remember the elephant as a permanent roommate in my upstairs bedroom: he hung out with Knocky, my Pinocchio doll, with whom I slept every night.

The next day Peter returned to the city only to find it occupied by another alien force: "base wallahs," meaning the vast, and usually slow-moving, military bureaucracy of staff officers, secretaries, clerks, and gofers who tortured junior officers in the field with forms to be filled in in triplicate and sextuplicate as if to reassure everybody that the work of killing and being killed was as boring and tiresome as any other job on offer at the labor exchange. In barely forty-eight hours the bureaucracy had occupied all the better hotels and restaurants of Rome, placarding them with "Out of Bounds to Troops" signs, for base wallahs believed themselves to constitute an elite that should keep clear of the begrimed and muddy-booted soldiery that had liberated the city in the first place. Gerry Scrivener would have none of this, and he and my father gate-crashed their way around Rome, thereby saving themselves from the ignominy of having to take their own "haversack rations" with them every time they visited the city. After a few days, on Major Kerr's initiative, the Sixty-Seventh Field Regiment commandeered its own Italian restaurant in the center of town near the Pantheon and, following the example of the base staff, placarded the windows with signs prohibiting the entry of outsiders. The regimental restaurant turned out to be an unqualified success and survived a divisional HQ closure order issued a couple of days after its opening.

The American Fifth Army and the British Eighth Army passed through Rome at speed in order to harass the Germans who were flee-ing northward to Florence and Tuscany, leaving a wide trail of blown-up bridges and mine-infested roads behind them. But the British First Division was ordered to stand down in Rome for rest, reequipment, and reinforcements to replace the losses it had suffered at Anzio. The division stayed in the city or on its outskirts from the first week of June until the first week of August, long enough for the men to become adoptive citizens of the place, which was far more congenial to them than their last protracted stop in Tunis had been.

ENSA (officially an acronym for Entertainments National Service Association but more widely known as Every Night Something Awful) put on shows to jam-packed audiences. Peter attended one that quali-fied for the "something awful" category, a one-man performance by the BBC talent show host Carroll Levis, who, conscious that he was speaking to servicemen, talked down to them with a foul-mouthed display of sexual innuendo. Luckily for him, no BBC executives were present. More to my father's taste was another ENSA production, Noël Coward's *Blithe Spirit,* which my parents had seen on its first London run at the Piccadilly Theatre in 1941, when they spent a night at the Dorchester Hotel. Seeing the play in Rome three years later gave Peter the chance to reminisce tenderly about that earlier evening when he and Monica were newlyweds. The great Welsh actor-writer Emlyn Williams was in the Roman production, and he "made a very nice & homely little speech at the end which was very touching in its sincer-ity," Peter wrote to Monica, "but I needed little reminder of home and you, Dear Heart, as I was filled all evening with the memories of that lovely time in London."

For my father, Rome became a city of music. On first arrival there he narrowly missed, to his considerable chagrin, a Beethoven recital. But he did get into Irving Berlin's *This Is the Army,* with Berlin him-self singing "Oh! How I Hate to Get Up in the Morning" as Sergeant Irving Berlin (nearly everyone involved in the production wore their army ranks on their program notes). After that he attended a medley of opera arias, drawn to the performance by the presence of Benia-mino Gigli, only to find that Gigli wasn't present because the managers of the Rome Opera House had canceled his appearance on the grounds that he was a Fascist and a German sympathizer, a favorite of Mussolini who had made a recording of the Fascist national anthem, "Giovinezza" ("Youth"), in 1937. Peter to Monica, on June 22:

> We had hoped that Gigli, of world fame, would be performing. However he had blotted his copybook apparently by having been pro-German, & it was found necessary to cancel his services which had been offered free, as those of all the other performers. He couldn't have done us much harm by being allowed to appear—it shows the nasty type of narrow-mindedness, but there it is.

Peter's taste in music wasn't shared by Monica, who claimed to be tone-deaf, and left the drawing room every Sunday afternoon after Peter's homecoming when he had a private date with the *Sunday Symphony Concert* on the wireless. However, in Peter's wartime absence she wasn't above switching on *Music While You Work* and *Workers' Playtime* (BBC programs, the latter broadcast from factory canteens all over Britain), both of which supplied what Peter decried as "dance music," which ungentlemanly subalterns played at full volume on the wind-up gramophone in the mess, and sometimes jitterbugged to it too, a cause of great frowning annoyance to my father.

In Rome, Peter sought out operas with household names—*Madame Butterfly, La Traviata, The Barber of Seville,* and *Tosca,* among others—and made rather commonplace observations about the behavior of their Italian audiences, who hissed and booed performers who didn't catch their fancy, gave standing ovations to those who did, and interrupted the action of the piece to call for an immediate encore of any favorite aria. As someone who believed that all feelings should be kept discreetly hidden behind a stiff upper lip, he judged his fellow opera-goers to be childishly incontinent and came out into the street after the long melodrama of *Tosca,* in particular, feeling rapt but suffering from emotional exhaustion, probably brought on by the effort it took to mask his emotions with a face of faintly amused indifference.

He was never far from the vast, if flabby, ecclesiastical network of Church of England priests, and in Rome he was more entangled in it than ever. He visited the redbrick Gothic-revival church of All Saints'

on the Via del Babuino ("extraordinarily nice inside—all the furnish-
ings are so pleasing & the architecture too"). The chaplain there was
the same man who had officiated at Holy Eucharist on Easter Sunday
near Amalfi; turfed out of his Roman parish by the German occupation, he had reclaimed All Saints' just the week before. "The padre
has roped me in to meet the Bishop of Lichfield"; a sherry party beck-
oned. Enlisting not just one but two of his fellow captains, Gerry and
George, to provide moral support, he ventured onto more dangerous
ground when he visited the very heart of Roman Catholicism:

> [We] went to St. Peter's to attend High Mass, for interest,
> but I'm afraid I wasn't impressed—the church is undoubtedly
> magnificent, in its way, but to our minds more like a museum
> or large decorative hall, with no chairs or pews so that the
> congregation stand about or walk around from chapel to
> chapel, taking their choice, & in general there's little connection
> between the actual celebration of Mass (very poor singing, I
> thought, & not nearly so impressive as many an English church
> service): cut out the disciplinary side & the customs & to me
> there seems very little "religion" left. I said the congregation
> stand around—actually the "natives" tend rather to sit or lean
> against the pillars, or the railings that surround the crypt of the
> Popes, or even against the railings surrounding the high altar
> (in the centre, & which was not being used at the time). But to
> us, the countless protestants who were attending, like us, out of
> interest, showed far more interest and concentration than the
> Catholics—all very peculiar & disappointing . . . we came back
> gloomy & dulled by it all after expecting so much more.

A bit more is going on here than meets the eye, I think. Peter's
upbringing as an Anglo-Catholic put him in danger of conversion to
the Church of Rome, and he needs to say that he was proof against
the temptation offered by the Vatican. Hence the belittling tone of
his letter and his assertion that he only visited St. Peter's "out of interest," like any other tourist. He wasn't to know this then, but after his
father died in 1959, Peter found among his papers an official-looking
scroll announcing that H. P.—who went in for the entire Romish
works of tinkling bells, genuflection, incense, Latin, candles—had

been secretly ordained into the Roman Church by a self-appointed rogue bishop named Ulric Vernon Herford, who claimed his apostolic succession from St. Thomas, a.k.a. Doubting Thomas, via the Syro-Chaldean Catholic Church in southern India. This was an upsetting discovery for my father, understandably, but its sheer nuttiness greatly amused me.

My mother wrote to Peter describing the special treat she had given to me on my second birthday. He responded:

> Darling, J did have a wonderful birthday, and I've enjoyed it too, forgetting with the help of your letters, that I wasn't there too: I can see him every moment of the day, hardly knowing what to do next, & his various parties—you must have been tired out by the end of it all, Dearest! What a lovely idea of yours of the train journey to Sculthorpe—I can already hear & see [him] quite speechless with the efforts of trying to describe his day's voyage of discovery and scientific study into the process of "puff puffs"—he just won't have enough arms and legs to show the motions of actually being in the train when it went under a bridge with the countryside moving past him. What a day!!!

I wish I could remember this outing, but the pungent stink of steam and coal smoke now in my nose, and the urgent metrical rhythm of the train wheels passing over the expansion joints between the rails and talking in nonsense verse, may just as easily have been drawn from a hundred later railway trips.

The journey from Fakenham to Sculthorpe is just two and a half miles, the perfect distance for a two-year-old's attention span, and, as my father said, a lovely idea of my mother's. It's also a melancholy reminder of how intricately and well Britain was connected up before Dr. Richard Beeching came on the scene with his still-controversial reports of 1963 and 1965, meant to restore the British rail system to profitability by ripping up many thousands of miles of branch lines, and damaging the country's social cohesion beyond likely repair. In 1944 Fakenham had two railway stations, each owned by a different company, the Great Eastern and the Midland and Great Northern lines. Now, like Sculthorpe, it has none.

Chapter 32

KELLI RETURNED FROM her brief Caribbean vacation looking lithe and tan while I was sleepless, pasty-faced, in need of a haircut, and hollow-eyed, like a raccoon with a nasty hangover after a night spent communing with the dregs of liquor bottles among the trash cans. I asked her if she'd had a chance to read David Foster Wallace's piece on cruise ship tourism on her travels. She said yes after a hesitation just long enough to convince me that she hadn't, and I didn't push it further. In the week she'd been gone, I had progressed to "walking" along the corridor between the ward and the gym, clinging for dear life to the handrail, fearful that my right leg might at any moment collapse under me and precipitate a dangerous fall. No foot trolley for me now, so I couldn't just drag the leg behind me as I'd done the previous week; I had to try to swing the damned thing forward as best I could, plant it squarely on the floor, transfer my weight to it, then step ahead with my good left leg. Seven or eight steps like this were as many as I could manage before calling for the wheelchair and one-handedly massaging my painfully aching calves.

I've always had a deep aversion to any exercise of an organized and regular kind. There used to be a popular TV show in Britain called *Superstars,* in which well-known athletes from various countries in Western Europe competed in whimsical and sometimes wacky games designed to test their physical agility. This program was not at all my usual television fare, but I used to tune in whenever I caught sight of a racing driver among the assorted runners, jumpers, swimmers, gymnasts, and so on. These drivers were rewarding to watch precisely because I couldn't associate them with any conventional "exercise" at all. They probably had lightning reflexes, cool nerves, and a talent for instant calculation of opportunity, limit, and risk; but did they have to do workouts in the gym? I thought not, and greatly admired them for holding their own against sprinters and other Olympian types because the drivers' working lives were essentially sedentary; strapped into a bucket seat behind the wheel of a Formula One race car, your body would be subjected to stresses galore—the air streaming past your ears at more than two hundred miles per hour, the howl of the engine, the roar of the tires on tarmac, the constant jolting of your spine imparted by the car's stiff suspension as it registered the smallest imperfections of the track—yet none of these called for athleticism in the usual sense. So it was a wonder to see how fit and able every driver seemed to be, and what a fine excuse they made for my own regime of no particular exercise except for everyday walking and driving, along with sailboat handling in the more clement months of the year.

I saw the stroke was going to change all that. In nearly all the stroke-related books that I was reading, either the author or the author's patient underwent a heroic and grueling program of relentless exercises to restore themselves to full working order. I also remembered seeing, as a boy, the movie *Reach for the Sky*, starring Kenneth More as Douglas Bader, the RAF pilot who lost both his legs in a flying accident that nearly cost him his life, then returned to the service walking on twin prostheses without a stick. As the epigraph to the film says: "Douglas Bader has become a legend in his own life time. His courage was not only an example to those in War but is now a source of inspiration to many in Peace." I had no plans to become a courageous example to anybody, but I couldn't help recalling the scenes of Bader in rehab where Kenneth More, surrounded by men in white coats, tried to walk on his new "tin legs" but succeeded only in toppling on his face time after time.

My objectives were modest. When I got home from the rehab ward, all I really wanted was to be able to return to a life of solitary scholarship, of reading and writing. Sailing and hiking were activities I could readily forgo, and so were driving, eating out in restaurants, and shopping (what else was Amazon for?). When I boiled my life down to these bare dimensions, I needed to learn just three things: to be able to walk a bit, to make competent "transfers," and to negotiate stairs. Anything else would be gravy on the side.

With this in mind, I was able to concentrate on the exercise at hand, and stumble a little farther along the corridor with Kelli walking just behind me and making encouraging noises as I went. "You're getting it—weight on the right leg, yes, that's it!" Basking in her praise, I made a continuous thirty steps along the corridor before asking her to fetch the wheelchair. With thirty steps accomplished, I graduated to making a circuit of the big (roughly twelve-by-fifteen-foot) padded bench in the main gym, using just the flat of my left hand to keep my balance as I made what felt an epic hike around this formidable blue rectangle, always with Kelli in very close attendance.

Next up was to walk with a "four-pronged cane" as my sole support, though this object wasn't a cane and didn't really have prongs. It was, rather, an adjustable black aluminum thingummybob with a sponge-wrapped handle, and at the bottom a metal plate to which four extended legs were attached, each ending in a nonslip rubber foot. Three of these feet stood firmly on the floor, but the fourth stood very slightly higher than the rest, which gave the cane an unsettling wobbly feeling as one leaned on it, and I'm sure I'd've felt more secure with an ordinary walking stick.

We were in the smaller adjunct to the gym, where, holding on to the armrest on the wheelchair, I levered myself up to a standing position and gingerly transferred my left hand to the handle on the cane. (I have it here beside me as I write, and the wobble is minimal— I can slide an envelope containing my monthly bank statement between the offending foot and the floor—but even that small imperfection was enough to make my standing feel dangerously precarious.) With only the cane to balance my weight, I was in a panic, expecting at any moment to crash to the ground. Kelli tried to soothe me, assuring me that she was there to catch me if I began to fall, and I managed to slide my left foot forward a few inches without losing contact with the floor. The inches felt like a triumph to me, as I dragged my other foot to join its partner.

Breaking into a sweat, I shuffled forward, taxing increment by taxing increment, toward the small padded bench ahead—a distance way too far for my taste. An image came to mind of the many beggar amputees I'd noticed in Arabia, men who'd lost their legs in wars or accidents, who scooted around the place on wheeled wooden boards, propelling themselves with their hands, and I found myself rather envying them for having found such a safe and simple means of transport. When I eventually made it to the bench I collapsed on it, exhausted by the effort.

"Five minutes' rest, then we'll do it again."

"You're joking."

But we did do it again—and again—and again. When our session ended, flushed with what I felt was justifiable pride in my progress (I hadn't fallen and didn't need to be awakened from the effects of concussion or worse), I thanked Kelli profusely for her help in achieving it.

"It's what I'm here for. Tomorrow, I thought we might try stairs."

Stairs were part of the reason why I spent so long in the rehab ward. Someone from the hospital had visited the house I lived in, with Julia for three and a half days a week and alone for the other half, as per the joint parenting agreement in our divorce settlement, and had counted the exterior steps leading to the second floor, seventeen in all, and had guessed that the stairwell from the second floor to the third would contain about the same number. So I became a problem case, because the rehab ward was reluctant to part company with me until I became adept at climbing and descending stairs without assistance from anyone else. The phrase "assisted living" was tried on me by nurses and therapists, usually with the accompanying phrase "just as a halfway house"—which was what I thought the rehab ward was supposed to be. "Assisted living" became a daily threat, certain to violate if not destroy my cherished autonomy and the right to live on my own.

So I became a keen student of stairs. Sitting or lying on the big bench in the main gym while Kelli patiently made me exercise my dud right leg, I watched fellow patients working on the double ziggurat of six steps up and six steps down, just across from the bench, hauling their weight up with their good hand clinging to the banister, then— much more tentatively—finding their way down on the other side, leading with the bad foot followed by the good one. Going downstairs was obviously a great deal more difficult for them than going up, and, from a few yards away, I vicariously felt their fear of falling, sharing their vertigo as they made their unsteady descent.

With Kelli's help, I could at least now brace the muscles in the knee of my starboard leg, though I was still much afraid of entrusting any real weight to it—an unnecessary cowardice, or so Kelli said. I've always been a physical coward and could only too easily imagine my leg turning back into jelly when the critical moment came. But in the struggle between my fear of painful and damaging collapse and my terror of assisted living, terror won hands down over mere fear.

We were at the foot of the practice stairs. I levered myself out of the chair and made a grab for the handrail of the ziggurat. One of my panic dreams has long been the moment when, as a parachutist, I've had to commit myself to the thin air below the open door of a plane, with the ground lying several thousand feet away. That is how I felt about my first stair—pure funk and dither. For less than a second I lifted my left foot from the floor and immediately slammed it down again.

"Don't stop breathing," Kelli said.

The daunting height of the stair astonished me.

"Try again."

I did. Result: same.

"Might it help if I held your knee?"

"I think it might—psychologically at least."

With Kelli cupping my knee with both hands, I was at last able to shift my weight onto my right side, and with that shift, I was able to lift my left foot onto the stair. Given the fuss I'd made over this simple maneuver, success at last came as an anticlimax. The thing was easy, and the difficulty I'd had with it was all in my mind, not my body. Kelli let go of my right knee and told me to repeat the action with my left leg, which I did, but at a camera-shutter speed because I couldn't count on my right leg to hold me for more than a fraction of a second. The foot flew from floor to step, and then from step to floor again as it expressed no confidence at all in its enfeebled counterpart.

Chapter 33

HIS TWENTY-SIXTH BIRTHDAY, on July 4, 1944, found my father still camped within walking distance of central Rome and its opera houses. Parcels from my mother had arrived to mark the day: one was full of books (titles unmentioned); another an assorted care package that included Veganin tablets for pain relief, film for his camera, various ointments and powders, and a new toothbrush; another a birthday cake baked by Monica in the White House. Meditating on his age, Peter wrote: "I'm still the third youngest officer in the Mess, which is quite an achievement, being the second senior captain in the Regiment at the same time."

He had just returned from a solo road trip that lasted nearly two days, following the coast road south past Anzio to Naples and beyond, with instructions from Major Gunn not to return until he'd found sufficient cans of paint to smarten up the battery's vehicles. So, with a trailer hitched up to his jeep, and a bottle of Scotch to ensure his welcome, he had gone in search of an American battery whose officers he'd befriended when they had all been positioned in the Padiglione Woods on the beachhead. He'd met with a "more than cordial welcome especially when they smelt the W.," and enjoyed a lavish birthday lunch with the Americans, who supplied him with enough paint to fill his trailer. He had then set off on the long drive back to Rome.

"It was a very enjoyable birthday Darling because I was more easily able to be with you in our thoughts together in the comparative solitude of the Jeep than if I had been here all the time." I know exactly what he means. As one drives alone on uncrowded roads, eyes and hands fully occupied, the mind floats free in untethered reverie. The motorcar is a fine machine for thinking and imagining in, and my father's pleasure in long-distance driving was a big factor in his choice of the first civilian job he took on after being demobilized: a regional secretary for Toc H. His love of driving lasted him until the end of his life in 1996, when he was mapping a route on minor roads from Minneapolis to Seattle in a rental car at the time of his death.

At the end of July he was transferred from 265 Battery to 446 Battery, and on August 3 the regiment moved on from Rome to Florence, following the route taken by the British Eighth Army back in June and July. The landscape they passed through, dotted by farms and little hills, was bucolic and unspoiled because the German troops had beaten such a rapid retreat. The bridges they had blown up behind them had nearly all been replaced by portable Bailey bridges assembled by Allied sappers, and the roads had (mostly) been cleared of mines. My father had mixed feelings about his transfer to 446. As he wrote to my mother on July 29:

Thank you very, <u>very</u> much for three grand letters that arrived today, Dear Heart—they have helped me a lot, Precious, as I feel rather in the dumps. As you will see I've changed my address—not yet, in point of fact, as I go to the other battery tomorrow evening, but still the last evening in this one can never be exactly a happy one after well over five years. The change-over is, I suppose, my own fault and, from one point of view, to my benefit, as I had to ask as long ago as early in May that I should be given a different job—OP work was getting me down as I found the constant strain was beginning to tell (I'd never mention it to you, Beloved, as there was nothing you could do except to worry all the more)—it was the cause, in part anyway, of my skin trouble again, just as in Africa, and now here's the answer, that I'm going to 446 as Battery Captain which is a purely administrative job and, by rights, that of a senior captain. This is the only thing that justifies my going; and I can only square myself up with the reminder that I've done more OP work than any other officer in the Regt. and so am due for a change. I'm afraid 265 has always been my only interest—however . . . it's no use getting maudlin, & I know you'll excuse me if I get a little drink inside me when I've finished this, Darling—not enough to make it disgusting, but just so as I can forget the worst & get into a frame of mind where I can see the rosier side which is <u>very</u> definitely there: the one where we shall <u>both</u> have a lot less to worry about, Precious.

It's good to know that Peter could admit to being seriously rattled by his duties at the observation post—the most dangerous job in an artillery regiment because it was closest to and sometimes ahead of the front of foxholes and barbed wire. Because the OP was invariably located at a high and therefore visible point in the landscape, it was a prime target for enemy snipers and field guns, and just behind his modest, reassuring remarks here I can see him crawling along a wadi at the beachhead to his post for a forty-eight-hour shift of calling the shots down to his troop, always frightened by the thought that this time he wouldn't make the return journey alive. Although the acronym for his condition had not yet been coined, he was plainly suffering from PTSD.

Peter's transfer to 446 Battery was sweetened for him by the fact that Gerry Scrivener was going there too ("he has just been posted to this battery, & is, as a result, very fed up I imagine . . . as he's now a surplus captain, without a job, & only the rank as a 'gratuity'"). My father's sympathy for his friend seems untainted by schadenfreude: since North Africa he'd been saying that Scrivener's lack of promotion was unfair. In a letter sent the next month, on August 17, he wrote:

Gerry Scrivener came along last night as I'd invited him & we sat on the garden wall, the house is right on top of a hill & the wall drops from the lawn, a full twenty feet from the hillside, so that we looked out over all the orchards and packed olive trees to the other side of the valley, & talked until nearly 1am! I then drove him back in my Jeep to his abode about a mile away (I told you yesterday he'd just come to this battery as a spare captain!?) You can guess we had a lot to talk about—it's really most amusing; we've worked together, worked against each other, fought each other over the minutest details—argued, haggled and criticized George (poor George!) for over three years—(265 must have heaved a sigh of relief when the trouble-makers departed!) and now here we are again, the heavenly twins, both determined to have our own <u>separate</u> ways in this battery. We are both agreed in the first place that it can do with a lot of shaking up, & he's already trying his dear old arguments on me that he used to try on George! (And me!) We shall be both quite ruthless, particularly as neither of us cares an iota what anyone else thinks of us and I can see the stick in the muds, the polloi that infest this Battery getting a little shaken!

Polloi that infest! After nearly three weeks' residence in 446, he'd clearly found no amiable acquaintance in the new officers' mess, which he seemed determined to regard as a mannerless assortment of oiks. Unlike several of the officers at 265, they hadn't apparently been to public schools or graduated from Oxford or Cambridge. It's true that 265 held at least one authentic future pillar of the Establishment in the person of Kenneth Jupp, 1917–2004. In 1939 Jupp interrupted a prize-laden undergraduate career as a classicist at University College, Oxford, to enlist in 265 Battery, with whom he served at Dunkirk, North Africa, where he won the Military Cross, and Anzio, where he was severely wounded and invalided back to England. In Anzio, in an echo of Peter's experience, he had been promoted from captain to major in a different regiment, the Nineteenth Field; indeed, the question may well have been put to both of them on the same day. He would go on to become a barrister, a Queen's Counsel, and then a knighted High Court judge—all this besides standing for Parliament in Canterbury as the Liberal candidate in the 1950 election, in which he came in third, and marrying and fathering four children, though my father described him as a "confirmed bachelor" when he knew him.

If he thought his transfer to 446 was a disappointing social come-down, he was cock-a-hoop about his duties as battery captain there.

This is the type of Army life that I like . . . I'm quite on my own, with about 30 chaps . . . a law unto ourselves with a certain amount of work to do tho' most of it is individual stuff where every man does his own particular job. My time is my own & I go just where I want to when I want to . . . I must try

to improve my Italian as I'd be able to get a lot more for the
chaps that way tho' everything is scarce. It's a poor "do" that
I haven't yet got myself (won) a wireless set, but the Germans
took <u>everything</u> (with much gesticulation!)

Preparing for the move, he bought himself a hardbound Italian desk
diary with AGENDA 1944 in gold letters on its oil-and-coffee-stained
green cloth cover. There's a full page for every day, and for every day
a patron saint. When my younger brother Colin brought this book
with him to Seattle in 2012, I opened it eagerly, though he warned me
that it was the most boring diary he had ever read, and he was right,
unless one happens to be fascinated by, say, the correct tire pressures
for all of 446 Battery's vehicles (there were around twenty of them),
or the daily consumption of government-issued tots of rum (191), or
to which wave bands Peter had recalibrated his (newly acquired) wireless. Most of AGENDA's pages are blank, except for those in which
the day's work allowed my father to indulge his affection for numbers
for numbers' sake. The most interesting entry by far is for Settembre,
Sabato 2, St. Mansuetus's Day, which reads in its entirety as follows:

Moved WL's fwd to 834686.
Lts. Gyles, Beadle & Holbrook killed & Gnr. Tummey, on
    Recce by driving over a Tellermine in their Jeep.
Heavy thunderstorm @ night.

The brisk—and brusque—arithmetic of warfare. But, more than
fifty years later, in 1995, when Peter was making notes on his own war
service, Lieutenant Gyles was treated to a more friendly recollection:
"Freddy Gyles was a warm and open-hearted fellow and his death, by
a road mine north of Florence, was a great blow to us all."
By September 1944, three months after the fall of Rome, the Italian campaign was no longer news. Every war correspondent wanted
to be in France to witness the liberation of Paris and follow the Allied
armies to Berlin and the end of the war in Europe. Winston Churchill
found himself alone in his demands for more troops and matériel to
be sent to Italy. Andrew Roberts in his fine and capacious 2018 biography of Churchill says that he was "rowing badly with the Chiefs of
Staff over the Italian campaign, which he wanted reinforced but which

they, by then rightly, saw . . . as 'a secondary front.'" My mother was on Churchill's side: she found the dearth of news about what was happening in Italy almost impossible to bear.

Far from sending reinforcements, as Churchill wanted, the chiefs of staff, American and British, insisted on a strategic depletion of Allied troops in Italy after the capture of Rome. Whole divisions were withdrawn from the Italian theater and shipped to northern France, their departure making Churchill's ambition to cross the Po Valley, enter Austria via the eastern Alps, and seize Vienna ever more improbable.

General Clark's Fifth Army (to which the British First Division was now attached) took Florence on August 4, 1944. The next city to be conquered was Bologna, just sixty-seven miles to the north, on a road that I well remember traveling in the high summer of 1974, when it was a pleasant and often exhilarating two-hour drive over the northern Apennines, those fold-and-thrust "recent" mountains of the Neogene (twenty million or fewer years old), largely made of granite and limestone, full of sheer precipices, narrow, steep-sided valleys, and mountain streams that overflow their banks and become raging torrents at the first hint of serious rain. Richard Whitfield tells of how the ever-intrepid Major Bill Kerr and his driver tried to ford one such stream in their jeep: they had to be rescued by the Royal Engineers with a breeches buoy, and the jeep was carried away downstream, never to be seen again.

Meanwhile, my father was engaged in the less adventurous pursuit of billets for his battery HQ. First he parked himself in a "very comfortable" house belonging to a retired professor and his wife, both in their eighties. His only complaint there was that his bedroom, with a fine view from the window, was ostentatiously "Victorian." When he took his leave from his professorial hosts a few days later, they "shed tears . . . it was most touching." Later that day, after a short drive north, he found a much grander country house with only a young wife (her husband, a count, was temporarily absent) and a staff of servants in occupation—the wife too young, he thought, to deserve having a battery of English soldiers visited upon her, so he spared her the mass of gunners and lance bombardiers (who, presumably, put up their tents in the gardens) and limited access to the house to commissioned officers, sergeants, and full bombardiers. He set up his office in the massive ground-floor dining room with its refectory table as his desk, and slept in a divan bed beneath the main window, from where he could see "various sofas & deep armchairs to lounge in when I've got the time!" He admired the high vaulted ceilings, oak-paneled walls hung with ancestral portraits, coats of arms painted above the fireplaces. In return for this lavish haute-bourgeoisie hospitality, the battery had brought with them a six-cylinder electric generator, picked up in Rome, with which they lighted the entire house ("the Ities are very pleased, tho' I have to chivvy them a little about blackout & so forth!").

This was, almost certainly, the house where, according to Whitfield, a "housemaid told us that the 'Tedeschi' [Germans] had been there until the previous night and she had been dancing with them outside in the garden to gramophone music. She also told us that she was a virgin and longed to be otherwise, or words to that effect. Which fact was duly noticed and acted upon."

My father believed that the family were Fascists, on the grounds that their silverware and antique china all appeared to be intact and hadn't been looted by the retreating Germans. If so, his young hostess was a skilled diplomat: on the second day of Peter's stay in the house, she took him to have tea with some near neighbors who were yet another Italian count and his American contessa, who together ran a turkey and olive oil farm.

The Allies were now facing the Gothic Line, General Kesselring's last fortified and entrenched defensive front in Italy. They were also facing the unusually early onset of a bitter winter as September gave way to October and the mountains were drenched by a succession of rainstorms that turned most of the Apennine landscape into mud. Photographs of the area taken in the late fall of 1944 make it look like the battlefields of Flanders in 1917: Indian muleteers coaxing their sodden animals uphill, hocks buried in the slurry; soldiers, as if sculpted in wet clay, trying to extricate a foot from the suck and squelch of what's below; corpses littering a hillside, limbs turning into earth before our eyes; a tank so thoroughly immobilized, first by mud and then by frozen snow, that its only useful function now will be as a static artillery piece until the spring returns and sets it free.

This impasse was as bad as or worse than the previous winter's stalemate at Anzio. Between October 1944 and April 1945 the opposing lines of German and Allied troops barely shifted, though men on both sides were dying without point every single day, and "morale," never high since the conquest of Rome, sank to record lows, prompting an epidemic of desertions. Many men quit the lines for the criminal allure of the thriving black markets of Rome and Naples, and joined the gangs of hijackers who held up trucks and trainloads of military supplies and sold off their contraband at stalls in the cities. Some of these, especially the Italian Americans among them, were effortlessly absorbed into the Mafia. Otherwise law-abiding deserters simply melted into the shadows, returning to their former civilian occupations in a foreign country that was in such social turmoil and upheaval that it was hard to recognize almost anyone as an intruder or outsider.

My father never mentions the deserters in his letters, though I did find one entry about a gunner with a bracketed "AWOL" beside his name in the AGENDA diary, but Whitfield notes (in a generally friendly way) the disappearance of several of his mates. In Britain, the death sentence for desertion was abolished in 1930 by Ramsay MacDonald's Labour government, and Churchill's National Government of 1940–45 held firm on its abolition, despite pleas for its reinstatement from a wolf pack of generals. In the United States the penalty of "death by musketry" remained on the books, but only one misfortunate private, Eddie Slovik, a twenty-five-year-old ex-con from Detroit, was actually executed for the offense: all other deserters who were found, detained, and tried by the military authorities had their sentences commuted by presidential order—usually to a short spell in jail.

One of my father's friends, Major David Shepherd, the commanding officer of 266 Battery, went missing sometime in early December. Both men had joined the regiment in 1939 as raw subalterns, and both were "sons of the cloth," Shepherd's father being the archdeacon of Dudley, another parish in the Worcester diocese. As Peter wrote to Monica at the end of the month:

> By the way I've not yet told you that David Shepherd has been taken prisoner—a patrol caught him whilst he was up with the infantry & quietly hustled him off in the darkness whilst he was visiting his OP, or rather returning from there. I'm afraid I don't know Doreen's address if you should feel you ought to write to her tho' I don't think there's much you could say to her if you did—it's rather hard to know what one <u>would</u> say! Luckily

that sort of thing is most unusual—tho' she will be relieved, no doubt, he will be absolutely furious: we have all been speculating on the difficulties any interrogation officer would meet in trying to get him to "talk"!

Doreen might have been Major Shepherd's mother, the archdeacon's wife, or, judging by Peter's tone here, I think it much more likely that she was the same "young woman" mentioned in my father's 1995 notes, who was "found" by Shepherd in Sleaford, Lincolnshire, where she took him in and "offered him every home comfort." "I think that her husband was elsewhere in the Forces," added my straitlaced father.

In *The Eyes and Ears of the Regiment,* Whitfield gives a fuller account of Major Shepherd's disappearance in the Apennines:

Major Shepherd of 266 . . . went out with Major Rose (2IC Gordons) to visit the Rovine OP. They went together—Major Rose to the left-hand company, Major Shepherd to the OP. An escort was arranged to bring Major Shepherd back, which he did not wait for as the journey back was only 600 yards. At Tac HQ and at the company a scuffle was heard but no shots. When Major Rose returned there was no sign of Major Shepherd. A Gordons' search party was sent out and found Major Shepherd's tin hat lying on the track. He was reported missing, presumed captured. Subsequently we learned that Major Shepherd's grave was found at Ferrara where he died of wounds on Christmas Day.

Missing? Dead? Deserted? The unavoidable ambiguities of war bring home the anguish of not knowing, not being able to know, sometimes temporarily and sometimes forever, endured by the families and lovers of soldiers, sailors, and airmen in combat. Major Shepherd's actual fate was not discovered until after the war, when he failed to return from the German POW camp to which his fellow soldiers had so confidently sent him.

As it happened, the entire British First Division was pulled out of action in Italy in the second week of January 1945. Whitfield paints a pretty good picture of the miserable weather conditions and other details of how the move was conducted:

On the 5th a thaw set in rendering the tents and cookhouses a morass. Heavy rain followed making everything once again a sea of mud. It then turned very cold and this was followed by heavy snow the depth of four inches by evening.

Rumors were rife that we were moving soon.

For the next two or three days the heavy snow continued and the temperature dropped to minus 17°. There were snowdrifts 20 feet deep and all the roads were marked out with tall poles. Our vehicles were started every hour during the night and the guns recuperator systems padded up.

For people who have visited northern Italy only in the heat of summer, its brutal winters can come as a shocking surprise. The Sixty-Seventh Field Regiment was well out of it. The original objective, Bologna, only fell to the Allies on April 21, barely two weeks before Germany's unconditional surrender on May 7. It had been one hell of a long, bloody, cold, wet, alternately snow- and mud-bound sixty-seven miles from Florence.

Chapter 34

IN MY OWN life, September 28, 1944, was a momentous occasion, though I have no distinct memory of that date at all. It was the day on which Granny at last moved into her own house, Notch Hill in Sheringham, and also the day when Lucy, who became my intimate confidante, moved into the White House. My mother wrote to Peter:

> Two <u>lovely</u> letters have come from you and I feel you as very near me, Darling and, Dearest, we have also acquired a new addition to the family!—We've got a "puppy-darg"! as Jonathan calls it! He hasn't seen it yet but I promised it him before lunch & only went out to fetch it afterwards, having fallen in love with it and bought it, all by twelve o'clock in about five minutes time. I had never even remotely considered buying a dog, but Darling this was in a hatch outside Mr. Coll's with all its brothers and sisters and quite irresistible. When he wakes up I shall take it up for him to see.
>
> I'd better hurry up and introduce you to the lady, for lady I am afraid she is!—Tinker Bell, Tinker for short I think her name shall be and she's a smooth fox terrier and marked like a hound with brown eyebrows and black ears divided by a neat line of white running up her nose, and a black tail and all the rest is white.
>
> Can you see her, Darling? Her muzzle is white and there is a

white division up her head and there is just a touch of tan low down on each side of her cheeks—She _is_ sweet!

Lucy, as she was rechristened the next day, was seven weeks old and still in the waddling stage of puppyhood. I remember her, fully grown, with her long, lustrous, floppy black ears, and hazel eyes rimmed with black, set in an expression of sympathetic inquiry, as absorbed as I was in anything I did. A week after her arrival at the White House, we took her in the train to Sheringham, where she puddled all over Granny's carpets, failed to make friends with Granny's dogs, Timmy and Charlie, who terrorized her, miniatures though they were, and after two days of this had to be sent back in disgrace to Fakenham, riding the train inside the guard's van in Timmy's crate. My mother had arranged for a dog sitter, a Mrs. Dennet, to pick Lucy up at the other end, and phoned her that evening from Notch Hill to find out how things were going. As Monica reported to Peter, "Mrs. Dennet remarked how perfectly sweet she is!—She is, you know, she's a lovely little dog." I was, apparently, utterly disconsolate at the prospect of not seeing Lucy again for more than two weeks—an unimaginable age.

Chapter 35

I HAD JUST finished using the bathroom and a nurse was interrogating me about my stools.

"Were they runny? Soft? Hard? Were they well-formed?"

"I'm afraid I paid them no attention at all."

"You must have some idea."

"This is the rehabilitation ward. Can you please explain to me how my damn stools have anything to do with my neurological rehabilitation?"

"We're just trying to build a picture of your general health."

"Do you stand over the toilet and investigate the character of your own stools?"

"Sometimes, yes. I do."

"Okay, then. Mine are always paragons of their kind. Perfectly formed pieces of shit; i.e., they were *normal*—the Platonic ideal of the shit world."

The nurse left my room in a huff.

All right, I am a squeamish prude, a serious character flaw that I put down to my all-too-English upbringing, which foisted on me the convention that the inner workings of one's digestive, sexual, and excretory functions were not fit subjects of conversation, except between parents and young children. Even now, after more than a quarter of a century of living in the United States, I quail from the ceaseless barrage of TV commercials for pharmacological solutions to erectile dysfunction, irritable bowel syndrome, "leakage," and piles; DIY home tests for colon cancer; and all the rest, as much for their annoying whimsy as for their violation of an irrational taboo.

But the point here, about the nurse's cheerful discussion of my stools, is that talk of bodily functions took so much precedence over talk and treatment of neurological symptoms in the neuro rehab unit that the real fears of stroke patients were almost totally neglected by the nursing staff. On my first day there, when I was introduced to Dr. Clawson, the commanding officer of the unit, I asked him for his opinion about my prognosis "as a neurologist," and he responded, "I'm not a neurologist: my specialty is sports medicine." The only connection between sports and neurological rehab that I could see was that both tended to take place in gyms and dealt with patients who hobbled along on sticks and had trouble with their arms and hands. I never saw Dr. Clawson wearing a white coat; his preferred medical uniform was a tracksuit and trainers, authentic symbols of what the neurological rehab ward actually did.

What I really wanted was a friendly neurologist; someone who would explain to me in terms I understood what had happened to my brain during the stroke. All I knew for certain was that a double hemorrhage had taken place in the left hemisphere of my brain, an event that ought to have damaged, if not wiped out, the faculties of reading, writing, calculating, remembering—all the skills, in short, that enabled me to do my job. I did recognize one loss, or "deficit" as the dim psychologist chose to call it: I was having trouble with the simplest maths; additions and subtractions that I could once do in my head without conscious thought now had to be written out on paper, then checked and rechecked. I found myself reciting the multiplication tables in my head, from two twos are four to twelve twelves are one hundred forty-four, often stumbling, then recovering, as I reached the higher numbers like nine nines.

All stroke patients need to know, as exactly as possible, what they have lost to the stroke, and how much of that loss may be potentially recoverable. At around three in the morning of June 17, 1783, Dr. Samuel Johnson, a lifelong hypochondriac, woke to find his power of speech had gone and quickly diagnosed himself as having suffered a "paralytick stroke." He then set himself to take an ingenious intelligence test—to compose in Latin a prayer to God, begging the Almighty to spare his reason. In a letter to his friend Mrs. Thrale (from whom he was temporarily estranged), Johnson described the test and its result:

> I was alarmed and prayed God, that however he might afflict my body he would spare my understanding. This prayer, that I might try the integrity of my faculties I made in Latin verse. The lines were not very good, but I knew them not to be very good, I made them easily, and concluded myself to be unimpaired in my faculties.

"But I knew them not to be very good," and that negative judgment is held up as proof that Johnson's critical intelligence was still intact.

Despite the hideous-sounding and ineffectual treatment inflicted on him by his team of physicians who were also his close friends (it consisted primarily of "blistering," applying cantharides, a concoction of crushed "blister beetles," otherwise Spanish fly, to his skull, throat, and back, in order to raise blisters on his skin), Johnson made an astonishingly rapid recovery from his stroke. His voice returned to normal after a few days, and so did his physical health: twelve days after the stroke he reported to Mrs. Thrale, "I climbed up stairs to the garret, and then up a ladder to the leads, and talked to the artist rather too long, for my voice though clear and distinct for a little while soon tires and falters." This visit to the (unnamed) artist strikes me as an accomplishment comparable to an ascent of Everest for a stroke victim. Lucky Johnson!

Compare this with Sheila Hale's account of her husband's voice in *The Man Who Lost His Language,* three years post-stroke:

> John's non-language has, in fact, become more comprehensible since, three years after the stroke . . . *da woahs* was interspersed with more *ers, urns, ohs, ahs, aarghs, gahs, nos* and *oh my Gods.* His voice is now less fluent. He pauses more often as though searching for a word. His slight stutter has returned: the utterance sometimes splutters out as *d-d-d-DA woahs.* He is more frustrated than he was by his inadequate powers of expression. When he sees that we don't understand, he tries more often to rephrase his comments, enunciating more slowly and emphatically. These are good signs.

Sir John still liked parties and performed sufficiently well at them for other guests to tell Sheila Hale how much they had enjoyed their conversations with him. Throughout the book, Hale talks of her husband's "histrionic" talents: in his life as in his lectures he was always an extravagant actor. In her afterword ("John died peacefully in his sleep next to me in bed at four in the morning of 12 August [1999]"), she writes of his seven years spent as a stroke victim as if they were a master class in the art of acting:

> Five weeks short of his seventy-sixth birthday, he had continued to act the part of a man in the prime of life. He played the role so convincingly that he fooled us all: his doctor, his family, his friends, and above all me. I would like to think that he fooled himself, but I'm less sure about that.

Her conclusive ambiguity seems exactly right: Sir John's performance, she suggests, was at once a sincere and unselfconscious state of being and a cannily calculated act, and its balance of those ingredients can't be exactly measured, even by the person who knew and loved him best.

One last example: Henry James, who in his late phase wrote his books by dictating them to his devoted secretary and the author of *Henry James at Work,* Theodora Bosanquet, had a stroke on December 2, 1915. James's speech remained normal but he was paralyzed on his left side, and his mind appeared to be confused. Leon Edel, his biographer, published an essay titled "The Deathbed Notes of Henry James" in 1968, in which he tried to analyze the few fragments of writing that James dictated to Bosanquet in the days following the stroke. The first fragment is rather more straightforward than the ones that follow; James is describing his stroke:

> I find the business of coming round about as important and glorious as any circumstances I have had occasion to record, by which I mean that I find them as damnable and as boring. It is not much better to discover within one's carcase new resources for application than to discover the absence of them; their being new doesn't somehow add at all to their interest but makes them stale and flat, as if one had long ago exhausted them. Such is my

sketchy state of mind, but I feel sure I shall discover plenty of fresh worlds to conquer, even if I am to be cheated of the amusement of them.

A familiar joke about Henry James, variously attributed to both Philip Guedalla and Rebecca West (my money's on West), says that his work falls into three periods: James I, James II, and the Old Pretender. All the fragments show at least faint traces of James in his Old Pretender phase (i.e., *The Golden Bowl* and subsequent novels). The vocabulary and elaborate syntactical structures both sound right. His voice is there, even if his logic is scrambled.

Two days after dictating the first fragment, James had pneumonia. Edel writes: "Miss Bosanquet wrote in her diary, 'Mind clouded this morning and he has lost his own unmistakeable identity—is just a simple sick man.'" But the next day he asked Bosanquet to take down further fragments:

On this occasion moreover that having been difficult to keep step, we hear of the march of history, what is remaining to that essence of tragedy the limp? We scarce avoid rolling, with all these famished and frustrated women in the wayside dust . . . mere patchwork transcription becomes of itself the high brave art. We [word missing—the typist apparently could not make out what he said] five miles off at the renewed affronts that we see coming for the great, and that we know they will accept. The fault is that they had found themselves too easily great, and the effect of that, definitely, had been, within them, the want of long provision for it. . . . They pluck in their terror handfuls of plumes from the imperial eagle, and with no greater credit in consequence than that they face, keeping their equipoise, the awful bloody beak that he turns round upon them. We see the beak sufficiently directed in that vindictive intention, during these days of cold grey Switzerland weather, on the huddled and hustled campaigns of the first omens of defeat. Everyone looks haggard and our only wonder is that they still succeed in "looking" at all. It renews for us the assurance of the part played by that element in the famous assurance [divinity] that doth hedge a king.

Enough! (All parentheses are Edel's.) You get the point. The best comparison I can think of is with Noam Chomsky's "colorless green ideas sleep furiously," his memorable example of a grammatical nonsense string. Edel describes these fragments as "a kind of stream of consciousness of a fading mind still in possession of its verbal power and the grandeur of its style." More fragments, about Napoleon Bonaparte, are on offer in the essay. I see what Edel means but I'm also in sympathy with James's family, who tried to suppress the deathbed writing as, Edel again, "too tragic a record of a mind in disintegration." James lived on for another eleven weeks; George V awarded him the Order of Merit on January 1, 1916, and he died not long after, on February 28.

In the case of my own stroke, I've now spent more than eleven years asking myself two questions every writing day: What have I lost? and Am I fooling myself? But I find both questions maddeningly unanswerable.

Chapter 36

IN THE REHAB ward, I continued to find common ground with some of the Ethiopian, Eritrean, and Somali cleaners who showed up each day in my room with their mops and buckets. We were all relatively recent immigrants, our characters shaped by cultures in lands far away from the West Coast of the United States. Whatever these cleaners had been doing in their home countries, here in Seattle they were standing on the bottom rung of the American labor market, and their primary ambition was not for themselves but for their children. Most particularly, I shared with several of them the besotted anxiety that grips parents of children who are coming up to college age, when SATs and GPAs become the thieves of time and stuff of nightmares. College admission is a cruel and wayward lottery, depending as it does on the whims of the admissions department in whichever school the student is applying to.

In the UK, sixth formers apply directly to the academic department for a place in which they hope to "read" their chosen subject, and they're chosen or rejected by members of faculty who teach that subject, so would-be physicists are judged by teachers of physics and would-be philosophers by philosophers. In America it's very different: a bachelor's degree normally takes four years, of which the first is spent dipping into sample courses from the enormous array of academic subjects available to any admitted student, who will eventually choose a "major" and begin to specialize in that sometime in their second or sophomore year. The admissions departments aren't staffed by academics but by people in the slippery field of human resources, whose time is spent trying to balance intellectual prowess or the lack of it with such extracurricular activities as team sports, arts, clubs, languages spoken, volunteer work, and helping old ladies cross roads. Canny sociopaths have a pretty good idea of what admissions officers are looking for and consequently devote a substantial chunk of time in high school to joining clubs and organizations that will look well on application forms and present the applicant as an admirable all-round human being and not the blinkered swot he really is.

Listening to the mothers' stories—one involved a seventeen-year-old son laboring at the kitchen table under an unshaded sixty-watt bulb to finish his homework long past his bedtime ("I worry for his eyes," his mother said)—I tried to share their ambitions for their progeny. I also had a tip for them: don't fall into the trap of being intimidated by the extravagant tuition fees and costs of residence at America's private universities and liberal arts colleges, where tuition alone starts at $50,000 a year, but such prices are only for the rich or rich-ish. Stanford, for instance, the college I now knew best, charges nothing for tuition to families earning less than $125,000 a year, and it operates a "need-blind" system of admission, as do its fellows in the private sector, from Harvard and the other Ivy League universities to liberal arts colleges like Williams and Amherst. Going to a top-notch private college can actually be cheaper than going to the nearest public university because the private schools are so much better endowed than public ones and can offer many more "full-ride" scholarships.

The hospital cleaners' children all had an ideal subject for the personal essay that is the key part of an admission form, if they could write how, when, and why they'd come from the Horn of Africa to the United States. Knowing damn all about the Horn of Africa except skimmed headlines of wars, civil wars, AIDS, and famines, I doubted if college admissions departments knew much more than I did; the cleaners' children would have much to teach them—and earn scholarships in the process. As for their mothers, it was a pleasure to see their habitually noncommittal faces brighten when I brought up the subject of their children.

Chapter 37

JULIA VISITED ME when she could, in the off-hours from her job with the Fund for the Public Interest, sometimes in the evening, sometimes looking in on a therapy session during the day or catching me reading alone in my room—Swedish Health Services apparently had no set visiting hours. She had grown bored of raising money to (slightly) extend Mount Rainier National Park and was now making the pitch for ending federal corn subsidies to corporate agribusiness in the Columbia Valley and on the Columbia Plateau in eastern Washington; a much tougher sell on the doorsteps of Seattle but an intellectually more interesting one.

I applauded this switch because eastern Washington had been a personal obsession of mine since I had first come to live in the Pacific Northwest. Everything in it is so very different from its western counterpart that it feels as if one has entered another country if not quite landed on another planet. It begins at Snoqualmie Pass, a fifty-minute drive from Seattle, which marks the abrupt transition from temperate rain forest (one hundred inches of annual rainfall) to sagebrush desert (nine inches or less); from predominantly Democrat in politics to overwhelmingly Republican; from no poisonous snakes to rattlesnakes everywhere; from one of the three most secular cities in America (Seattle ties for first place with Portland, Oregon, and San Francisco) to this landscape of believers and their competing sectarian congregations.

Driving east one summer twilight into the encroaching darkness, I picked up an English-speaking radio station from the medley of

Spanish-speaking voices on the FM band. A phone-in show was going on, with the host performing live exorcisms on his callers: in his commanding basso profundo, he ordered the evil spirit that had taken up lodgings inside a youngish-sounding woman's heart to be on its way at this very instant. The woman—whether she was the exorcist's collaborator or his victim I couldn't tell—answered with shuddering banshee howls, giving the impression that we were listening to a protracted on-air rape. The fast-failing light and speeding sagebrush gave their own sinister context to the drama on the car radio, and that broadcast from long ago has haunted my view of eastern Washington ever since.

Geographers have a term for the topography of this part of the state—"channeled scablands," meaning that the landscape was formed by a succession of cataclysmic floods that swept the region through the Pleistocene epoch and continued into the most recent ice age, between twelve and fifteen thousand years ago. Each flood would cause the collapse of the ice dam at the western end of a huge and very deep (two-thousand-foot) historic lake, named by the geographers Lake Missoula, after the Montana town situated on what used to be the lake's bed, where now the trouty Clark Fork River runs. Whenever a strong warming trend occurred, the dam blew, and the great onrush of ice and water, traveling at more than sixty miles an hour, would scour the Columbia Valley, leaving behind such relics of its passage as dry waterfalls, giant ripple marks (some nearly fifty feet high), and "erratics," boulders the size of semitrucks, carried on or inside gargantuan blocks of glacier ice from their origins in Montana's Rocky Mountains. If eastern Washington looks like another planet to a newcomer, planetary scientists have confirmed that impression by calling the scablands the nearest terrestrial equivalent we have to the Martian "canals" (otherwise "current outflows").

Although farmers and fruit growers who settled on land close to the Columbia had been pumping water from the river to irrigate the soil since the 1850s, humankind didn't manage to seriously improve on nature until the 1930s, as part of Roosevelt's New Deal. What began as a great, wild, untamed river of waterfalls, rapids, whirlpools, boils, was transformed into a series of tame reservoirs, locked in by a total of fourteen concrete hydroelectric dams, from the pharaonic masterpiece of the Grand Coulee, five hundred feet high, to the Bonneville, about four hundred river miles downstream. The Bonneville Power Administration commissioned Woody Guthrie to write a sequence of propaganda songs, providing him with a car and driver for a month (his driver complained about Guthrie's body odor and his failure to ever change his clothes or take a bath), along with a hotel room and a one-off payment of $262. The songs promoted the whole electrification-and-irrigation project as a coming paradise for small farmers and workers, with lines galore like "The Coulee Dam's the biggest thing that man has ever done" and "Roll on, Columbia, roll on," when the whole point of the BPA exercise was to stop most of the Columbia from rolling freely ever again.

The first beneficiary of the hydroelectric scheme wasn't the small farmer but the Manhattan Project, which was searching for a suitably isolated spot in the United States where it could have an endless supply of cold water to cool its reactors and cheap electricity to develop the war-ending nuclear bomb. The Hanford Site on the Columbia River looked perfect for the job. First of all, though, the small farmers whose land lay on the Hanford Reach had to be evicted. They were given a month to pack and leave. The plutonium that fueled the bomb that fell on Nagasaki on August 9, 1945, was produced by Hanford's B Reactor. Now, cleaning up the mess left by the bomb makers on the Hanford reservation, where irradiated jackrabbits set Geiger counters clicking, is forecast to take another fifty years and the people who live downwind and downstream from Hanford continue to blame their cancers and birth defects on the Manhattan Project.

Another hush-hush government enterprise was, until a very few years ago, the "listening station" operated by the National Security Agency, nicknamed by journalists the No Such Agency for its extreme reticence and secrecy. In 2004 I had no difficulty finding it on Google Earth—a compact array of white pylons, domes, and dishes whose purpose was to intercept emails, calls made by mobile phones, and other electronic communications, as part of the George W. Bush administration's "war on terror." It used to lie on a US Army firing range about forty-five miles west of Hanford. In early 2019 I looked for it again but it seemed to have gone, just like the small farmers of eastern Washington.

In 2008 I took a long and lazy three-day drive around the Columbia Basin and Plateau, wondering if I had the gall to set a book in eastern Washington and its temptingly paradoxical human geography. Fiction or nonfiction? I had no idea. At Quincy, a small, unlovely, single-story farm town on the eastern side of the river, where the telephone poles towered above the buildings, I stopped the car and reached for my notebook. A couple of years before, Microsoft had installed a "cloud farm" data center in Quincy, whose architecture of white steel and aluminum sheds blended in perfectly with a branch of Washington Tractor and the other businesses in town. Since my visit the Microsoft farm premises have grown to just short of half a million square feet. Who knew that storing digital data could take up such a quantity of physical space? As a long-term user of Kindle, I've often been innocently struck by the fact that you can download a ton of triple-decker Victorian novels without adding a single milligram to the weight of the device—the thing brazenly defies physics, except, apparently, in Quincy, Washington, where data storage eats hydroelectricity by the terawatt and needs a backup system of a multitude of air-polluting diesel generators, just in case there's a hiccup down at the Grand Coulee Dam.

I headed south on a road as true as a line of longitude. This was a landscape empty of farmhouses, empty of fences, let alone walls or hedges, but full of "walking johnnies"—irrigation sprinklers up to half a mile long, apparently stationary, actually trundling very slowly on their triangular, wheeled undercarriages, around a central pivot, their engines powered, of course, by low-cost, subsidized hydroelectricity. The dust-fine beige soil turned briefly black beneath them as they trundled, watering these enormous circular fields. Every few miles there was a "facility," set a long way back from the road, which conformed to the architectural standards set by Quincy: same white steel and aluminum, same single-story spread, same absence of windows, same vast car lots. Each facility possessed a string of loading bays big enough to accommodate eighteen-wheeler refrigerated trucks and projecting from the main building like the individual "gates" of an international airport.

A huge harvest of, say, potatoes would enter the facility from the back and emerge at the loading bays transformed into machine-cut, parboiled, pre-fried, flash-frozen french fries bound for the fast-food outlets of America. All these industrial enterprises were owned by corporate agricultural giants like Conagra and J. R. Simplot, and all of them, especially in the summer picking season, employed some of the worst-paid workers in the United States—a ragged Hispanic army of migrant farm laborers from Mexico, Guatemala, El Salvador, Honduras, Nicaragua, who doubled and tripled the populations of small Spanish-speaking towns in the valley and on the plateau like Mattawa and Othello in high season.

Here was my problem. *No hablo español,* and I could hardly write about people with whom I couldn't talk; I'd be the grinning simpleton, barely understanding a word they said.

That had been my main problem then. Seen from the rehab ward, where I was dining alone off soggy chips and impossibly overcooked fish clad in some kind of brown batter, along with my single glass of prescription red wine, it seemed the language barrier had become the least of my worries. To travel successfully one needs a high degree of personal autonomy. You have to be able to double back on your tracks at will, change plans on a whim, make no advance bookings, go with the flow, poke your inquisitive nose into other people's business on impulse, be free as a feather adrift on a thermal of air. That's why "isolation" is listed as a synonym for "freedom" in *Roget's Thesaurus:* I've tried traveling with a companion, and it has never worked, at least with another adult—if I'm not already driving my companion mad, I'm in a fret of anxiety that I'll push them over the edge with my next aberrant move.

Driving with Julia was my one exception, and it went back to her babyhood. Both of us looking ahead through the windshield and not at each other loosened our tongues, whether we were driving to school or Mexico or the Grand Canyon or across England. That slight impersonality, not making eye contact, liberated free association experienced nowhere else except in the car and its passenger seat. I loved our road trips for the conversations they enabled, and was aghast at the prospect of my stroke killing them.

I didn't know if I'd be able to drive again. Certainly a stick shift would be beyond me, so the Mazda would have to go and an automatic take its place. A paralyzed right arm and a semi-paralyzed right leg and foot were going to turn driving even an automatic into a tricky and maybe dangerous performance. Sitting at the table in my room, I took my left hand off the imaginary wheel and swung it right, across my chest, to grab the imaginary gear selector on the center console, at the same time reaching with my left foot for the imaginary gas pedal, only to find that I could barely do it because my right knee firmly obstructed my left leg. I felt like Dr. Johnson's dog walking on its hind legs, "not done well; but you are surprised to see it done at all." Fat chance, I thought, that either of these movements would ever become instinctual and unconscious as they should.

But how would I refill this car with gas? Or transfer my overnight bag from the trunk to the motel room? How often would I have to stumble and fall without being able to protect myself with my right hand? The more I speculated, the more I convinced myself of the odds against my ever traveling on my own again.

I thought of a bus I used to see sometimes at Fishermen's Terminal, which I visited regularly to buy cigars from the tobacconist there and talk with the fishermen and go aboard their boats. The bus, owned by a tour operator, was designed for the old and infirm; its front steps, across from the driver's seat, converted at the push of a button into a wheelchair lift. I bet this bus, or one of its siblings, went on tours of boutique wineries in the Yakima, Columbia, and Walla Walla Valleys.

I imagined the interior of the bus into being. It was a custom-built "luxury coach," according to the company, designed to carry twenty-four passengers at most. At the back, the floor was open, with sufficient space for up to four wheelchairs and enough in the way of belts and straps to anchor them securely in place. Forward of the wheelchair area, two gender-specific toilets, distinctly wider than those on airplanes, faced each other. Then came five rows of two-by-two seats, each plushly upholstered in Beaujolais nouveau–colored velveteen, with ample legroom and "upright" and "recline" buttons; all the seat backs had folding snack tables made of varnished teak, along with black netting kangaroo pouches for books and magazines.

In my present phase of rehabilitation I couldn't tell whether I'd be in the back of the bus with my fellow wheelchair users or if I'd have graduated to a seat of my own. Included in the price of the tour (just under $1,000, as I discovered, after some Googling) were two nights at the Marcus Whitman Hotel and Conference Center in Walla Walla, on which the tour operator must have negotiated a hefty discount for the block booking. Walla Walla, which began life as an incorporated city in the 1860s, was easily the prettiest town in eastern Washington, whose temperate microclimate (eighteen inches of annual rainfall, compared with nine inches or less elsewhere) attracted both winemakers and home-buying retirees, and whose small but well-thought-of private liberal arts college, Whitman, gave the place an important touch of faux-antiquity. Whitman College, founded as a seminary in 1859 before it became a nonsectarian institution in 1882, modeled its campus on those of its older East Coast counterparts, like Amherst (1821) and Williams (1793), which were themselves unabashed copies of much older colleges in Oxford and Cambridge.

Once our air-conditioned, double-glazed, sound-insulated bus would have merged into the eastbound stream of traffic on Interstate 90, our tour lecturer would get up to speak. I pictured him in his early thirties, round-spectacled and dressed in Brooks Brothers casual—plaid flannel shirt, open at the neck, and freshly pressed khakis, with a mini-microphone clipped to a shirt pocket. The small black perforated vents above our heads, which I'd taken to be parts of the AC system, turned out to be loudspeakers.

The Oenophile in his welcoming remarks told us that we were in for a treat, that Washington wines were now challenging not just those of California and Oregon for their excellence, but those of Burgundy and Bordeaux. That was true enough, but the Oenophile's voice wasn't; it over-enunciated every syllable and had the tone of a grown-up addressing an audience in their first or second infancy. What I heard was the struggle between manner and matter, for the stuff the lecturer was trying to communicate was technical to the point of being recondite, but none of the people around me seemed to share my discomfort. Some flourished pens and notepads, and everyone looked engaged and indulgent.

"Terroir," the Oenophile said, then, "Loess."

Loess!

We'd just crossed Lake Washington and were still in Seattle's eastern suburbs, and already I wanted to bail out of this trip, but my stroke-induced infirmities made that impossible. My only other option was to hole up in the hotel with my Kindle and a notebook for company to escape the intolerable condescension of the tour guide's voice, up with which I could not put, to quote Churchill, supposedly.

But Julia could freely nip over Snoqualmie Pass in her mother's old car (now fast becoming her own), inspect her territory on the Columbia Plateau, taking in the look and smell of the massive farms on which the federal government was showering subsidies, and be back in Seattle in time for dinner. How I envied her.

Chapter 38

My FATHER WAS on his way to Palestine. Army censorship forbade him to mention place-names or troop movements in his letters. So he was required to maintain the fiction that he was still up in the mountains of northern Italy, with descriptions of the weather there whenever called for, from January 12, 1945, until March 7, when he was officially allowed to blow the gaff:

> My Very Own Most Beloved Darling,
>   At last I'm allowed to give you my new address, from which you may deduce that we are out of action & just enjoying ourselves for a change. It's been very difficult in my past letters to give an impression of "status quo"—snow & mud & all the rest of it—when in fact the only cloud on the horizon has been the day or so of seasonable rain followed by sunshine & warmth. . . . I'm not allowed to tell you <u>where</u> I am, Darling, but it's a pleasant spot close to the sea, with sand mostly in the right places except when the wind blows too hard! The whole, or most, of the Middle East is interesting & this part just as much as any other.

Peter's letterhead contained three pieces of news: he had moved from the Central Mediterranean Force to the Middle East Force; he had left his temporary position as battery captain of 446 Battery and returned to 265, his original battery and full of old friends; he had also been promoted to major and was now the battery's commanding officer.

Richard Whitfield, in *The Eyes and Ears of the Regiment*, supplies plenty of details about the move from the Apennines to the Middle East from an NCO's point of view. Escaping the Apennines in mid-January was in itself a hazardous operation: the mountain passes were snow- and ice-bound, and the regiment's vehicles—jeeps, trucks, quads, field-gun limbers, and the rest—went slipping and sliding all over the road. Whitfield describes the conditions:

> When we did start visibility was nil—windscreens and goggles were thick with snow and ice, and boy was it cold. The roads were inches thick with ice and every new layer of gravel was covered in and frozen within a few minutes. One jeep driver whose side shields were torn away almost immediately was wearing a leather jerkin over a greatcoat, over his battledress, over two thick sweaters, over a thick woolen vest and shirt and after an hour the snow had penetrated to his undervest.

In at least one instance, a gun was towing its quad backward down the steeply sloping summit of a pass. This was in pitch darkness and in the middle of a blinding blizzard. Presumably for security reasons (not advertising their departure to the Germans), the convoy had set off at eight in the evening on January 12. By noon the next day, writes Whitfield, "all except three of the battery's vehicles had arrived at B Echelon area, near Fiesole where we spent the night in comparative comfort."

Dusk on January 14 found the three batteries assembled at Magione, a small town on the eastern shore of Lake Trasimene, where they billeted themselves on a cement works, a cinema, and an old Crusader castle. My father's battery (he was still captain of 446) drew the short straw and got the unheated, drafty, and intensely cold cement works, where it was determined that Christmas Day would be celebrated on January 19. Peter in his role as quartermaster of supplies had to buy the turkeys, and was given the address of a reputable and fairly priced turkey farm that lay nearly two hours away by road. On the sixteenth, he and a fellow officer, Peter Mennell, set off in a pair of jeeps to find the turkey farm, only to discover that it was the same one where he'd been taken to tea and made friends with the count and his American wife. He and Mennell were lavishly welcomed, made to stay for a "first class lunch," "a quiet afternoon partly spent listening to gramophone music of the semiclassic style," shown the family's olive oil presses, and sent back to Magione with several ten-pound turkeys at two pounds, fifteen shillings apiece.

The postponed Christmas dinner, held in the frigid basement store-room of the cement works, was a success, according to Whitfield, with "plenty of turkey, plenty of pork, plenty of plum pudding, apples, and nuts, but not plenty of beer"—whose loss was made up for by drinking ample "red and white vino" in pint-size beer mugs, which resulted in a lot of bad hangovers on the morning of the twentieth.

After that, the troops hung around in Magione for day after day, waiting for their kit bags to be restored to them from Naples, where they had been sitting since January 1944 and the embarkation for Anzio, and then for the regiment's guns, vehicles, and other matériel to be taken over by the Second Field Regiment in the British Fifth Division, which was replacing the Sixty-Seventh on the Italian front. The arrival of Royal Army Service Corps trucks laden with kit bags occasioned what Whitfield calls the "Magione black market," in which the men sold off unwanted personal possessions to the locals (blankets were a particular prize because they could be converted into overcoats), and some soldiers came away a hundred pounds richer from the impromptu market, "a lot of money in those days."

Finally, the RASC trucked the regiment to the railway station at Castiglion Fiorentino, "to start our journey to Taranto by train":

Accommodation was the usual cattle trucks, lined with straw—30 men per truck and bed was the only place to keep warm. It was a most unpleasant journey. Movement Control supplied occasional meals of stew and tea on a journey taking three days and as far as I remember there was snow all the way down Italy.

"The usual cattle trucks, lined with straw"? Whitfield illustrates this with a photo of troops jumping from what are clearly cattle trucks, with no carriages for passengers in sight. My father says nothing of this in his 1995 notes, but talks of a pleasant if overlong journey in a first-class sleeper with a dining car attached. It is extraordinary how the British class system became grotesquely exaggerated in the army's treatment of its officers and men. Many democratically minded Americans were morally offended by this, as they were by the batman system of assigning a personal servant to every officer (a practice phased out after the end of the war), although it has to be said that many English men and women were equally shocked by the attempts of American staff officers to impose racial segregation on English pubs and hotels. Some of these attempts were successful, others honorably rebuffed by pub landlords and hoteliers.

Arrived at a transit camp in Taranto, troops changed their Italian lire into pounds sterling, then embarked on a French ship named the *M. V. Erida,* once a luxury "motorship" (at its launch in 1928, steam was giving way to diesel) that ran between Dunkirk and Australia via the Suez Canal. In 1942, the *Erida* was captured by the Americans from the Vichy French and sent to England for conversion into a troopship. Its captain, crew, and onboard staff remained French for the duration of the war.

Again, Whitfield's experience was very different from my father's. Whitfield writes of the ship being "grossly overcrowded and unbearably hot. . . . Food, what there was of it, was pretty horrible." My father notes that he shared a comfortable cabin with one other officer, and that the French meals in the officers' dining room were "very pleasant." Both men agree that the sea was smooth and the sun shone from a cloudless sky all the way. The *Erida* briefly dropped anchor off Alexandria so that one man who was seriously ill could be taken ashore to a hospital; next day the ship docked at Haifa, Palestine.

Why Palestine? Whitfield believed the regiment was sent there for rest, recuperation, exercises, courses, and to be restored to full strength with replacements for troops that had gone missing, or been killed or injured between Rome and the Gothic Line, and he expected to be back in Italy soon. My father feared that Burma might be the next destination. In the meantime, there was policing to be done in the British mandate of Palestine, where tension between Jews and Palestinian Arabs was growing by the day. At best, soldiers don't make good policemen, and it's hard to see how a regiment of Royal Artillery gunners, fresh from real warfare, could play a useful role as peacemakers in this increasingly troubled and anarchic patch of ground.

Just three months earlier, in November 1944, two hit men from the Jewish terrorist group the Stern Gang had shot to death Lord Moyne, the resident minister of state in Cairo. Moyne was an Anglo-Irish heir to the great Guinness fortune, Winston Churchill's close friend and political ally, and by no means an anti-Semite. For Churchill, a self-proclaimed Zionist,* Lord Moyne's assassination was a tragic outrage. On November 17, he addressed the House of Commons:

> I have now to make a short statement about Palestine. On Thursday last, my right honourable friend the foreign secretary gave the House a full report of the assassination of Lord Moyne. This shameful crime has shocked the world. It has affected none more strongly than those, like myself, who, in the past, have been consistent friends of the Jews and constant architects of their future. If our dreams for Zionism are to end in the smoke of assassins' pistols and our labours for its future to produce only a new set of gangsters worthy of Nazi Germany, many like myself will have to reconsider the position we have maintained so consistently and so long in the past.

At least partly as a result of Churchill's personal involvement in the case, the two assassins were hanged together on March 23, 1945.

My father claims to be grandly impartial on the Jewish/Arab question when he offers my mother his first impressions of Palestine, which include two ready-made stereotypes of the money-grubbing Jew and the thievish Arab, and decides evenhandedly that there is nothing much to choose between them. The mountains hereabouts, he writes,

> are very craggy with boulder outcrops & a barren look about them. The plains, at this time of year, are carpeted in green corn, & wildflowers when the soil is too thin or sandy for

---

* Churchill was among the first to recognize the monstrous enormity of the death camps. In a letter to Anthony Eden, the foreign secretary, dated July 11, 1944, Churchill wrote: "There is no doubt that this is probably the greatest and most horrible crime ever committed in the whole history of the world." Eden was unmoved. His private secretary noted in his diary that "AE loves Arabs and hates Jews."

anything else. The staple population is Arabic & primitive
to an extent except that a very posh saloon car will flash past
one on the main roads full of burnoosed Wogs. The Jews
congregate into colonies & build for themselves such towns
as Tel Aviv, Haifa & the new Jerusalem which are nothing
better than tawdry imitations of Brighton—the shops all at
"Cut down prices" & a general air of cheap lavishness in large
lettering & gilt to cover very poor and cheap materials. There's
nothing more permanent about them than the permanency
of "quick easy money." Once in a Jew's shop, you have to be
rude to the point of bluntness in refusing to consider to buy
anything, tell the proprietor that his wares are junk & cheap
& bloody expensive at that & just walk out! The Arabs are
rogues—but smiling ones—& cause just as much trouble as our
"International Friends" in that theft is their hobby & livelihood,
so I really have no ready answer or partiality for either side in
the Palestine problem! I'm told there are some very nice Jews,
and wogs too, but it all depends on one's own preference, &
mine is for neither.

More than a month later, on April 22, he describes how he and
George Blyth visited a city (unnamed but obviously Jerusalem), where
he was bowled over by what he saw in the souks—not just by the
intricate craftsmanship of the commodities for sale by the Arabs, but
by the demeanor of the Arabs themselves.

I got there more of an atmosphere of the Orient than I've had
before out here—the Arabs were somehow more Arabic, clean
looking & finely cut faces, upstanding, & after a false start
when George guided me in the completely wrong direction,
we eventually found the old shopping streets—the "Souks" to
which we'd been recommended to go, one shop in particular,
for brocades—which we found and marveled at—brocades
that are classical in their design and workmanship & world-
famous—the shop that supplies London's more famous shops,
that supplies royalty & so forth, & the prices are almost in
proportion though, in relation to the quality and rarity, are not

anymore than is to be expected. We spent well over an hour in there looking at all they had to offer & were very sorely tempted.

After tea at "the ubiquitous & invariably drab officers' club," the pair headed out again in search of the silversmiths' and goldsmiths' quarter, where they spent another hour or two

chatting with the various Arabs who spoke English & were most insistent on showing us their wares and how they made them. Can you imagine the Birmingham market hall choc a bloc with desks & small glass counters with narrow paths between . . . behind the counters a man sitting waiting for customers & one or two others sitting at a bench making another brooch, bangle or whatnot . . . fezzes, European, Arabic & a mixture of clothes and colours . . . small boys bringing even smaller cups of coffee, thick and sweet, to you . . . black-veiled women, & your hand permanently on your pocket where the cash is to get early warning of a pickpocket!? For £5 I got you a bracelet, flapjack & small brooch all done in fine silver filigree work . . . which is very "dainty" & consequently almost too pretty-pretty by itself, but should look quite well against one of your black frocks or evening dresses . . . & I'm still debating brocades, Darling.

If this highly enjoyable shopping trip helped convert my father to the Arab cause in Palestine, his anti-Semitism, in all its ugliness and banality, only became more entrenched. Jews, he remarked, were like "bloodsucking lice on the backs of swallows."

After the German surrender, boats carrying immigrant Jews, many of them survivors of the death camps, unloaded their human cargoes at every Palestinian port on the Mediterranean, vastly exceeding the meager monthly quotas imposed by the British mandate. Temporary camps were built to accommodate the overflow, with the stipulation that no barbed wire should be used in their building, for obvious reasons. Meanwhile the competing Jewish terrorist organizations like Irgun, Haganah, and the Stern Gang designated the British occupying forces as their chief enemy, a colonialist power in illegal possession of the land sanctioned by holy scripture as the ancient home of the Jews. With this justification the terrorists killed British troops and sabotaged their chains of supply and communication, especially the railways, as well as carrying out punitive raids on Arab villages, meant to encourage their inhabitants to flee eastward.

On November 1, 1945, my father wrote:

After hearing the news tonight, I'll have to send you a telegram tomorrow, Dearest, even though I'm afraid when you first see it you will think it bears good news: I <u>do</u> wish, above most other things at the moment, that the papers & reports & comments given would retain some sense of proportion, & realisation of what effects those reports will have at home. How nice they must think it to be for you to hear that [an unidentified] major was wounded north of Jerusalem . . . blast them. I suppose they were correct in saying that it was a night of terrorist activities—but why give it an air of headline news & give the bloody Jews just the advertisement they want.

. . . I shall never meet a Jew again, if I think he appreciates the English language, without letting him hear the usual epithet that throws doubt on the legality of his birth—they are bastards in every sense of the word, & there's not one of them any less guilty than any other—English, American, European or Palestinian—they're Jews. Gentlemen of the Black Markets, the Ghettos & Chicago gangsters . . . Swine. A little deportation instead of immigration wouldn't be a bad idea—on the basis of a 1000 for every murder, & 500 for every other casualty, Arab or British, that they have caused. It's too early yet to know what the outcome is of last night's episodes: but they can't keep that pace up . . . they had the advantage of the initiative & took the first steps against no opposition. It will be different in future . . . & it may only have been a demonstration. But I'd like to know just how Congressman Cellar [Emanuel "Manny" Celler], in Washington, was able to state in a speech yesterday that today was the Jewish D-Day in Palestine. Did you know you'd got an Anti-Semitic husband, Darling?!

In her reply to this letter my mother rose, rather timidly, to the defense of Jews:

> I agree, more or less, with all you feel about the Jews, my Sweetheart, all except wholesale condemnation of 'em as a race, I'd never agree with that—nor do you really, do you, my Sweetheart—or do you?

Because this exchange took place months after the liberation of Belsen, Auschwitz, and the other death camps, it perhaps needs to be said that the great majority of contemporary newsreels and reports failed to mention that the people killed were primarily Jews, and only a handful of reporters (Richard Dimbleby of the BBC is one example) dared to say that what they had witnessed was a genocide on a mass industrial scale. It took years for the dreadful truth of the Holocaust to become generally accepted public knowledge.

Winston Churchill lamented that the British Army was predominantly pro-Arab* and anti-Jewish in its views, but since the Jewish militias were waging an asymmetric war against the British occupiers, to whom the Arabs were appealing for their protection, it seems naive of Churchill to have affected surprise at these prejudices. More ruthless and far better organized than their Arab counterparts, the most militant groups of the Jewish fighters (which included many survivors of the German camps) cast British troops as their chief enemy, and the troops responded by falling back on their default position of routine English anti-Semitism.

No one stated this more clearly than Hugh Dalton, the Eton-and-Cambridge-educated chancellor of the exchequer in Clement Attlee's Labour government, in August 1947. Urging on the prime minister the importance of Britain relinquishing its Palestine mandate at the earliest possible opportunity, Dalton wrote:

> The present state of affairs is not only costly to us in manpower and money, but is, as you and I agree, of no real value from the

---

* British Arabism had a long history that culminated in figures like C. M. Doughty (*Travels in Arabia Deserta*, 1888) and T. E. Lawrence (*Seven Pillars of Wisdom*, 1926). Edward Said's book *Orientalism* (1978) is a deeply skeptical critique of Western Arabism.

strategic point of view—you cannot in any case have a secure base on top of a wasps' nest—and it is exposing our young men, for no good purpose, to abominable experiences and is breeding anti-Semites at a most shocking speed.[*]

True as this almost certainly was, I don't think that being stationed in Palestine was the root cause of my father's anti-Semitism. That lay in our surname, Raban. In September 1953 when I was eleven, in my first week at the boarding school that my father had attended twenty years before, an older boy stopped me in a flagstoned corridor of School House (same house as my father, where I found his name neatly chiseled into a stone window frame in the junior common room). The boy asked me, in a voice of deceptively disinterested curiosity, "Ray-Ban's a funny name; are you a Yid, Ray-Ban?" I can't believe that my father wasn't taunted with the question in the 1930s.

The association persisted: seven years later, when I was a freshman sorting through my first tranche of university mail in my new pigeon-hole, the only interesting-looking item, addressed to me in pen and ink and not in typescript, was a welcoming invitation to join the Jewish Society. By that time, I had grown used to and entirely tolerant of this assumption. After King's School, I went to two state grammar schools, where I had been nicknamed Oscar, for Oscar Rabin, the Jewish leader of a dance band that was omnipresent on the BBC Light Programme. (Recently I've learned that William, one of my three brothers, was given the same name by a tutor at St. Martin's College of Art in London, though the Oscar Rabin he was called after was a very different kettle of fish from mine: a Jewish Russian dissident and expressionist painter who became an exile in Paris in the 1970s.)

My father was a stickler for the "correct" pronunciation of this "uncommon patronymic" (as Evelyn Waugh terms it in his autobiography, *A Little Learning;* his mother was a Raban and a somewhat

---

* Quoted in Tom Segev, *One Palestine, Complete: Jews and Arabs under the British Mandate* (2000). Hugh Dalton, yet another son of the cloth (his father was chaplain to Queen Victoria, canon at Windsor, and tutor to the future George V), was one of a substantial clutch of patrician Englishmen in Attlee's cabinet. He also earned a mention in Anthony Julius's *Trials of the Diaspora: A History of Anti-Semitism in England* (2010), for describing Harold Laski, professor of political science at the London School of Economics and an influential Labour Party intellectual, as "an undersized Semite."

distant cousin of ours). Peter insisted on abolishing the second vowel altogether and sounding the name as Rab'n, stressing the first syllable (Ray) and swallowing the second, in a vain attempt to eliminate any Jewishness with which it might be associated.

He became an obsessive genealogist, and not for the usual reason of tracing a rapidly diminishing trickle of blood that might connect one to nobility or celebrity, but to justify his assertion that "we come from yeoman stock—good yeoman stock." In other words, that we were not Jews. Half my childhood summers were spent in rural churchyards, where we had to scrape the moss off tombstones to read the names of long-dead ancestors, or sitting with my father in the dusty basements of county record offices, transcribing the births, marriages, and deaths of ancient Rabans and their multitude of relations who went under different names.

I remember Peter's rage one afternoon in the 1950s, when Cousin Barbara came to lunch at the parsonage in order to pick my father's brains on the subject of Palestine and the Holy Land, for which she had booked herself on a package tour. The tour company had sent her a questionnaire, and she disclosed that she had answered "Don't know" to the question, "Are you Jewish or of Jewish descent?" My father's fury was unconstrained, and Barbara left the house very shortly afterward, leaving him to mutter, "Stupid woman! Stupid woman!" in her wake. Barbara's recently deceased father had been the Reverend Cyril Raban, vicar of Crawley, so she was hardly unschooled in the distinctions between Jews and Anglicans, and her "Don't know" must've been the product of honest thinking, not indifference to the question.

As for the gentile yeomen, my father found them in the village of Penn, Staffordshire, where they flourished, by 1569 at least, when surviving parish records began. A Walter Raban is listed as one of the two churchwardens of St. Bartholomew's Church, and numerous Rabans, variously spelled Rabon, Rabone, Rayban, crop up in these pages, which come to an end in 1754. (The Staffordshire Parish Registers Society published a transcription of the Penn register in 1921; I snaffled my father's copy on the day of his funeral in June 1996.) In the appended list of vicars of the parish, John Rabon appears as the incumbent from 1674 to 1709, and is credited with having an MA degree from Magdalene College, Cambridge—a sign, I'd guess, of how the family was making its way into the professional middle class, where they regularized the spelling of their name as Raban in the mid-eighteenth century. If, as Alexander Waugh claims in his *Fathers and Sons,* the family was "anciently Jewish," it must have been an awfully long time ago. My father's "yeoman stock" seems a more likely bet, but who knows?

Peter's prejudices on matters of race and class ran deep, but when he vented them to my mother in letters, he consistently acknowledged that they violated social taboos ("I'm an awful snob"; "Did you know you'd got an Anti-Semitic husband, Darling?!"), and I can find no sign that he ever translated them into action, except in his craze for genealogy. On Jews, for instance, he mentions how boring his desk work is by telling how a Jewish refugee and a photographer by trade was found inside the camp by an NCO, touting for business among the gunners by offering cheap portraits for them to send home. When the man was brought before him, Peter told him that he should have entered by the front door and asked permission first instead of trying to sneak in around the back, then wrote a permit for him to continue his work, having satisfied himself that the photographer was not a spy.

On his professed loathing of the feckless working class, it has to be said that Peter showed nothing but loyal affection, and admiration, for his two successive batmen, Tench and Ransome, the first of whom was deemed by the regiment too old for service overseas, and the second stayed with him, apparently happily, through North Africa, Italy, and Palestine. And then there is the case of Gunner Strachan of 446 Battery, who became a joint project of both Peter and Monica that lasted long after Peter became commanding officer of 265 Battery.

Gunner (actually a driver) Strachan's story was and is a common enough one in every foreign war. In January 1943, two weeks before the regiment embarked for Algiers, Strachan married his girlfriend, who lived with her parents at Hempton, Norfolk, just a few doors away from the White House. The newlyweds wrote steadily to each other through 1943 and 1944—when, in September, she went silent on him. By late in November the gunner was frantic, and approached my father, hoping to be granted compassionate home leave. No leave was granted; my father said that army regulations expressly forbade it in Strachan's circumstances (the British Armed Forces would fall to bits if such leave were given on the grounds of wives, fiancées, and girlfriends failing to answer letters). But Peter did enlist my mother's help, asking her to write to Strachan's mother-in-law, Mrs. Wright, and tactfully suggest a meeting.

Monica immediately recognized the name, and the girl in question, whom she had interviewed for the job of housemaid when we moved to Hempton—"a bit dirty, but nice," as she described her. My mother wrote to Mrs. Wright and heard back from her by return of post, saying that her daughter was currently living with a friend in the nearby village of Little Snoring. A day later Monica and Mrs. Wright walked together from Hempton into town, taking the longer "back way" from the ruins of Goggs' Mill along the footpath that ran beside the left bank of the Wensum, where the river ran fast and shallow, clear as gin, over long tresses of weed in wavering motion, with here and there the silvery-gold flash of a fish diving for cover beneath the greenery. Mrs. Wright ("a very good sort") broke down into tears several times in the walk, and it seems that Monica was the first person to whom she'd told what she knew of her daughter's story. She couldn't tell her husband, she said, because he was recovering from an illness, and the shameful news might finish him off. Mrs. Strachan (and my mother never gives her a first name) was pregnant, her due date was in May, and Mrs. W. didn't know who the father was. She said of Vic (Gunner Strachan) that "she thinks the world of him," and the tears she shed seemed to be as much for him as for her daughter, my mother wrote.

Mrs. Strachan's baby brings home the wagging tongues and unavoidable public scandal that attached themselves to "illegitimate" children in village communities as small as Hempton, as it does the ubiquitous collection boxes for charities like the Salvation Army and the Dr. Barnardo's national network of orphanages, all those conscience-salving loose pennies and threepenny bits with here and there a silver sixpence. For my parents the whole affair succeeded in drawing Palestine a little closer to Fakenham as they colluded together on the fate of the unfortunate baby.

Monica had begun by delivering the news she had gleaned on her riverside walk with Mrs. W., saying, "It is most rotten and tragic as far as I can see it," but five weeks later she was writing in elation:

Mrs. Strachan has just gone, at ten to ten & she came at five! We've talked quite a lot in that time. She was looking very well, very happy & very pretty and told me as soon as I opened the subject—I let the conversation ripen for an hour or so before I did—that he [Strachan] was going to take her back, that she had been a silly little fool & that she had written several times to tell him so and how much she wanted to go back to him. And she looked in love, she looked so happy and proud that he should still want her—Oh Darling I _am_ glad! I told her so too, I felt most moved.

We discussed even the baby, interspersed with less intimate topics—in fact we discussed the baby quite thoroughly—it's coming in May and she is going to try to get it adopted.

I think that her sacrifice, which she firmly intends to carry out because it wouldn't be fair to him, shows there is good stuff in her too & certainly an all out effort to atone—of course in her heart she wants to keep it, it's not <u>natural</u> for any mother to go through childbirth and then have to part with the baby, and she obviously adores children.

She is quite right too, it wouldn't be possible for her to ask her husband any more—I kind of wish he would, though, be so super Christian & forgiving as to offer to keep the child too.

A month later, the grandparents, Mr. and Mrs. Wright, volunteered to adopt the baby when it came, and keep it within the family—a move that my mother warmly endorsed, but my father did not, on the grounds that the Wrights would thereby appear to condone their daughter's adultery. Such austere moral logic, with its stern indifference to the child's well-being, was deep-rooted in my father's character, as it was in the church in which he had grown up, not to mention that in rural Norfolk, in the fifth decade of the twentieth century, the scarlet _A_ was still in vogue as a powerful symbol of public dishonor and disgrace.

The Strachan affair was discussed in more of my parents' letters than I can count. My father dealt with the Welfare Office in Jerusalem, my mother with its counterpart in Cromer, Norfolk, and eventually, in July, the War Office in London rubber-stamped my father's application on Strachan's behalf for one month's home leave, with due acknowledgment of my mother's assistance in the situation. For both Peter and Monica, Strachan's misfortune was a godsend, and their enthusiastic collaboration over his welfare only helped strengthen the ties of their own rock-solid marriage. Vic Strachan himself can have had little or no idea of the enormous quantity of ink being expended in England and the Middle East on the subject of him and his wandering bride.

As it turned out, Mrs. Strachan showed more independence of spirit (or, perhaps, plain foolishness) than was generally considered seemly in a "fallen" woman. From the outset she said that she wanted to have the baby at home in her parents' house, and brave the village gossip, rather than be banished to a two-month exile in a Salvation Army home for unmarried mothers-to-be, located in some distant county where the baby's birth could be kept more or less secret. On the matter of adoption, she played her hand close to her chest by pretending to agree with whatever advice was being offered to her, pro and con.

Late in August, when the baby, a girl, was three months old, Gunner Strachan came home from Palestine. My mother spotted him in the garden of the Wrights' house, where she was going to pick up an empty basket that she had lent to Mrs. Strachan a few days before, full of apples from our overproductive trees. Strachan himself was shoeless and wearing his khaki shirt outside his trousers (which my mother thought "rather an innovation"). "I thought he looked very happy & beautifully, glamorously brown—are you that lovely, apricot tan, my Darling?"

> I hope against hope still that he will father the baby—it's such a pretty little thing, and a girl & good too! It would be such a fine thing to do—and they say, and I think it's true, that the people you make benefit are the people you love, rather than the other way about.
>
> But I expect he'll make sure she has another and this time his, pretty quickly. I didn't see Mrs. Strachan but <u>oh</u> she must be happy to have him home!

When Strachan (this time with his shirttails tucked inside his pants) paid an evening visit to the White House, he cut a woebegone figure:

> Mr. Strachan came tonight & stayed about an hour and we talked. . . . I liked him so much, my Darling, and I'm awfully afraid that in spite of the impression of happiness I had when I

first saw him for a brief exchange of words across the Wrights'
back yard, things aren't going too well. He is very hurt by a
lack of warmth & right feeling in his wife. She doesn't act as
though she owed him anything at all & is completely tied &
wrapped up by the baby which she is continually nursing—
and they have nowhere to sit but in the midst of the family in
that beastly squalid little house. He has no way of getting "at"
her & piercing through her complete absorption in herself &
the child. And a fortnight of his leave has gone—Darling it's
terrible!

 . . . We talked a lot even apart from Mrs. S & the baby, and
Dearest he had a lot to tell me. . . . He talked to me about
Anzio too, my Darling . . . of men going off their heads with
the shelling, and about the infantry. . . . About the letters
from home that hurt with their complacency & utter lack of
imagination as to what it felt like to expect death all the time—
letters that didn't even try, little selfish letters—My Darling I
don't think any of us who haven't lived in the midst of death
& in hourly expectation of death, can realise what you went
through—I don't think I ever realised or ever shall—what you
suffered. I imagined. . . . I was desperately afraid—sick with
fear for you, sometimes, but I shan't ever know <u>quite</u> what
hell it was. . . . He told me he'd never known another officer
quite as cool as you, my Cherished Love, except when you lost
your temper when the trucks weren't bringing up "ammo" fast
enough!

To my mother's first, optimistic letter about Strachan, Peter replied:

I thought you'd like him. He is a very nice chap indeed—very
straight, & cheerful too until he first got news of the trouble.
I expect that there's a very good chance now that they will
keep the child—they'd only really had 2 weeks of married life
together & life will seem quite different now with this break. I
hope for your sake, Darling—& I expect he will—that he talks
about the Regiment a little. . . . Just life in general, he wouldn't
have much to say about me unless he tries to be too polite
because I always was a bit of an enigma in 446 . . . he was one

of the handful of men there whom I got to know well, as we lived in the same conditions & in the same spot.

And, responding to Monica's report of Strachan's visit to the White House:

I must say, Darling, that I smiled to myself when I read what Strachan had to say about being "cool in action"! He's never seen me in action, in a slit trench, wishing it was 3 times as deep—he has seen me lolloping up roads to the gun position, & generally trying to urge ammunition up quicker, hence the loss of temper occasionally.

He is a nice lad, & I'm very sorry that things aren't going as well as they appeared to be—very sorry indeed. I only hope he does manage to get compassionate leave—he must go & get Mrs. Barclay (is it?) to recommend that he should be granted an extension—get her to write a very strong letter to the AG 4 A. at the War Office, claiming undue hardship & the necessity of an extension to achieve the aim of the leave, quoting you, the wife of one of his officers, as having been in close touch with the whole case & knowing the full circumstances. Perhaps she's done it already. They must get away & leave the baby with her sister—I sense that Mrs. W is the centre of all the difficulties, thoughtlessly, & immorally, championing her daughter's cause & encouraging her. The girl is fundamentally all right, so far as I can make out, but her parents aren't—they're a bad lot with insufficient intelligence to see beyond their own smug selves.

The common humanity in both these letters belies Peter's innate class snobbery, and points toward his eventual career as a clergyman in the Church of England—a career he resisted until it was almost too late. But his summary judgment of the Wrights, made at a great distance, foretells the habitual class condescension of so many pastors in action, like actual shepherds chivvying flocks of actual sheep via intermediaries of actual dogs.

As the Strachan correspondence illustrates, the war was rapidly turning into the postwar well in advance of the official celebrations of V-E and V-J Days (May 8 and August 14, 1945), both of which turned out to be anticlimactic events for Peter and Monica. In the late evening of May 8, Monica took her bicycle to inspect the bonfires on Hempton Green and in Fakenham, and kept her nightly ten o'clock "tryst" with Peter:

> I leant on my bicycle a way off & kept our tryst, but instead of comfort in your nearness, I felt a wave of pain so keen, Darling, that it took my breath, because we couldn't be seeing this together. Oh my Own, my Darling, pain and love indescribable—perhaps that too at that moment we were sharing? as we share at other times the communion of our thoughts, I expect we were, since at that time of all times we are as one, in all we feel and think.
>
> I went too & watched for five or ten minutes in the market square in Fakenham—weird war dances between servicemen & civilians, lit spasmodically by brilliant ground flares that made the shadows of the long snake of dancers leap grotesquely like the shadows of a race of giants, nearly as tall as the house fronts on which they played.

I too saw the Hempton fires, long past my seven-thirty bedtime, standing at the bedroom window in my pajamas, and deeply resenting my exclusion from the festivities, confined to the house with only Vicki (an airman's wife temporarily billeted with us) and Lucy the dog for company. I didn't like Vicki, suspecting her of witchcraft and worse, and longing to be one of the village boys, wicked imps racing around the green, setting fire to the dry gorse with flaming torches.

My father was in Damascus for V-J Day and, preoccupied with the humid heat of the Syrian summer and foraging for dressmaking materials in the souk, wrote: "Very sticky indeed, in that VJ Day hasn't very much meaning at all, as compared with the tricks of this climate," which is well said; we all know how the contingencies of our personal here-and-now have the capacity to obliterate the importance of great international events.

The big shift in tone of my parents' letters to and from the Middle East in 1945 is their concentration on the immediate future, both the future of the nation in Churchill's snap election in July, and my father's future in civilian life, beginning with the overwhelming question of

when he'd be coming home. In the letters, Palestine—and Syria—
become increasingly represented by inter-battery and inter-regimental
cricket and football matches, by the welfare of the troops, as my father
wrote on average three applications a week for compassionate home
leave for individual gunners, and by the days "wasted" in preparations
for ceremonial visits to the camps by First Division military bigwigs—
colonels, brigadiers, and the occasional major general. In the inter-
stices between such duties, Peter became a conventional tourist in the
Holy Land, floating like a porpoise in the blood-temperature Dead
Sea, photographing the excavated ruins of Jericho, making the obligatory trip to Bethlehem (a predictable disappointment), and shopping,
shopping, shopping. As long as I knew him, my father was a man who
did his best to avoid all shops except tobacconists' and those that sold
secondhand books; his appetite for Arab souks and the materials for
women's clothes in the last year of the war apparently satiated him for
the rest of his term on earth.

Chapter 39

I'd BEEN IN rehab for nearly a month now when I had a breakfast-time phone call from my friend Mike Wollaston, asking me if I'd yet begun suffering from cabin fever. I told him that my case of the disease was so far gone as to make me wonder if it might be terminal. He suggested that we meet for dinner the next evening at a restaurant and bar on the Ship Canal, close to both my house—which I'd bought from him in 1991—and his new digs at the marina. Date made, I suggested to Kelli a change to our usual curriculum, proposing that we concentrate on getting in and out of cars, using the life-size mock-up car in the gym.

Julia would pick me up from the hospital and join us for dinner. She came to my room at six, having parked her car on the circular drive at the hospital entrance. As we prepared to leave, a physical therapist materialized out of nowhere and insisted on escorting me off the hospital premises, saying that was a rule that had to be obeyed. So, under his critical eye, I made the transfer from wheelchair to car—a matter of reaching for the overhead strap above the passenger seat, standing upright, swinging around through ninety degrees, then projecting my ass backward before lowering myself into a sitting position and hoisting both legs inside the car. My five-stage maneuver was poor but adequate. Julia folded the wheelchair, stowed it along with the four-point cane in the trunk, and we were off, with the hospital diminishing in size in the mirror.

I felt inside the breast pocket of my jacket, unworn since the day of my stroke, and my fingers found the cigar that I'd been smoking on our drive to the hospital in Edmonds. For the last four weeks 1 had been getting by with Nicorette patches on my left shoulder blade that had taken care of most of my nicotine pangs. But now I wanted to smoke as a formal symbol of my temporary release from the hospital.

"You don't mind, do you?"

"No, just open your window a crack, can you?"

So I sat, smoking pleasurably, gazing out the window at the city streets, their hard edges blunted by the heat haze, and at the people, themselves on temporary release from their office blocks, going about their private business. As we turned and ran alongside the west bank of Lake Union, I watched the sailboats, most lallygagging about with limp sails on the glassy surface of the lake, and, here and there, a single boat that had found a riffle of wind, raised, as if by magic, from thermal imbalances in the warming/cooling architecture of the city and its traffic. I had sailed on Lake Union long enough to know how to seek out these urban zephyrs and was at least sometimes lucky, but, looking at myself now, I doubted if there'd be much sailing in my future.

Julia parked her car temporarily in front of the restaurant, Ponti Seafood Grill, so named because it was tucked beside the blue-and-orange-painted Fremont drawbridge over the Ship Canal. She retrieved the wheelchair from the trunk, unfolded it, and positioned it by the car's passenger door. Getting out of the car safely was a good deal trickier for me than getting into it: I had to lower the window to get a handhold on the sill, stand upright on the road, face the wheelchair, swivel 180 degrees, then deposit myself on the seat, while Julia held the car door steady and readied herself to grab me if I started to fall. The simplest movement becomes a hazardous adventure when you're crippled, and I was relieved to see that the restaurant worker whose job was to park customers' cars was absent from his post that evening so didn't witness the heavy weather I was making of the car-to-wheelchair transfer.

Waiting for Julia to park the car in the lot, I sat and watched the traffic on the canal and listened to the horn signals from the bridge, which was unusually busy because this was a Friday evening; with only thirty feet of clearance over the water, Fremont was the lowest of all the lifting bridges on the canal, and every tall-masted sailboat in Seattle appeared to be headed westward for the Ballard Locks and the freedom of Puget Sound. The bridgemaster was pleasing nobody: frustrated motorists in long backups blew their feeble horns at him, and equally frustrated yachtsmen jostled in the scrum of boats waiting on the Lake Union side for the bridge to lift. The bridgemaster, sternly impartial, went on with his job. For the idle spectator, a hot July Friday evening at Fremont Bridge always lays on a mildly misanthropic entertainment, with a repeat performance a mile or so later at the Ballard Locks.

Ponti had opened in 1990, the same year that I moved from London to Seattle and was living in a rental house two short blocks from the restaurant, up the steep slope of Queen Anne Hill. As soon as Ponti opened its doors for the first time, I became a regular there for lunch, for dinner, for drinks at the convivial bar, where a wood fire blazed from late autumn to early spring, and the restaurant became my favorite place to meet journalists and others whom I was a little leery of inviting home. There was a private dining room at the back which I never saw, but some of Seattle's mega-rich, like Jeff Bezos and Paul Allen, regularly used it for business discussions. (Ponti closed in 2016, and reopened as an Elks lodge.)

Julia rejoined me and we entered the restaurant; I insisted on wheeling myself inside, which slowed our progress but, I hoped, asserted my autonomy. Mike was already seated and had brought along Mark, the Irish carpenter who lived in the ground-floor apartment at Mike's moorings. A bottle of local, Columbia Valley chardonnay was already open on the table. Richard, the owner-manager, was making his usual rounds of familiar customers at the restaurant, and we had barely said our hellos before he reached our table.

I'd always had mixed feelings about Richard, who in the past had addressed me with a combination of condescension and flattery (not an unusual trait for a restaurateur, but Richard did it in spades or spadefuls). He was also afflicted by some kind of allergic eczema or psoriasis that on some days so reddened his face that it looked as if he was suffering from the Great Plague ("ring a ring of roses, a pocket full of posies, atishoo, atishoo, we all fall down"), but on that evening, at least, he was plague-free.

He stood behind me, leaning slightly forward, and I realized that he must be gripping the handles of my wheelchair. Someone, Mike or Mark or possibly I, dropped the word "stroke" into the conversation, and I felt rather than saw that the word registered with Richard as a synonym for "brain damage," for his tone changed, and he began quizzing me not only as a half-wit but as a deaf half-wit, asking me in a foghorn voice questions in words of one syllable. Reluctantly I submitted to this treatment, hoping that the sooner it was done with, the nearer we'd come to our escape from Richard's attentions.

"Well, good luck!" he shouted at me. "I'd never have noticed if you hadn't told me."

I was watching the dining room windows, where masts were passing; the sill of each window lay at table-level, and viewing them from across the room, one could only guess at the hull and superstructure of any of the boats, let alone the canal water on which they were afloat. A sturdy old wooden mast, freshly varnished, went by, followed, a few seconds later, by its matching, much slimmer and shorter companion, a mizzenmast. The pair put me in mind of a Thames barge, blown far off course and many thousands of miles distant from its natural habitat.

So, at the table, we talked of the fabulous voyage of such a barge across the Atlantic to the West Indies, through the Panama Canal, and up the west coast of the Americas to Seattle. Mike's various accomplishments included a master mariner's ticket, and he had firsthand knowledge of all these tricky waters. Our fanciful craft wholly improbably survived, with pleasant stops at the Azores, the Bahamas, Havana, and beyond; we came nearest to disaster when crossing the Gulf Stream in a severe gale with the wind against the current. The entire fantasy was my attempt to escape from the nondescript gray horizon seen through my rehab ward window and gingerly set foot in a wider world.

I felt like a temporarily released jailbird. Never have oysters on the half shell and grilled halibut tasted better, or the long, slow-gathering evening light fading to darkness looked so piquant, as they did that evening. But when we were at last leaving the table, noticing that Julia's glass of chardonnay remained untouched, and that my own was barely half-empty and hadn't been topped up since the meal began, I marveled at my own extreme sobriety. This onset of unintentional temperance put me in mind of *My Year Off* by Robert McCrum, in which he noted how his own consumption of alcohol had fallen after his stroke—an unexpected health benefit of catastrophic hemiplegia. A dozen years later, I'm still drinking only a fraction of what I used to consume before the stroke intervened.

Chapter 40

Back in England, on May 18, just ten days after V-E Day, Clement Attlee, the leader of the Labour Party and Churchill's deputy prime minister in the wartime coalition government, telephoned Churchill from Blackpool, where the Labour Party was holding its annual conference, to say that the coalition must end immediately, even though the war against Japan still continued. On May 23, Churchill visited King George VI at Buckingham Palace twice on the same day, the first time to offer his resignation as prime minister, the second to accept the royal invitation to form a new government, consisting only of Conservatives, that would be known as "the caretaker government," and would hold office only from May 23 until July 5, when a general election would be held.

Clement Attlee seemed an unlikely person to be Churchill's nemesis. When the Labour Party elected him as leader in 1935, Hugh Dalton noted in his diary, with a sardonic nod to the prophet Isaiah, "And a little mouse shall lead them." Attlee's clerkly mustache and homely manner belied his keen political intelligence and his ability to say very little but do very much. Despite his record as Churchill's loyal deputy, presiding over the war cabinet in Churchill's frequent long absences abroad, his name was barely known in the country at large. Churchill's own verdict on Attlee was "a modest man, who has much to be modest about."

Churchill believed that his own popularity as the hero who had just won the European war would be sufficient to lead the Conservative Party to victory in the election. In May 1945 his approval rating stood

at 83 percent, and had never fallen below 78 percent in the previous
five years. Had Britain been a republic and had Churchill been running for president, he could hardly have lost, but he was dragging the
enormous, negative weight of the Conservative Party behind him. In
April the Conservatives had lost the Chelmsford, Essex, by-election
to an upstart party of the libertarian left called Common Wealth, the
Tory share of the vote dropping from 70 percent in the last general
election (held in 1935) to just 42 percent in 1945. Even more omi-
nously, an opinion poll conducted across the country in February had
shown the Conservatives lagging 18 percentage points behind Labour.

On June 4, Churchill delivered an election address to the nation on
BBC radio; a speech that he insisted would be regarded in future years
as one of his best. The bit that everyone remembers is this:

> No Socialist government conducting the entire life and indus-
> try of the country could afford to allow free, sharp, or violently
> worded expressions of public discontent. They would have to
> fall back on some form of Gestapo, no doubt very humanely
> directed in the first instance. And this would nip opinion in the
> bud; it would stop criticism as it reared its head, and it would
> gather all the power to the supreme party and the party leaders,
> rising like stately pinnacles above their vast bureaucracies of civil
> servants, no longer servants and no longer civil.

It was very warmly received by at least one member of the officers'
mess at 265 Battery:

> Churchill's Election Speech has just been broadcast, or rather
> the recording re-broadcast, & I think that a copy should be sent
> to every man & woman in the country—absolutely first class
> & it has about it the touch of the 1940–41 days—a fighting
> speech where one almost expected him to suddenly say "That
> low fox—Mr. Attlee" or "That jackal—Herbert Morrison"!
> Anyhow, nobody hearing it can have many doubts as to where
> his duty lies at the election!

The "Gestapo speech" as it came to be known has been blamed by
some for losing Churchill the election, though the June opinion polls

contradict that by showing a distinct uptick for the Conservatives after the speech was made. Its critics hold that painting Attlee (so recently Churchill's close colleague) as a Hitler in sheep's clothing was a patent absurdity, beyond the pale of civilized political discourse, but when one reads it now, especially in the wake of Donald J. Trump's time in office, it's hard not to feel at least a mild twinge of nostalgia for the political bite and wit that went into its composition.

Peter had first written to Monica about the election on May 23, the same day that Churchill paid his two visits to the King.

> I apologise, Dearest, because I <u>know</u> you never did say you
> would "obey" . . . !—about this coming election, I've done
> all the business, some time ago, of filling in blue postcards &
> what-not & I appointed you to vote by proxy for me, & when
> you do, I want you to vote Conservative, whoever the candidate
> may be. I expect you agree about that, but in case you've got
> your doubts may I guide you to do the same!?!

Between the Beveridge Report of 1942 and the Butler Education Act of 1944, the Labour Party's election manifesto was already written, and only really needed to be savagely edited for length. Sir William Beveridge went far beyond his original dry remit, which was to survey "social insurance and allied services," and instead addressed what he called the "Five Giant Evils"—squalor, ignorance, want, idleness, and disease. His extraordinary report met with equally extraordinary reviews. The archbishop of Canterbury, William Temple (who is also credited with coining the phrase "welfare state"), wrote that it was "the first time anyone has set out to embody the whole spirit of the Christian ethic in an act of Parliament." *The Times,* in an editorial, called it "a momentous document which should and must exercise a profound and immediate influence on the direction of social change in Britain." The Beveridge Report was published at the beginning of December 1942, and by the end of the month had sold more than a hundred thousand copies, an astonishing figure. As for the Butler Act, already partially implemented, it greatly enhanced the chances of working-class children to go on to (free) university education by way of the "eleven plus" exam and (free) tuition at grammar schools. It raised the school-leaving age from fourteen to fifteen, and promised a tripartite system of secondary schools: grammars for the academically gifted, technical schools for aspiring craftsmen and women, and "secondary moderns" for the rest. So few technical secondary schools actually emerged from the scheme that in effect a fortunate minority of children went to the grammar schools and all the others landed up in secondary moderns; again, just like the railways, first or third.

Churchill was not entirely unfriendly to the proposals of either Beveridge or R. A. Butler (a fellow Tory in the National Government war cabinet); he had, after all, twice crossed the floor of the House of Commons—first to leave the Conservatives and join the Liberals under Lloyd George, and then to join the Conservatives again. So there was a Liberal (and liberal) side to his character, imperialist though he undoubtedly was. But Churchill, fighting exhaustion and preoccupied with the war and international diplomacy, had only skimmed Beveridge and the Butler Act; in any case, his instincts were gradualist and he thought that the Labour program went far too far and far too fast for a country verging on bankruptcy at the war's end.

When the results of the election began to be broadcast on July 26, my father wrote in his AGENDA diary: "Socialist gains all round—devastating!" On the same day, my mother began a letter with "State control! Ugh!" and went on to forecast the abolition of private schools and the establishment of "state doctors now too, I suppose?" She proposed that we all go into exile in British Columbia.

My father's reply, written on July 30, is both more thoughtful and, as it has turned out, prophetic:

> There are two coincidences in your today's letter, my own,
> & one is that you mention British Columbia as a possible
> escape! Because, our local rag, with a sly dig or not, had a full
> page article on that very colony on the same day as the first
> results came out! But I understand the cost of living is rather
> high out there! No, Darling—I rather fancy we shall stay at
> home & either help work the Labourites on their way back
> to the opposition benches, or else live our own lives more or
> less as usual but with the steady decrease of the prestige of the
> British Commonwealth an ever present reality as we kowtow
> more & more to the lesser socialist nations of Europe. I don't
> honestly know what their policy is going to be, & how far they

are going to take it, but I don't think that it will go as far as all that, Darling. Nationalisation won't go to the full limits of making us <u>all</u> civil servants. I think that private schools will still go on much the same as usual except that they may be made to have a certain number of State aided children in their numbers. Equally, tho' all or most doctors may have to have a panel of patients, they will still be allowed to have their own private "rounds"—they must be otherwise the whole system & supply of doctors would fail in a very short time. On the other hand, nationalisation of electricity, say, would probably benefit everybody by giving basic rates all over the country and decreased costs. My own reaction is that when the populace realise exactly what they have voted themselves into—& seen this party at work for a year or so, helping us to founder rapidly in International policies, they'll react very strongly!

In other words, the new "socialist" government was going to make a very British fudge of things, with two lines, two classes, public and private, running alongside each other. The National Health Service would cater to one set of patients while the same doctors and surgeons would treat a different clientele that had the money to pay (through their insurance companies) for more prompt, comfortable, and deferential service. Similarly with schools: Eton, Harrow, and Winchester would thrive as ever, while poorer (in every sense) schools, like King's, Worcester, would be thrown a lifeline by the state in the form of a "direct grant" in exchange for opening their doors to a total of 25 percent of non-fee-paying pupils who had passed the new eleven plus exam.

Such compromises and trade-offs reflected the character of Attlee's first cabinet, which looked like England in its diversity and mix of social classes. The prime minister himself had gone to a public school, followed by Oxford University, and was the son of a solicitor. His deputy, Herbert Morrison, was the son of a reactionary-minded policeman, and had left school at fourteen to become an errand boy. His chancellor of the exchequer, Hugh Dalton, son of a Church of England canon and tutor to the royal family, went to Eton, Cambridge, and the London School of Economics. His minister of education, Ellen Wilkinson, daughter of a self-educated insurance salesman, went to Stretford Road Secondary School for Girls and the University of Manchester. Wilkinson was "as far removed from being a bore as it is possible for any human to be," her fellow MP and feminist Thelma Cazalet-Keir once said of her, in a broadcast election speech.

More decisively socialist measures would probably have been quickly abolished by the next Conservative government, but, seventy-plus years later, the NHS continues to stagger on,* and so do the multitudinous inequities of the education system, both victims of the fudges and compromises that attended their birth. The Attlee government was never "the Attlee terror," as Evelyn Waugh delighted in calling it.

---

* It's worth noting that the single most effective—and utterly misleading—slogan of the Leave campaign that led up to the 2016 British referendum on whether the country should leave or remain in the European Union was coined by Boris Johnson: "We send the EU £350 million a week: let's fund our NHS instead." Inspired by Beveridge and implemented by Aneurin Bevan, the National Health Service is still very close to Britain's heart.

Chapter 41

GOING FOR DINNER at Ponti left me pining for release into the outside world. When I first saw Swedish Health Services, it evoked troubling memories of School House at my hated boarding school. Both had been built within a decade of each other in the 1880s; both were of the same raw redbrick construction; both had deep ecclesiastical roots, one Anglican, the other Catholic; both felt like prisons to me. By now I was the longest-serving inmate of the rehab ward (after about five weeks of residence), and, though I was properly grateful for the lessons I had learned there, I badly wanted to get free from the clink.

The problem was the seventeen exterior wooden steps that I would need to climb—and descend—between the yard and the top two floors of my house. Going up them would be a lot easier than coming down because I'd have to lead with my dud right leg on the descent, trust my full weight to it, then lower my good left leg to join its mate on the same step while clinging for dear life to the railing. That each step leading to my second-floor deck was two or more inches higher than the steps I had been practicing on in the hospital gym was a further deterrent, again especially on the downward trip.

Mike Wollaston had evidently been thinking along the same lines because he phoned me a couple of mornings after our dinner to make a generous proposal. He'd been talking to Mark, the Irish carpenter, who lived in a single-story, single-bedroom cottage in Mike's compound on the Ship Canal; Mark had agreed to move out, into one of Mike's several oceangoing tugs that lay in his marina, for as long as it took me to move back into my own quarters a couple of hundred yards up the hill. Julia could take the bedroom at the back of the cottage, while I could use the bed in the large, combined living room, dining room, and kitchen. Problem solved. We'd make the move in three or four days' time.

When I came awake in the small hours in these last few days of my stay in the ward, I'd listen to gurneys and trolleys rattle past my curtained window and to the infrequent, color-coded alerts broadcast from the nurses' station, and would be pleasantly reminded of my chronic insomnia in the dormitory of my boarding school in Worcester. There the sound was always of the cathedral bells ringing the quarters of each hour, powered by their windup carillon machine and its giant hammers striking brass, while I lay awake, my head beneath the single blanket, reading a book by the light of a steadily dimming torch, whose batteries were an essential item of my economy. By day I barely noticed the cathedral clock, but by night the bells were my intimate companions, the distance between the dormitory and the bell tower shrinking from perhaps two hundred yards to almost nothing in the still, before-dawn air as I listened to every note of the "Westminster" chimes and savored the suspensive pause between the last minim of the quarters and the sound of the big, bass, B-flat bourdon bell counting the hours. The book might be the memoir of a solitary escape from a German POW camp, or one of Michael Gilbert's Detective Chief Inspector Hazlerigg novels, or Thomas Hughes's *Tom Brown's Schooldays,* or W. A. Darlington's *I Do What I Like,* a great and influential favorite of mine. What it would never be was a book on the school curriculum.

It was a Friday when I left the rehab ward. Julia was unpinning her prints from our road trip to Stanford from the walls of my room, which was beginning to crowd with my favorites among the hospital staff: Kelli, Richard, Robert, Kathy . . . With Kelli a warm hug, with the others mumbled thanks, slightly embarrassed handshakes, and friendly goodbyes. I was in street clothes and in need of a haircut. A gurney was piling up with stuff to be taken to our new temporary digs in West Ewing Street: the new electric razor, with which I'd never managed to establish a satisfactory working relationship; Kindle; electronic notebook; Paul's gift of a half crate of red wine, as yet untouched; a dozen or so books; assorted clothes stuffed into a holdall; a corkscrew; Julia's pictures, rolled up in a loosely tied scroll; the usual shabby disorder of a haphazard traveling life. There are people who are meticulous about packing, but I'm of the school that doesn't give a thought about what to take and what to leave until a few minutes before the taxi arrives to take me to the airport. Whatever gets left behind can always be replaced at the next stop if necessary, or you can just do without.

Mike's compound on the Ship Canal, Ewing Street Moorings, had been a home away from home for me since September 1990, when I came back to Seattle after three weeks of nosing my way around British Columbia in a sailboat for which I needed to find a permanent berth. Before we introduced ourselves in his snug, dingy, dog-smelling office, I noticed Mike was reading the new paperback edition of Bruce Chatwin's posthumous essay collection, *What Am I Doing Here.*

"I knew Chatwin in London," I said.

"Yes, I thought you probably did," was his faintly disconcerting reply.

His moorings were sui generis, a floating maze of mostly old, mostly wooden sailboats, houseboats, tugboats, where a pair of long-established beavers swam around between the craft. Mike had inherited the place from its founder, Captain Maurice Reaver, in the 1960s, when counterculture names like Timothy Leary and Ken Kesey had hung out here, finding its easygoing strain of libertarianism in tune with theirs. Later, in my own time, there was the commandingly tall figure of Fendall Yerxa, an octogenarian when I first met him, who had fought at Okinawa as a company commander in the Marine Corps, then gone on to a career as a journalist, writing for the *New York Herald Tribune* in its 1940s heyday, anchoring the ABC TV evening news for two years in the early '60s, then becoming the Washington, DC, bureau chief for *The New York Times* before resigning from that job to come west to Seattle to join the faculty of the University of Washington as a journalism professor, a post he occupied for twenty years, while simultaneously pursuing his alternative avocation of sailing on Puget Sound. When Fendall died in 2014, aged 101, I wanted to credit his longevity, at least in part, to his life at the moorings and his regular's stool at the far right-hand end of the Ponti bar, a walk of less than a half mile from his houseboat.

In person, Fendall was a man of exceptional courtesy and gentleness. His *Seattle Times* obituarist brought out one aspect of his character that I recognized immediately, his distaste for quarrelsomeness of any kind. Robert H. Phelps, a former colleague in the *New York Times* Washington bureau explained in his memoir, *God and the Editor,* why Fendall had quit his job there at a time when the *Times'* editorial staffs in New York and Washington were habitually at one another's throats: "Yerxa had little stomach for dissension and wanted out." Another former colleague, this one at the University of Washington, remembered how she and he had emerged from a faculty meeting that Fendall remarked was "like a bunch of seagulls fighting over a pile of manure," a simile that nicely describes all faculty meetings in my limited experience of such things.

Mike Wollaston was the moorings' genius of place, and he ruled it with gruff, poker-faced humor. It was down to him that as you stepped from solid ground onto the dock you felt you were just sufficiently "offshore" to have put the strict conventions of the land temporarily behind you. I've never known a marina where this was so palpable a sensation, or where the small human community it harbored was so various. My incalculable number of visits there, always met by the reliable smell of fir shavings and sawdust, paint, diesel oil, and sweaty labor, invariably put me in mind of Kenneth Grahame's *The Wind in the Willows* and the water rat's observation to the mole, "Believe me, my young friend, there is *nothing*—absolutely nothing—half so much worth doing as simply messing about in boats."

All this came back to me as Julia and I moved into the small cottage just across the street from the moorings. Ewing Street itself was short, narrow, dusty, with as many potholes as surviving scraps of tarmac clinging to the stony, khaki-colored ground. At the cottage Mike had laid a line of wooden planks over the concrete steps at the front door to make a wheelchair ramp that proved too steep a slope for Julia and me to navigate, and I had to lever myself out of the chair, grab hold of the rail, and sidle crabwise up the ramp to the top step (the ramp was doubled in length later that afternoon). This was my first real-world test of wheelchair accessibility, and one I passed only by the skin of my teeth.

The cottage was snug but commodious. A narrow corridor ran along the side of the house, leading to Julia's bedroom by way of a bathroom. Another bathroom was attached to the open-plan kitchen/ dining room/living room, where a made-up bed had been pitched for me on the lee side of a wall of books (more Mike's than Mark's). So I and my daughter could live under a single roof without bumping into each other unless we chose to do so (which we did, frequently). Mike's quarters lay behind the cottage across a small courtyard: he'd quarried a second-floor studio apartment out of a disused industrial building, to which he'd moved from a grand, 1920s Tudor-style mansion on Capitol Hill with a full-size ballroom on its top floor. His maritime museum, including a collection of vintage marine diesel engines, extracted like wisdom teeth from deep inside old tugboats, stood next door. He had lately set to contracting his life down to its essentials, and restoring abandoned things like antique diesels to working order was high on his agenda, as it had always been. His kindly attempt to rescue me from the rehab ward was another such project.

That evening people kept dropping by. Drink was taken. The occasional cigar was smoked. I was woken at just before 6:00 a.m. in my new surroundings by the clank and rumble of a procession of trucks negotiating the potholes of Ewing Street on their way to work at the Foss shipyard next door to the moorings. I welcomed the noise—so much better than the intervention at the same hour of a lab worker in search of a blood sample. It was the sound of the real world going about its daily routine.

Foss was the biggest tug company in the Pacific Northwest by dint of having swallowed nearly all its smaller competitors. Before the activities of the timber industry were more closely regulated, the single most common sight on Puget Sound was a Foss tug towing, a long way behind it, a raft of "logs," meaning a horizontal forest of freshly clearcut Douglas firs, stripped clean of their branches. In the summer of 1991, I hitched a ride on a Foss tug from Bellingham, Washington, to the state capital, Olympia, a voyage of days, not hours, because we traveled at a snail's pace of just two knots to save our giant log raft from breaking up. Vulnerable to every tidal current in the sound, and they are legion, we spent much of our time at anchor in windless shelter-holes with the tree trunks gathering loosely around the hull of the tug as if by natural affinity, while the crew brought out fishing rods, hoping to snag a salmon for dinner. I remember passing six hours like this, less than a mile short of Deception Pass, where at full tide the current rages through at up to twelve knots and "slack water" is more a hypothetical idea than a practical fact. I'll never forget the captain's face as he fed his tow into the pass, studying the water and checking his wristwatch, his neck continuously swiveling from ahead to astern, forgetting to breathe. Our murdered forest appeared to contract to fit the narrowing channel, the water still roiling with the swirls of leftover current as the ebb switched to flood, the captain tensing for unexpected disaster. As the last of the trees came clear from under the road bridge, the captain allowed himself to exhale and say "Miller time!"— a forlorn wish because American tug fleets are as prohibitively teetotal as the US Navy.

After my Foss wake-up call, I struggled to sit upright in the bed, trying to get leverage by holding on to one of the handles at the back of my wheelchair, which stood, wheels locked, beside me. Failed attempt followed failed attempt, but eventually I succeeded, then made an easy transfer from bed to chair. Note to self: buy bed assist rail.

Chapter 42

My FATHER's FUTURE. Throughout 1943 and 1944 his consoling day-dream was that he'd become a farmer after the war. He read and reread *The Story of a Norfolk Farm* by Henry Williamson, also the author of a series of broadly autobiographical novels for adults and an impressive stream of articles and columns for newspapers and magazines, including the *Daily Express*. Williamson's farm was at Stiffkey, a village just fourteen miles from Hempton, at the point where the River Stiffkey empties into the Wash, and its chalky soil was of a piece with Hempton's own.

Williamson was an oddball, spiky, stubbornly opinionated mentor. His farm book presents his uncompromising character even before he reaches the first page of the first chapter. A prefatory note complains that Faber & Faber, his publishers, have censored him: "The publishers have told me that certain passages, including an entire chapter, 'are not essential to the story of the farming venture, and they are likely to excite a controversial interest at odds with the main theme of the book.'" He hopes "that they may be restored to the text in the happier and healthier age following the end of the War." He dates the note November 11, 1940. Given what we know of Williamson's politics, it's a tossup to decide whether this happier and healthier age will dawn under German or British sovereignty.

Then there is the main epigraph to the book, which begins, "We count it a privilege to live in an age when England demands that great things shall be done." The author is Sir Oswald Mosley, leader of the British Union of Fascists, who in 1940 was safely under lock and key, in accordance with the terms of Defence Regulation 18B. Mosley's name alone would have been enough to shock prospective readers of the book, including my father. But Williamson's tendency to be at odds with public opinion was counted by him as a badge of honor.

Reading *The Story of a Norfolk Farm* now, it's tempting to see it as a fascist parable in which Williamson buys on the cheap (£2,250) a 235-acre fragment of England, sunk in decadence, degeneracy, and decrepitude (its roads impassable, its fields full of thistles), and by a great effort of will, aided by the wonders of modern machinery, restores it to a pristine state even as the mocking locals jeer at his methods. It is a story of blood, toil, and soil, half a how-to book and half a testament to the author's dogged courage and his powers of close observation as a naturalist. If the missing chapter and the other cuts made the political theory of the book explicit, then Williamson's editor at Faber was serving the author to his best advantage, for the book's implicit politics make it a work of teasing ambiguity.

Williamson came to his Norfolk farm as a novice and a visitor from his home and writing hut in rural Devon—a move he describes in racial terms, as he drives his fast, open-topped Alvis Silver Eagle across the country:

The road was straight, and with the surface it had probably had since the end of the [1914–18] War. The sunset was plain and simple, like the character of the people, almost one-dimensional, as linnet, hare, thorn, or partridge. The northern blond invaders' blood tamed by the climate and immingled with the Saxon or Celt, the little Celts who were always defeated but made the best-humoured slaves. In Devon the Celtic blood dominated the strains of blue-eyed Nordic and hard-dark Norman; in East Anglia, the Nordic strain was clearest. And musing thus, I came to Breckford.

In other words, Stiffkey is as close to Hitler's Germany as you can get. Williamson had served in World War I as a supply officer. He enlisted as a private, applied for and got a commission, but never rose above the rank of lieutenant except in his personal stationery after the war, on which he styled himself Captain Henry Williamson. His relatively safe war job in his infantry regiment was to send horse and mule trains of food and ammunition to the front lines. In the celebrated and heavily mythologized "Christmas truce" of 1914, said to have included international games of football in no-man's-land, he claimed to have experienced an epiphany, discovering that both German and British troops were fighting for their country's freedom and for their one true God. Williamson's lifelong belief in the "cousinship" of the English and Germans was grounded in his own ancestry: his paternal grandmother was Adela Leopoldina Lühn from Bavaria.

For Williamson in the 1930s, Hitler was a hero to be worshipped; others in his pantheon included T. E. Lawrence, an admirer of *Tarka the Otter,* with whom he'd made friends. In 1969, as the week's guest on the seemingly eternal BBC radio series *Desert Island Discs,* the host respectfully asked, "Between the wars you were a, er, nonconformist?" Williamson went on to deliver one of the strangest epitaphs on Hitler in its mixture of reverence and repudiation: "A man of that tremendous artistic feeling should never be in charge of a nation because he was a perfectionist—and once you begin to force perfection on other people you become the devil."

The villagers of Stiffkey were still enduring the comic notoriety brought on them by their former rector, the Reverend Harold Davidson, the self-proclaimed "prostitutes' padre," who in 1932 had been found guilty of immorality and neglect of his parish by a consistory court (the Church of England's own criminal justice system) in Norwich. The evidence brought before the court on the immorality charge was flimsy, and an incriminating letter from a seventeen-year-old prostitute was probably faked. Davidson, who had always hankered for a stage career, protested his defrocking by putting himself on exhibition in a barrel on Blackpool's "Golden Mile" and later moved across the country to the seaside resort of Skegness in Lincolnshire, where he reenacted the tale of Daniel in the lion's den by entering a cage with two live lions. On July 30, 1937, either one of the lions mauled him to death or a doctor killed him by treating his minor wounds with an overdose of insulin. Several thousand people showed up for his funeral at St. John and St. Mary's Church in Stiffkey.

In *The Story of a Norfolk Farm,* Williamson claims to have witnessed the crowds at Davidson's funeral on August 3, but this seems improbable. In any case, Williamson's arrival in Stiffkey was not met by the villagers with an effusive welcome. He was an outsider. He disdained local advice. He painted on the front of his new farmhouse (built by knocking three derelict laborers' cottages into one) the encircled double lightning flash that was the logo of the British Union of Fascists, which can still be seen there, so I'm told. For him, this was a symbol of the progress he meant to bring to the village; for the villagers, it was a signal of his alien and dangerous political intentions toward them. After having a Soho prostitute in the rectory, they were getting a raving Nazi on Old Hall Farm (renamed in the book Old Castle Farm, as Stiffkey is renamed Creek, and Wells, Whelk—all these rechristenings are lazy). The villagers waited, watched, gossiped, and on June 14, 1940, after Dunkirk and with the invasion scare accelerating fast, they reported Williamson to the police at Wells-next-the-Sea, five miles from Stiffkey. Anne Williamson, Henry's daughter-in-law and biographer, says that the villagers' "evidence" included accusations that his handsomely improved farm roads were designed to assist the invading Germans and that a recently installed fanlight above the stairs in the farmhouse was a signaling device, presumably to communicate with overflying enemy aircraft.

The Wells police came to the house, examined Williamson's books and papers without unduly disturbing them, and, in general, were (in his words, quoted in Anne Williamson's biography) "very kind." But they drove him back to their police station, locked him in for the weekend, under the same provision in the Defence Act that had led to Mosley's internment in Brixton Prison a month before, and allowed him to put the finishing touches on *The Story of a Norfolk Farm* while sitting on the narrow bed in his cell. On the Monday morning the police took him to Norwich, "where the Chief Constable, Capt. van Neck [not a pseudonym, though it sounds like one], said I was to be released, as nothing found against me."

I've enjoyed the book, trying to read it as my father read it, against the war-savaged farmscape of Italy, and the smaller Arab subsistence farms of Palestine, as he, in his turn, tried to dream himself into the peacetime future. He seems not to have noticed the book's political undertones because he wasn't looking for them, and they are easily overlooked. (The Mosley epigraph is just an excuse to smuggle Sir Oswald's name into the book; the paragraph itself is patriotic bombast of the kind that is far more artfully phrased by Churchill.) Peter liked Williamson's passionate nature-writing, and was greedy for his farming hints and tips.

There is, though, another aspect of the book: Williamson's fondness for strict accountancy in pounds, shillings, and pence. He probably cooked his actual figures in order to deter readers like my father from daring to emulate his unique, backbreaking, heroic achievements at Old Castle Farm. At the end of his first year as a farmer, he calculates that he is £769 11s. 0d. out of pocket, a sum just nine shillings short of the price of the White House. "When I made up my balance sheet, for the second year, I found I had broken even," and then lets on that over his two years of farming he had also written four hundred thousand words. If a (sometimes) best-selling author, *Daily Express* columnist, radio broadcaster, and writer of a screenplay titled "Immortal Corn" (never produced) could barely break even on his farm, what chance would Peter stand? Very little, it seemed, for in June 1945 he wrote to Monica asking her to cancel his subscription to *Farmers Weekly*.

A couple of weeks before that, Monica had said in a letter that she estimated their joint capital as a smidgen over £3,000, including the cost of the White House, which, she wrote, they could restore to its original function as a farmhouse. Its large back garden could become home for pigs and poultry; they could exercise their turbary rights to the green, and put goats out to graze there; then they could rent a nearby field or two, either for cattle pasture or as arable land on which to grow wheat or barley. She finished this proposal with the remark, "All I can see is pigs in the kitchen!"

"Pigs in the kitchen!" was, I suspect, the final nail in the coffin of my father's pastoral dreams. He was interested, very interested, in money. Throughout most of my childhood and adolescence, he would retire to his study every Saturday morning to read the weekly *Investors Chronicle* before he began work on his Sunday sermon. He abhorred the idea of being in debt; it must be cash on the nail, or nothing. Mortgages of any kind were another name for usury (an anti-Semitic code word), or "paying on the never-never." To attempt to farm Williamson-style would put him deep in hock to Lloyds Bank for the rest of his foreseeable future.

If farming was beyond his means, what else to do? He signed up for a War Office–sponsored correspondence course on the Fundamentals of Industrial Administration, "which may give me some ideas."

> At the same time, I'm trying to delve into Economics from the business point of view as I've got a fairly abstruse & comprehensive book on the subject; I curled up with it this afternoon & even though it is almost incomprehensible, the very fact that it needs careful & thorough reading to be able to grasp the argument, is a good thing!

He grasped at passing fancies—a managerial job at Colman's mustard factory in Norwich? A short-term (six months or a year) degree at Cambridge University? (He doesn't specify a subject, and I doubt if Cambridge, indulgent as it may have been to war veterans, ever granted a degree based on so short a period of attendance.) My mother suggested portrait photography as a career; perhaps he could join her friend Miss Priest in partnership? (Priest was a regular visitor to our house in her role as a Fakenham photographer, and she and Monica sometimes had supper and went to the cinema together; the few photos that I have by her are posed and composed to a reasonably professional standard.) Perhaps they could buy a country pub?—a favorite job for middle- and junior-ranking officers after the war. Every army padre Peter encountered seems to have nagged him about going into the church like his father, but he saw his lack of a university degree as an insurmountable hurdle. The civil service, if and only if the Labour Party didn't win the impending general election? It seems he would take any employment he could find so long as it was not the only job for which he was qualified: he wouldn't revisit his "year of hell" by teaching at a state primary school.

His informal qualifications were listed in a letter to Monica where he describes his "new friend" Colonel Robin Boyle, a regular soldier who had recently taken command of a neighboring unit, and enumerates their common interests as "a leaning to the church, politics and social affairs & all the rest of it." There's another clue in the book that he asks Monica to buy and send him, which he'd seen well reviewed in *The Listener,* the BBC's highbrow weekly. The book, *Rebuilding Family Life in the Post-War World,* was edited by the Reverend Sir James Marchant, whose other occupations included being the leader of the National Vigilance Association "for the enforcement and improvement of the laws for the repression of criminal vice and public immorality" (one such aim was to ban English translations of Balzac's novels) and the director of the National Council of Public Morals. He was also a keen eugenicist. Born in 1867, midway through the reign of Queen Victoria, Marchant embodied the narrowest, most puritanical version of "Victorian values" as adumbrated by Margaret Thatcher in the 1980s. I'm keen to find out what exactly drew my father toward this grim-sounding killjoy, and a copy of his book (in its first edition, now priced at $7.31, including postage) is on its way to me as I write.

For Attlee's new government, demobilizing the troops in far-flung foreign parts and bringing them safely home again was an enormously complex exercise. Four and a quarter million men and women had to be transported back to Britain at a time when there was an acute shortage of ships, a housing crisis in the homeland, and an overwhelming need to appear to be fair and equitable in the eyes of the BBC and the newspapers. As early as 1942, Ernest Bevin, then minister of labour and national service in Churchill's wartime coalition, came up with a scheme for demobilization. Servicemen who were categorized as Class A were demobilized by order of age and length of service (first in, first out). Those in the smaller Class B were given priority because they had had prewar civilian jobs that were considered essential for the reconstruction of the country. This seemingly workmanlike system gave rise to a multitude of unforeseen ambiguities and subcategories, and there cannot have been a single member of Parliament who wasn't deluged with pleaful letters of complaint from constituents, all of whom were desperate for their loved ones to come home and come home *now.* By this time Bevin was foreign secretary.

Peter wrote to the MP for Evesham, Rupert de la Bère ("rather an ass," as Peter described him to Monica), whose parliamentary constituency included Hadzor and Droitwich, congratulating him on holding the staunchly Conservative seat against the rising tide of socialists, and describing the plight of Territorial Army volunteers who had enlisted, as he had, in 1939 before the declaration of war. De la Bère promptly responded with a chatty, officer-to-officer note recollecting his own experiences in World War I, and added that he was drowning under piles of letters about demobilization from his other constituents. Neither he nor Peter seems to have noticed that in times of war the Territorial Army legally became part of the Regular Army and so would not be officially demobilized until 1947. Monica, who was staying with me at Granny's house in Sheringham, made four separate drafts of a letter to the Labour member for North Norfolk, Edwin Gooch, also the president of the National Union of Agricultural Workers, begging for her husband's return. She put it in the postbox as we were on our way in AUP 595 to a tea party at a house on Blakeney Point, where the know-it-all husband of our hostess told Monica that Gooch was off to an agricultural conference in Canada, and that he (the know-it-all) very much doubted that the MP would find the time to read a letter from the wife of a serving soldier. Sucks to him. Gooch did write back—a letter as friendly and unhelpful as Rupert de la Bère's.

Even before the end of September, Monica was distraught. She hadn't yet discovered the Benzedrine inhaler ("mother's little helper," as the Rolling Stones called it); that would arrive in the 1950s. But her letters betray her as a woman in the throes of a chronic anxiety attack. At one point she implores Peter to reconsider his decision not to return to primary school teaching, if a recantation would bring him home a single day earlier. At another, she offers to write him a suicide threat that he can produce as evidence to his brigadier. At another, she is riding a high tide of elation, all problems solved, only to sink, the next day, into depression's unfathomable abyss. She's off her rocker. Peter's replies are calm, measured, always understanding, and overflowing with love, as he tries to soothe her from far Palestine.

I have one firsthand memory of this agonizing time. It's September or October 1945. There's a Welsh dresser in the White House dining room that faces onto the street outside. The dresser is equipped with a deep drawer to the right, and I'm not tall enough to see over the drawer's forward edge, but I can feel inside it with my hand, which encounters something interesting—a sort of box attached to a strap, that feels as if it contains an object of some kind. I haul it out. The box is made of khaki webbing, and inside I find a fantastic article, commensurate with my highest hopes: a pair of goggles attached to a perforated snout, like the face of a not-very-friendly black pig.

I try it on. The three straps meant to secure it to my head are too long for me and the thing falls from my face, but if I hold the straps from behind and keep them tight, it all fits beautifully. I turn to my left and confront myself in the looking glass on the wall, whose silvering has worn away in spots and gashes. I am marvelously transformed! I am the bogeyman, the trickster, the unnameable!

I walk on tiptoe down the hall to the kitchen, where my mother stands with her back to me, peeling a potato. I say, "Boo!"

My mother turns. For a moment she is smiling, then she's not. Eyes, nose, and mouth somehow all get smooshed together into the ugliest face I've ever seen, and she is yelling at me. "Put that thing back where you found it!" She sinks into an upright wooden chair beside the table, hands covering her face, her shoulders heaving as she sobs.

By turns fascinated, bewildered, and greatly frightened, I stood in my dungarees, holding the gas mask at my side, and watched my mother cry. I'd never seen such a thing before. I didn't know that grown-ups *could* cry. But here was my mother weeping just like a child.

An age passed before she spoke, or gasped, again. "I'm sorry, darling. I'm not myself today."

Now I was crying. She opened her arms and I went to bury my face in her all-encompassing hug.

In Palestine, my father was driven to subscribing to Hansard, the official daily transcription of all business in the two houses of Parliament, in order to follow the ever-changing intricacies and adjustments to Bevin's original demob scheme. His own group—25—kept on being deferred then not deferred before being deferred again. Garbled reports in the papers exacerbated Monica's already shattered state of mind. In her letters she talked of sleepwalking, "throwing myself around the bedroom," but made no mention of my performance with the gas mask. On October 17, after hearing yet another deferment scare on the BBC News, she wrote to Peter:

My own Darling Sweetheart,
   Tonight's news was a terrible shock—I felt Darling it was more than we could stand, more than I can anyway Dear Heart, I just can't face it . . . <u>I can't</u>.

I am going to see Dr Meanley tomorrow, if Jonathan is well enough to come and not chesty—no Darling I'm going anyway, I've just run down to a neighbour to ask her to come if I have to leave J.

My Darling Heart, don't please think that because before, I didn't feel in myself there was justification for asking a doctor to write me a certificate saying my nerves were going to pieces, that it isn't true now. There is a breaking point for everybody. Dear Heart, you know I wouldn't malinger.

I can't keep on without you—this is no letter for you to show anybody, Sweetheart, if you should be thinking that, it's for yourself.

I wept when I heard the news, and later I went up to see Kitty and to ask her to ring up Dr. Meanley for me. She did, the dear, and told him I'd had just about all I could stand so long away from you, & with worry about Jonathan—that I never had a night's unbroken sleep—which is true, I haven't knocked myself about lately, but I still wake sometimes with a shout. Last night I was sitting up in bed shouting to Jonathan "to get up & stand up!"

His rather scared small voice woke me, asking "Do you mean it, Mummy?" across the pitch dark room—poor little fellow.

And then spells of tiredness when my whole body aches, and I only want to cry . . . it's not just physical tiredness, and I lose my temper too, and that's not natural to me.

This is a letter all about me, but Darling I've written so many telling you all was well with me—and I truly felt with February as a definite fixed date to look forward to, I could stick it just as you could, and I'd have felt much the same shame about pleading for compassionate leave, as you'd have felt apparently, coming home with the Class "B"s.

So now Darling I want you to know that I'd not plead now or ever if I could stick it without. I'm not putting on an act, Darling, that's one thing I could never do to you, in fact I'd not find it easy to do to anyone. . . .

Darling I can't go through the winter alone like this with no certainty as to when I shall see you again.

I've got to the point where I feel I can't go on any more, it's just disappointment after disappointment and what ever they promise us now, I shan't believe it.

The letter goes on for another page and a half in the same vein, breaking into French in its more extravagant paragraphs. When Monica writes, "This is no letter for you to show anybody, Sweetheart, if you should be thinking that," she inadvertently betrays that she knows exactly how the letter will be used, as evidence to be shown to third parties—Colonel Bill Kerr and the brigadier—and that she is aware that her audience is going to be bigger than Peter alone. It's hard to measure the exact balance between unselfconscious candor and conscious calculation, but the letter is clearly a mixture of both. She sent it off at noon the next day, by registered mail, including the newly signed certificate from Dr. Meanley.

Peter's response was swift and decisive. He got the letter on October 23, and was able to respond with real news a little more than twenty-four hours later:

My Very Own Most Precious Sweetheart,
   I have done, this afternoon, what I wish I had done weeks ago; if I hadn't been so blindly optimistic I'd never have had the fantastic idea that you <u>could</u> put up with the present circumstances. Oh! My Very Own, my Darling, I can <u>never</u> forgive myself for asking you to do the impossible—I know, now, what it has meant to you, to try to suffer in silence, & then, in final desperation, having to steel yourself into going to see Meanley. But, Beloved, I wish now that I'd insisted on your doing it before . . . that I hadn't fooled myself into thinking that we had to try to set an example . . . we've done that long enough already. I have seen Bill Kerr, written out my application in full, in every detail & with the doctor's certificate—he has approved of it, as I knew he would if I ever asked him to, & it's going on, personally by him, to the Brigadier tomorrow. I don't know how long it will take to get the answer, which I <u>believe</u>, confidently, will be in our favour, but it'll probably be ten days yet, & I shall, of course, send you another telegram immediately I hear anything. Even after that, it'll take time I'm afraid, my Precious—not wasted in doing

nothing, but in travelling & waiting & travelling again, the
journey from Egypt to England takes 3 weeks at the minimum
& may take longer, but, once the decision comes through I
should be starting my journey within 48 hours. Now, Darling,
we've just got to wait somehow, until we finally hear. . . . Army,
duty & anything else means nothing now—nothing at all.
We've given so much that we've given our all . . . too much, &
now we're going to take back a little to ourselves, take back all
we can. My Own Darling . . . the <u>whole</u> of my life is yours—it
always has been but I've tried to give what belongs to us, to
others . . . & I blindly thought we could stand it. My Precious,
I don't think I need to tell you that nothing in this World, in
life itself, is going to deviate me one iota from coming back to
You just as <u>quickly</u> as I can . . . & that won't be soon enough.

"Army, duty & anything else means <u>nothing</u> now." For Peter, this
must have been the hardest renunciation to make. Army, duty, setting an example to his junior officers and men, together with supporting his budding family at the White House and fortifying the dogged
tenacity of his belief in Christianity: these had been the five great pillars of his life for the last six years. Compassionate leave was for the
weaker brethren, and he was proud that none of his written testimo-
nies for the troops had been turned down. But writing an application
for himself must have felt like eating crow. To have come so close to
being demobilized in the natural if frustratingly slow course of things,
and to capitulate within sight of the final hurdle, was a severe blow to
his pride. Up till now, his career in the TA had been unblemished, but
whatever Bill Kerr may have said to reassure him otherwise, he cannot
have avoided feeling that he was letting the side down—and a true
gentleman, in my father's stoic definition, never lets the side down.
   He told Monica that he should hear back from the brigadier in ten
days. On November 5 there was no news. He wrote:

Every time the telephone rings, or the colonel wishes to see me,
I wonder if this is it . . . & tomorrow is Tuesday, my own . . . &
on Wednesday you will be expecting to have heard already, or
at any minute, & it may not come through for a few more days
yet . . . oh hell!

November 9, and still nothing.

I'd better tell you the whole "mechanism" of my application,
& that may help reassure you if you still haven't heard by
the time this letter arrives. Firstly I fill in a form which gives
all our relevant details, ages, number & ages of children &
so forth, then a description of the grounds for application,
together with the doctor's certificate, & that I passed on to
WHK [William H. Kerr] who added his recommendation, &
in turn passed it on to the Brigadier who adds anything he may
wish & forwards it to the Committee who sit in Cairo. The
Brigadier to whom this went is a very nice chap indeed, human
& understanding. He was livid anyway about the way the
deferment of officers had been announced & applied wholesale.
I do believe he gave the application a fillip on its way—& that's
not just a vain hope.
      The Committee itself is an "All-ranks" one with a Colonel as
chairman, a doctor in attendance in a consultative & advisory
capacity, & then I think 4 other officers, & 4 men (Sgts & so
forth). The case is read out to them, with no names mentioned,
& explained or expanded on as I think the doctor would be
called on to give a word about Coeliac disease, & then is put to
the vote for decision.

Quite how my father believed this elaborate bureaucratic procedure could be completed within ten days is impossible to explain, particularly since he had ample experience of writing such applications
on behalf of his men. At any rate, he and Monica waited on every
post and phone ring (a telephone had just been installed in the White
House, along with a flush toilet and a cesspit in the back garden, to
replace the Elsan and the weekly visits of the foo-foo man), day after
day after day. On November 13, a Tuesday, Monica wrote:

I've managed these last few days to keep tight hold on a
phylosophy [sic] of waiting, and just for the moment it still
works—I don't expect to hear today, I don't expect to hear
tomorrow and I know if it's good news it'll take longest of all,

good news always does! I'm even (at least I am today) prepared for the fact that Saturday even may come and go with still no news. And that's my phylosophy! I've beaten myself, & my hopes, down to believing it and I'm hanging on to it for all I'm worth.

Two days later, on the fifteenth, Peter, who by now seems to have abandoned my mother's philosophy, gives vent to his frustration:

As WHK had not rung up yesterday or the day before I went to see him this morning & got him to try on the spot, which he did, but then there was a "hitch" in the line & he couldn't get through, so told me to try this afternoon . . . which I've just done, & thoroughly lost my temper when a stammering subaltern officiously answered & pointed out they didn't work during the afternoons, & anyway the case would be going through the normal channels; so I've got to get WHK to ring up this evening when "they" are pleased to do work again.

In the middle of a paragraph on the division of furniture left to Peter and Nick by their mother, he abruptly draws a line across the page and begins again:

My own Sweetheart, I HAVE got a Birthday present for you! You'll have got it before this arrives in the telegram. . . . The Posting to the UK is through, approved, & I shall be leaving here in two or three days' time, just as soon as I can get things settled & handed over. It's such grand news that I can hardly realise it . . .
    . . . It will take a few weeks & I'm afraid you'll only be getting odd scraps of letters soon—from here I have to go to the Base Depot, and thence await further orders to proceed to the port, & then, after that, at least 2½ weeks travelling with stops at Toulon and Dieppe . . . but very soon now, my Precious, by our standards, you will be in my arms again & then time & the world & all but ourselves will just cease to be, & all that we've dreamed of, prayed for & imagined, will be OURS!

Arrived in Cairo, Peter met up not only with Bill Kerr but with Major A. O. McCarthy, now also a colonel, with whom he had escaped from Dunkirk in 1940; so his dinner hosts on three successive nights brought his war full circle. Kerr arranged for him to borrow a jeep, so that he could drive out to Giza and see the pyramids and the Sphinx before lunch at the Mena House Hotel, followed by a late dinner at Cairo's famous old Shepheard's Hotel—the war ended for him, as it had begun, with the soldier as tourist.

It also ended with a blaze of light after six years of darkness. At Alexandria, he embarked on a Dutch liner, the SS *Vanderam:*

> It is a change to be on a ship with lights on & shining unheeded out to sea—the old troubles and stringent orders about blackout forgotten so that I was able to take a pleasant stroll along the promenade deck last night after dinner, before going to bed! And no need to carry one's life saving jacket everywhere!

The *Vanderam* stopped at Malta to take on more homebound troops and went on to Toulon, now open for business again after the French scuppered their navy there in 1942 and British and American bombers largely destroyed the port in 1943.

The France that Peter saw through the begrimed glass of his train windows, from Toulon to Paris's Gare de Lyon and from the Gare du Nord to Dieppe, was a country of soot, bomb damage (nearly all of it inflicted by the Allies) and the bleak gray skies of November turning to December. Its years of being occupied by the Germans had left it with a scarred, hangdog look, as if it still awaited liberation. It was a country not yet fit for tourists and a journey more to be endured than enjoyed, although every hour brought Peter a few miles closer to the wife and child he hadn't seen for nearly three years. At Dieppe, he caught the Channel ferry to Newhaven in Sussex, and a train to London, where he reported to the main headquarters of the Royal Artillery in Woolwich (known to gunners as "the shop"). When the RA had finished with him (posting him as a supernumerary major, after his twenty-eight-day leave was over, to a regiment based at Thetford, Norfolk, where he had spent time digging up sugar beets in 1942), he took yet another train from Liverpool Street Station to Norwich, where he changed trains for Fakenham and was home.

Chapter 43

MAKING COFFEE, THAT first morning at the cottage, at the kitchen end of the room (Julia had bought some basic groceries the previous evening), I was maybe a quarter mile from our house, whose top floor was visible from the moorings and vice versa. The compact campus of Seattle Pacific University, a Bible college, intervened between the house and Ewing Street; I had used to be able to gaze down on the two masts of my moored ketch from the third-floor deck, to make sure that it was still afloat, which was why I bought the house from Mike in the first place, for its crow's-eye view over the Ship Canal and the airy redwood-paneled top floor that Mike had built with his own hands. Now the house on Queen Anne Hill was almost within touching distance, but would require a good deal of work before it became fit for a wheelchair-bound man to move back in.

Someone would have to fit grab rails in the bathrooms and missing banisters on the stairs. Mike introduced me to a meticulous ship's carpenter named David, who said he could reconnoiter the house and its needs and give me a rough estimate that afternoon. He had an infirm parent himself, so knew what should be done. Mike also mentioned a trained nurse called Jennifer, a liveaboard on her boyfriend's sailboat, who might be good for doing odd jobs around the house; he'd bring her over to the cottage at evening drinks time. The moorings' sixty-person settlement was an ad hoc community on whose help and various skills I'd be thankful to depend in the coming days.

David returned from his visit to the house with a nicely written estimate of the cost of raw materials and labor (which I noticed was way below the usual hourly rate for a ship's carpenter). I told him to go ahead as soon as he conveniently could. Jennifer, who presented herself to me as an eager, personable sufferer from ADHD, I liked sufficiently to entrust her with selecting an electrical supplies company to replace two space heaters on the second floor, and finding carpet layers to replace the carpet on the stairs that Julia's two pet canines had infused with their ineradicable stench of dog pee. I foresaw that my life from here on in would have to be more open to strangers, from therapists to food shoppers, than it had ever been before, and I didn't want my future visitors' first response to my quarters to be a disdainfully wrinkled nose.

The first such visitor, who showed up one morning when we were still living at the cottage, was a physical therapist from a nursing agency, arranged for by Swedish Health Services and paid by Medicare, whose most prominent, though miniature, physical feature was the small, square patch of cultivated bristles that he maintained between his lower lip and the beginning of his swelling chin. It was no more than half an inch by half an inch, painstakingly edged and trimmed. If it contained a message, I didn't know the code, but it struck me as the most affected piece of facial hair that I had ever seen. His name is lost to recall but I think of him as Mr. Barbula, Latin for "little beard" and for me, now, a byword for therapy at its most discouraging. When I asked him if he thought I could ever look forward to walking without the four-pronged cane his answer was a flat No, and when Julia and I met him at the house so that Barbula could supervise my first attempt to scale the double flight of steps to the second floor, he was equally crabby. Halfway up and making good progress by my own lights, I asked him how he thought the climb was going.

"It's not pretty," Barbula said. "But I suppose it gets the job done."

And fuck you too, I thought. My contention is that therapists should steel themselves to tell benign lies to their clients; brutal honesty is hard to take and the Barbula method is a surefire guarantee that progress will slow if it isn't halted altogether.

That first visit to the house was dispiriting. As soon as I managed to insert my wheelchair through the narrow doorway, scraping the paint on both sides as I did so, I was met by the smell of neglect, staleness, and dog pee, along with a whiff of fresh sawdust. At the rehab ward I had kept in communication via email with my twice-a-week housekeeper, Masguda, a recent immigrant from Tatarstan in the Russian Federation, who had been feeding the cat every other day of my absence and—I hoped—cleaning up the house for my return. Everywhere I looked there were signs of Masguda's recent activities, none of which unfortunately had involved the use of a vacuum cleaner. Rather she had concentrated on assembling every shoe that Julia and I had worn in the last twenty years, and making a neat pile of them on the floor of a closet, from where they appeared to gaze back at me with a silent glare of reprehension for my wastefulness. The finishing touch to this work was made by a pair of Julia's bright purple baby shoes that Masguda had placed, in careful consort, on a shelf of books in my workroom. Various boxes of what she considered junk had been laid out side by side against the wall stretching from my desk.

By contrast, David's work on the stairs and second-floor bathroom was elegant and tidy. The carpentry in the stairwell fitted perfectly with Mike's original structure there, done sometime in the 1970s or early '80s. I climbed the three steps to the landing so that I could see around the newel post to the flight that led up to the big open room on the third floor. Everything looked good and properly secure, and would have looked better had not the dog-piss reek obscured the view; Jennifer's carpet layers were due on Monday.

I wheeled myself into my second-floor bedroom, formerly my study, where Sammy the cat lay asleep at the end of the bed, having positioned himself exactly in the middle of the duvet with the strange obsession with symmetry that all cats seem to possess. He woke, turned his head, stared at me with narrowing eyes, then let out a shriek and scarpered past me at a hell-for-leather pace I hadn't seen since his long-ago kittenhood; I heard the snap of the cat flap, followed by the frantic slithering of paws racing down the outside steps. It was not an encouraging welcome home.

Epilogue

AT RATHER WIDELY spaced intervals throughout my rehab, I had fretted about Julia. Her summer job with the Fund for the Public Interest had her spending her days going doorstep to doorstep fundraising—a thankless task, mostly—and she was also faced with upheaval in the lives of each of her parents. Jean, with her second husband, Dan, and Julia's younger half sister, Susannah, was moving house, roughly a thousand miles down the Pacific coast, from Seattle to Los Angeles. Up until I went into the hospital Jean and I had been living in two houses a mile or two away from each other. Looking north across the ship canal from my top deck, I could have seen Julia's other house on Phinney Ridge had not the ridge itself blotted out the view, and, unless the Fremont Bridge over the canal was "up," I could be at the house in five minutes flat by car. This happy proximity took quite a lot of the sting from the grim arithmetic of the fifty-fifty "parenting schedule." As for her father, she had undoubtedly saved him from the worst consequences of his own imbecilic judgment; it was great good luck for me that the schedule had placed her at my dining table and not Jean's on that Saturday evening.

And none of this mentions Julia's rite of passage from high school girl to woman undergraduate at one of the very best colleges in the United States, or so the annual rankings assured their readers. I hadn't been surprised by her success at winning a place in the early action program, just relieved that she'd been spared the anguish and hysteria of her fellow twelfth graders as they competed with one another during the remainder of the winter and spring of 2010–11. Julia had received her notice of acceptance by email at 3:00 p.m. on Friday, December 10, the same time and date that all or at least most of the colleges offering early action places sent out their notices. In her own words: "I think the writing seminar discussion was serious that day so I very quickly/silently checked my phone and nodded to friends in class, I think we did manage to stay silent." She was sleeping that night in her mother's house, where I turned up at about 5:00 p.m., carrying champagne.

Fast-forward to mid-September the next year. Mike Wollaston is driving us both to the airport in his elderly Mercedes, and we're just a couple of miles short of our destination. The early-morning sky is uniformly gray. Having ceded the front passenger seat to me and my hemiplegia, Julia's sitting in the back, keeping herself to herself, taciturn to the point of being mute. When she does speak, it's to Mike, and it's an order. She's going to be sick. Mike glances at the rearview mirror, then applies the brake; the car may be old but its brakes feel new, and we skid to a standstill, seventy miles per hour to zero in a very few seconds. Julia makes her escape onto the verge of sparse, oily grass and a shallow drainage ditch running through it.

Mike said, "Just minding my upholstery," referring to our emergency stop.

She was standing with her back to the car, leaning over the ditch and retching. I'd never known her to be carsick before. Watching her heaving shoulders now, I see, or so I think, this wasn't carsickness at all, but a great upchucking of all the tensions she'd been bottling inside her during our weird summer, when both of her parents were lost in preoccupations of their own, Jean with her move to southern California, me with my stroke, both prime examples of bad timing.

On this remorseful note (for me), Julia returned to the car, looking paler but a little happier than when she'd left it. I was glad for her that she wasn't going to be thrown into the deep end that day, but would be joining SPOT, short for Stanford Pre-Orientation Trip, in which the entire graduating class of 2015 was already divided into groups of half a dozen or so students, and each group would settle in a small timber house on one of the many organic farms that are sprinkled over the length and breadth of Silicon Valley. By day they'd help out with farmwork, and in the evenings they'd have informal seminars on life and study in the university. This would last for the inside of a week; then the students would be transported to the Stanford campus and the hard stuff would begin.

Bidding Julia goodbye through the rolled-down passenger window, I was ruefully thinking of all the many things that had been left unsaid between us, the unasked and unanswered questions, and, as Mike's car wriggled out from the double- and in some places triple-parked curb of the departures floor, I was feeling a bit sick too.

Editor's Note

Father and Son was the culmination of twelve years' work by Jonathan Raban. By the time we met to go over the manuscript, in Seattle in the autumn of 2022, he knew every page, every phrase, the location of every bit of research that went into the book. While typing was difficult for him, the thinking involved in composition was not, and he wanted this book to stand alongside his others: a map of inner geographies, this perhaps the closest to home. There was one element of this terrain he planned to address: he had recently acknowledged that many years ago, he had fathered a son, Alex Reeve. During the last years of his life, he had just begun to get to know Alex, a happiness he spoke of, and he was drafting a chapter of *Father and Son* about this fact when he died. I want to thank Alex for his generosity in reading this manuscript, as well as Colin Raban for his crucial corrections, and Julia Raban for her kindness and editorial labors, for making it possible for Jonathan Raban to finish this last book.

—J.F.

A NOTE ABOUT THE AUTHOR

JONATHAN RABAN is the author of the novels *Surveillance* and *Waxwings;* his nonfiction works include *Passage to Juneau, Bad Land,* and *Driving Home.* His honors include the National Book Critics Circle Award, the PEN/West Creative Nonfiction Award, the Pacific Northwest Booksellers Association Award, and the Governor's Award of the State of Washington. Raban died in 2023.

A NOTE ON THE TYPE

This book was set in Adobe Garamond. Designed for the Adobe Corporation by Robert Slimbach, the fonts are based on types first cut by Claude Garamond (ca. 1480–1561).

Typeset by Scribe
Philadelphia, Pennsylvania

Printed by Berryville Graphics
Berryville, Virginia

Designed by Michael Collica